To Marcia y Mark

Next year in Mendoza, ok?

Enjoy.....

David

Bs. As

Nov 2011

# Dream On

David Smith's latest book will inspire undisguised envy among his former colleagues. Not only are we reminded of his distinguished career as a Foreign Correspondent, but then he represents the United Nations Secretary-General and fulfils the dream of a large slice of humanity – of owning a vineyard and a house in Argentina where his wife was born. To top it all, Smith is a brilliant writer.

SIR TREVOR McDONALD OBE

OTHER BOOKS BY DAVID SMITH

*Mugabe*

*Prisoners of God*

# Dream On

## A DEMI-MEMOIR

## DAVID SMITH

**QUARTET**

First published in 2010 by
Quartet Books Limited
A member of the Namara Group
27 Goodge Street, London W1T 2LD

A catalogue record for this book
is available from the British Library

ISBN    978 0 7043 7199 6

Typeset by Antony Gray
Printed and bound in Great Britain by
T J International Ltd, Padstow, Cornwall

*For Sonia, who inspired the Dream,*
*Mark, Matthew, Alegría, Nelson*

# Contents

# Acknowledgements

In my broadcasting days, I learned a life lesson. "You're only as good as others make you,' a craggy cameraman warned me in my first month on TV. 'Never forget it, young man, you don't do this alone.'

To say that I have been blessed by team-mates and tutors, colleagues and friends, teachers and mentors, is an understatement. Whether in my journalism years, or on the wine adventure that followed, I have been helped, encouraged, motivated, inspired by so many. Some have saved me from myself on more occasions than I choose to remember.

I owe an enormous debt to Sir David Nicholas, the man who hired me at ITN, and the Editor-in-Chief who supported me through the ups and downs of a quarter-century on TV. David was my boss, but also the friend who dared to tell me the truth. So many others at ITN deserve my thanks. A special mention to Richard Tait, Stewart Purvis, Nick Pollard, Sue Inglish, Andrew Macdonald, Mike Morris, Chris Shlemon, Gerry Seymour, Peter Wilkinson, Fred Hickey, and in Africa the masterful Mohinder Dhillon. They worked with me, and all of them taught me so much. The privilege was mine.

At the United Nations, a word of thanks to Sir Kofi Annan and Lord Mark Malloch Brown, my bosses, but also my friends. From the moment I joined them, they knew I was living a second chapter motivated by the causes we fought for. They understood the dream in the Andes, and they encouraged me to pursue it. Privilege indeed.

I was lucky to be able to ask old friends to read the draft manuscript, and all came back with incisive, thoughtful suggestions, corrections and challenges. My thanks to Bob Deans, a colleague from our days together in the White House Press Corps; Peter Reid, once of the Foreign Office, later Vice-President at the Carnegie Endowment in Washington DC; Patrick Brogan, longtime Washington Correspondent for *The Times*;

and Professor Stephen Gill, the man who taught me English literature at Lincoln College, Oxford, and my trusted confidant ever since.

Memory, as we all know, is far from perfect and this book is based largely on personal recollection. If errors remain, the responsibility is entirely mine.

Just as lucky, was the advice and support of two dear friends from reporting days, John Humphrys and Sir Trevor McDonald, who remained true to themselves, no matter how famous they became.

And in the world of books, how fortunate I have been to be re-united, a quarter-century after our first venture together, with the irrepressible Naim Attallah and my editor Peter Ford. I drew such inspiration from both.

One of the joys of my new world of wine lies in the people you meet. We were so blessed, at the outset, to have my wife's lifelong friend in Mendoza, Lorraine Mafi-Dodds, truly one of life's givers. Without her kindness, advice and equanimity, we would not have embarked on the adventure. Her mother, Shirley, guided us through the early days with a gentle eye. We will always be grateful.

Nicolas Catena, and his daughter Laura, not only inspired us to make our dream come true; they helped us start our vineyard and our wine. They didn't have to; conventional wisdom probably told them not to. But, as always, they broke new ground. To have worked with Nicolas and Laura, to have been given their time, advice, and wise judgement, is a privilege. They are true visionaries, and our debt to them both is limitless.

Everyone who has seen our vineyard will understand the special role played by Luis Reginato. He built everything from scratch with devotion, commitment and professionalism. He monitored the progress of our vines with the loving eye of a father. We have shared some triumphs, and some setbacks, but never lost sight of the mutual respect and friendship that entwines us. To have Luis, and his young family, spend a night with us in the vineyard has become one of life's treasured moments.

So many others helped us in Mendoza. My thanks to Alejandro Vigil, a genius of a wine maker and an inspirational coach; Jeff Mausbach, who always provided such valuable insights on the business side; Alejandro Sejanovic, who taught us time and again how the quality of grape determines the quality of the wine; Felipe Stahlschmidt and Manuel Martiarena, who showed such patience and understanding of our innocence.

On the land itself, we have been so lucky to have worked with extraordinarily loyal and devoted people. Our thanks to Gabriel and Marta Quiroga, Pancho and Olga Catalano, Daniel Favier, Ricardo and Margot Rojas. Likewise, to Aldo Monteverdi, Manolo Horno, Monica Navarro, Viviana Espina, Raul Battelini, and our lawyer, Daniel Esain. Back in Washington, a special word for Carlos and Cynthia Rojas, friends, architects, and excellent palates to boot. A heartfelt thanks to Pepe Almodovar, whose commitment to selling our wine made such a difference.

In La Consulta, a group of friends have made me feel uniquely at home 5,000 miles from London. Jorge and Cecilia Peterle, Lalo and Elizabeth Testa, Victor Martinez, Jorge Muzaveh. A special word to our Spanish neighbours in the Uco Valley, Jose Manuel Ortega and his wife Nadia. It's never lonely with their extraordinary spirits and indomitable energy, just a few miles down the valley.

Lastly, my families in London and Buenos Aires. My mother Pat and brother John could have been forgiven for questioning my sanity. Instead, they got on planes and came to the Southern Hemisphere to share the dream with us, showing us such love. My Argentine in-laws, Frans and Elsa, had their doubts, but embraced the adventure wholeheartedly, offering us wisdom and support when we needed it. So too Sonia's sister Ginny and her brother Frank. My children, all four of them, have been stellar supporters of Dad's dream. I cherish watching them play in the pool, understanding better than anyone perhaps how far it is from their grandmother's two-up two-down in suburban North London to the family plot in the Andes.

As for the woman I love, well she has been responsible for so much down the years. Chiefly, my happiness, my survival and creation of one, united family. Sonia nurtured this book from beginning to end. She performed major surgery on it just when it was needed, with a combination of grace, intellect and honesty that is uniquely hers. For that, and for so much more, this book is dedicated to Sonia.

Mendoza, September 2010

# Uncorked

I am not sure when I decided to kick the habit.

I do not recall one instant when I told myself that it was time to get off the drug.

Life was meant to shift in a blinding flash of inspiration. But it was not an epiphany. Instead, I recognized warnings. My addiction would kill me.

But until it did, I would keep going.

Fifty-five days after the 9/11 attacks in New York and Washington DC, I drove myself straight to a cardiac unit. Pains in my chest, enough to call my doctor. 'Pains in the upper left arm?' he asked, then paused. 'Get straight to emergency, now.' It was a crisp Saturday morning in Washington DC, sunny, cold and bright. By the time my TV network called to discuss the fifty-sixth straight story for the nightly news, I was on nitroglycerin in the emergency unit, with doctors and nurses hovering efficiently, monitoring the electrocardiac pulses and debating immediate surgery.

I recognized the role of addiction in my DNA. I never knew my father. As a young child, I have a few odd, blurred memories. But relatives revealed that he gambled away the earnings of a well-paid job as a printer with the *Daily Mirror*, leaving us walking the poverty line. I did know that he drank and smoked heavily. I remember him, cigarette in one hand, whisky glass in the other, a lanky tall man, dark haired with a rakish smile. Most of all, I remembered his death, forty-seven years old, from a massive heart attack. It was my first funeral. Neither my mother nor my older brother, who remembered him more clearly in life, wanted to face the pain of losing him a second time. But I had been too young to remember him leaving.

When it was my turn to be in the intensive care unit in my late forties, it was too late to change the past, to wonder, knowing this, what would I change if I could do it again.

For thirty years I had enjoyed a charmed life. All those datelines as a journalist. Madrid, Rome, Lisbon, Paris, Berlin, Nairobi, Johannesburg,

Harare, Kampala, Addis Ababa, Mogadishu, Beirut, Jerusalem, Cairo, Amman, Baghdad, Tehran, Islamabad, Delhi, Beijing, Hong Kong, Tokyo, Buenos Aires, Santiago, Lima, Mexico City, Bogotá, Moscow, Leningrad, Tashkent, Kiev, Tbilisi, Riga, Washington DC, New York, Chicago, New Orleans, Los Angeles.

All those moments. The end of the last fascist dictator, General-issimo Francisco Franco, in Europe. The deaths of two Popes within fifty-three days as summer turned to autumn in Rome. The sunset of the British Empire in Africa. The horror of famine. The battle for Beirut. The fight for the soul of Israel. The election of an old Oxford friend, the first woman to take power in the Moslem world. Massacre in Beijing. The collapse of the Soviet Union. The end of the Cold War. Democratic revolution in Argentina, Chile, Brazil. And then, in Washington DC, the Bush years, father and son. The Clinton eras, husband and wife.

Best of all, I had been paid for doing what I loved. I was not the only one. 'The best job in the world, Smithy, because it never feels like work,' was the gleeful view of Jon Snow, my co-conspirator at ITN and Channel 4 News.

Worst of all, I had paid a terrible price. One marriage lost. Two sons separated from me. Upheaval. Lost friends. Living with uncertainty. Every day for thirty years expecting the unexpected. An earthquake, an assassination or just another daily bite of a long-running story. Almost every day, scrapping plans with friends, yet again. I stopped making plans. Friends, family, everyone, sacrificed to work. I was ashamed to admit it, but I even missed my only brother's wedding.

Journalism was my addiction; the news, my drug. Singularly satis-fying, yet deeply addictive. Rarely, across the decades, had I said no when asked to cover yet another story. I went on the road, travelling to another continent, two days after my first child was born. I missed his first birthday. I would have missed his first steps, but Ugandan Airlines delayed a flight to Entebbe for twenty-four hours. In those hours, I watched Mark take his first fumbling steps, and cried, overwhelmed. Yet, instead of staying home, I did take that delayed flight. And the next plane. And the next. 'Trust me, David, I will get off a plane on the other side of the world, and you're either talking on the TV screen or there's a book of yours in the bookshop, or an article you've written in the paper,' a friend, Sir Trevor McDonald, remarked. Infectious industriousness, Trevor called it.

We all had it, the road warriors of the news business. Some told themselves it was a moral imperative, stories need to be told, the truth must be revealed, the wrongs of the world need to be righted. Bullshit. There were no more competitive animals on the road than reporters competing for a story. The reason, we all knew, lay in the ego-driven nature of the business. The 'me' factor in the business of journalism. On the road, we were rivals during the day and bar buddies in the evening. In Africa, my mentor, and rival was John Humphrys, a lean Welshman who later became the most influential radio journalist in Britain. 'No need to think too much about this, David,' John said. 'Journalism is a compulsive disorder, and we're all sick with it, loving every minute.'

At what price? My day of reckoning had arrived in Sibley Hospital, Washington DC. When I came out of an emergency angiogram, the surgeon looked wry. 'Good news, Mr Smith, you do not have your father's heart.' The bad news, a few months short of my fiftieth birthday, was that life was now on borrowed time. Change or die. What was there to celebrate? I wanted to disappear, from family and friends, from everyone, and escape to a hideout, preferably in wine country, California. Nobody had to tell me. I knew what I had to do.

# Temptation

Were we nuts? A British TV correspondent and a CNN TV anchor, both based in Washington DC. Our daily life one of deadlines, stress, screaming producers, the cellphone never turned off. Glamour, certainly. Cocktails at embassies, interviews at the State Department, the occasional evening at the White House. And yet. And yet. The reality of 24/7 was all work, all the time. Or, as my television-star wife concluded: 'Do your job well; and your payoff is – work on Saturdays, Sundays, and midnight as well.'

Why not just give it all up?

Live in a vineyard, miles from where we abided and worked, a world away from the cosmopolitan circles we moved in. Swap our natural habitat of newsroom, corporate office and diplomatic mission; change out of dry-cleaned suits into muddy boots and sunglasses. Sit back, sip our wine and watch the grapes grow. Ah, the temptation. Life would be good.

How could anyone resist? The hunt began, for a small plot of land, far away from it all, to grow vine.

'What, exactly, do we know about making wine?' asked Sonia, taking off her TV make-up.

'It's made from grapes,' I ventured.

'Red grapes for red wine; white grapes for white,' she agreed. 'What about rosé? Is that made by mixing them both up?'

I gave her a look I usually reserve for our children when faced with a why-is-the-sky-blue question.

Sonia, of course, was from Argentina. She viewed my enthusiasm for this grand adventure as a British eccentricity, an Arthurian quest, if you like, with no grounding in reality.

'And what, exactly, do we know about growing grapes?' she persevered across the dinner table.

This lack of faith was getting tiresome. 'Darling, grapes grow in the earth, from plants' – I started uncorking an everyday California Chardonnay, *squeak, squeak, pop* – 'and folks like you and me, after a shitty day at work, are glad to pour themselves a glass and drink it. That's all we need to know.'

# One Sip at a Time

'How do you make a small fortune out of wine?' (*Pause.*) 'Well, you start with a large one . . . '

In the wine world, that joke has done the rounds. You had to be a little naïve to own and grow a vineyard. Unless you were very savvy, and needed a loss-making investment to offset for tax purposes. We were in the naïve category. But it did not take long to find out the bleakness of the business plan. First, plant grape. Watch it earn little or nothing for at least three years. Once you can harvest, stake almost everything on making a wine. If it is a red wine, it will take another two years to be ready to sell. Then the going gets tough. It is not just the competition of thousands of new wines on the market every year. No, it is much simpler than that, and from a business perspective, more daunting. It is the law of supply and demand. There is too much wine in the world, way too much. The truth is that martinis are conquering the world, leaving the wine makers shaken and stirred.

Wine is made in more than sixty countries, almost a third of the nations on the planet. Leave aside production in Turkmenistan or Madagascar, the business reality is that the Old World is drowning in subsidized European Union wine lakes, while the New World is choking with new grapevines, from Adelaide to Walla Walla.

Still, the good news, from our perspective, was that we had sixty countries to choose from, to chase the dream of a vineyard.

We discussed what we would look for. Stability, both economic and political, might be a factor, yes? Constitutional safeguards about getting money in and out, yes? A safe investment climate, for sure. We would like to sleep knowing that our new home had a long history of peace and security, respect for individual freedom; in short, that our money was safe.

So what about France, 200-odd years since they stopped beheading leaders, right? Or Italy, a country known as the land of vines since the Romans ruled, even if it did have, shall we say, some unique business practices? Or the USA, land of the free – though perhaps, the not-so-free-to-drink-alcohol? After all, when an American under the age of twenty-one drank a Lite beer, he broke the law.

And yet, France, hmmm, already on the road to its own funeral, according to one of my Gallic friends. And then, Italy, drowning in European wine lakes of subsidized swill. Whereas in the USA it cost only half a million dollars for every acre in the Napa valley. Perfect for dot.com billionaires. Yet for us, of humbler bank accounts, that left . . . Argentina.

Argentina? Yes, we ended up choosing Argentina as the place to launch our dream of a vineyard. The same Argentina I first visited as a journalist back in the days when a military government murdered its young, making its opponents 'disappear'. A country I returned to later, in 1982, as a war correspondent, when my country fought for the Falkland Islands, or Malvinas. I survived the war, hospitalized. Unfortunately, not for a heroic war wound, but a humiliating appendix surgery. The very same Argentina I saw wracked by economic chaos in the late 1980s, with hyperinflation destroying wages by the minute. This was the Argentina that gave the world tango, gauchos, Maradona and Evita. A nation not for the faint of heart. A grand nation, with the heart of a diva.

# Valentine's Day

The search for a vineyard was not going well. I was sick in bed, with yet another bug doing the rounds of our daughter's daycare centre, staring at another bleak winter in Washington DC. But this time, as a peace gesture, Sonia bought me the Lonely Planet guide to *Argentina*.

'Check out Salta,' she said as she headed to another day in the TV studio. 'There's soup in the fridge.'

'Salta?'

'It's supposed to be beautiful. And it has vineyards, somewhere.'

A–ha. Now we are talking.

Salta, way up north in Argentina, close to Bolivia, with high mountains and colonial towns. It looked promising. Vineyards, highest in the world. Cafayate. I could see myself on a horse, with a poncho, viewing my vines. All I needed to do was get Sonia there, drive around, and we would find our land, I was sure of it. The Lonely Planet guide was refreshingly practical. Cafayate was only a four-hour bus drive from the nearest airport, Salta, which was a two-hour flight from Buenos Aires. There was no ATM machine in Cafayate, it warned, so bring plenty of cash. There was a place to stay, but it did not appear to have internet access. There was no car rental.

As my wife returned home that evening, I greeted her with, 'Are you nuts? Have you looked where Salta is?'

She gave me one of her Argentine, what-did-you-expect looks.

'There's always Chile,' I suggested.

'Never,' she vetoed. 'The Chileans don't like us.'

'Your brother lives there,' I reminded her.

'Yes, but he doesn't tell them he's Argentine.'

This was true. He told them he was a citizen of the Netherlands, not a son of Buenos Aires. But I knew how we could make a go of Chile. 'The Chileans love the Brits. They will love me.'

One look at my wife, and I knew I had made a mistake.

'The Chileans,' Sonia hissed, 'helped the Brits during the Malvinas.'

OK. Chile was out. Salta was out. My vision of myself in a poncho was not looking good.

But the British Empire was not conquered by giving up, I reminded myself. Maybe the Lonely Planet exaggerated.

And that was when the Lonely Planet guide changed my life.

'Darling, what about – Mendoza?'

'Mendoza?'

'It has vineyards,' I explained tentatively.

Sonia gave me another Argentine look, this time of where-have-you-been? 'Of course it has vineyards. It's wine country. Lorraine lives there; I spent every school summer with her, on her vineyard.'

It was my turn to give her one of *my* looks.

'In a vineyard?' I repeated, slowly.

'Of course. It's wine country.'

Unbelievable. We had been looking, dreaming, fantasizing about where to buy a vineyard of our own for three years by now, and not once, not once, had Argentina's most famous wine district been mentioned by my very Argentine wife.

And that was that. We knew where to look for our vineyard. It had to be in Mendoza.

# Don't Cry for Me

It is fair to say that, for me, there was one Argentina before Sonia, a country which gave me chills, somehow blending beauty and passion with torture and murder even before its generals went to war with my own. And then there was Argentina after Sonia, the country of my heart, my adopted home and the seat of my future dreams.

In between, the Argentina I saw as a journalist, the reeling nation dancing a wild tango from dictatorship to democracy, from juntas to Peronism, from war to peace. To love Argentina, as I discovered, was a life-long passion, which sometimes broke your heart. Not unlike my Argentine wife. Still, it helped that I played a very small part in ending the war between our two countries. The Falklands War, or Malvinas War.

From a distance, from my base as a young correspondent in Madrid, I had watched Argentina spiral into military dictatorship in the mid 1970s. As Franco died, and Spain transitioned peacefully to democracy, my colleagues in Buenos Aires reported the journey in the other direction. Blood-letting between left and right, death squads with names like Triple A, the Argentine Anticommunist Alliance, taking out student activists, union leaders, dissenting journalists, while on the left the People's Revolutionary Army kidnapped oil and car company executives, raising ransoms that broke the *Guinness Book of Records*. In March 1976, the military seized power in Buenos Aires and ousted General Perón's widow, Isabelita, who took over the presidency after he died. Like Evita before her, she was a nightclub performer who had caught Perón's roving eye, in Panama, and then outlived him to become his political heir.

Isabelita chose exile in Madrid, and it fell to me to keep an eye on her and her adviser-cum-lover, a true Machiavelli named José López Rega, as they settled into a fashionable suburb called Villanueva. From my distance, Argentina's drama seemed more farce than nightmare. Isabel, a cabaret performer with no claim to power except she had bedded General Perón after Evita died. López Rega, Rasputin to them both, a mason with ties to arms smugglers and death squads, the power behind the ageing Perón throne. The little we gleaned about them was equally bizarre. According to staff whom they had fired, they never ventured outside without consulting astrological charts, and they seemed to practice rituals normally associated with the occult. I concluded the sources were prejudiced by having been dismissed, and that there was no basis for filing a story on these two.

Little did we know, at that stage, what the mad couple behind the high wall in Villanueva had bequeathed to their country. A military dictatorship, acting it said in the name of God and Christian civilization, the very language General Franco had used down the years in Spain, moving against opponents with brutal impunity as Franco did decades before. Thousands tortured. Thousands murdered. Tens of thousands who disappeared, never to be seen again. In the name of the father, the son and the holy ghost, with the complicity of Catholic leaders, the military junta of Argentina kidnapped the country and murdered its young.

Looking back, what was so revealing was that the world turned a blind eye and went on doing business with the murderers, culminating in the staging of the World Cup in Argentina in 1978. No one boycotted that tournament, no country thought even twice about going, and while the media reported demonstrations in Buenos Aires by mothers seeking information on children who had disappeared, more headlines were generated by footballers behaving badly. In Britain, it was the saga of a Scottish player taking drugs, and the Scottish manager making delusional claims about his team's prowess. In Italy, where I was based by then, it was *la tragedia* of the national team's loss to Holland, with scant attention paid to the real tragedy of Argentina.

Sadly, the world only woke up to the reality of Argentina's catastrophe with the invasion of the Falkland Islands in 1982, and the subsequent war with Britain. For me, personally, it was a short campaign, dispatched to South America by my network. One dodgy ham sandwich, and I lost my appendix to a Spanish surgeon at a British hospital in Uruguay. Maybe it was the time spent convalescing, as the British Army stomped across the peat bogs of those distant islands, but I was haunted by one thought. Only General Leopoldo Galtieri of Argentina, a drunk who had little grasp of how the world worked, and Margaret Thatcher of Finchley, London, could have gone to war over those islands. Both leaders, facing trouble at home, seeking respite abroad. One needed the other to justify conflict.

First, the theatre. General Galtieri gave speeches on sovereignty and Argentina's geographic claim to the islands. Mrs Thatcher insisted war had to be waged to defend the rule of international law, and defend the world against dictators invading other countries. Galtieri strutted with his swagger-stick before cheering crowds. Mrs Thatcher emerged from No. 10 Downing Street to urge the nation to celebrate victory at sea. Britain's Boadicea teaching a lesson to wild Johnny Gaucho. While the general was responsible for starting the conflict, Mrs Thatcher was not for turning once she had dispatched the task force to the South Atlantic. Conversations down the years, with the key US intermediaries, the likes of Henry Kissinger, Alexander Haig, Jeanne Kirkpatrick, confirmed that my Prime Minister refused to consider a diplomatic solution once she had set her course against the general. One key mediator, Peru's President Fernando Belaunde Terry, insisted when I visited him in the late 1980s, that Mrs Thatcher had knowingly 'torpedoed' a peace settlement by ordering the sinking of Argentina's warship, the *Belgrano*.

She also made sure the British public would not get television news images of the battles. As the fleet headed south, the two main British TV networks, the BBC and ITN, worked together furiously to enable teams embedded with the British Navy to beam back pictures to London from the flagship carrier, *Hermes*. An irrepressible geek of a man named Peter Heaps, a brilliant ITN engineer who made the impossible seem work-aday, devised a satellite path that would have meant same-day pictures from the war, as long as the Navy shut down communications from a sizeable warship for a few minutes. The decision went to Downing Street, and the Prime Minister said no. Politically, a sound decision. Because if Britain had seen same-day pictures of its sailors and marines dying, as they did die, in agony, and chaos, and despair, in defence of territory 5,000 miles from London, it was debatable how well public opinion would have held up. As it was, it took two to three weeks for the pictures to reach Britain. By then the fighting was over. Considering that same summer we broadcast Israel's invasion of Lebanon, live from Beirut, or that thirteen years before we all watched live pictures of the moon landing, I would never again say that censorship was exercised solely by dictators.

Winners write history, and Margaret Thatcher buried the generals of Argentina. From that war on, I had assumed that any British national would not be particularly welcome in Argentina. I was wrong.

In fact, after Mrs Thatcher dispatched the generals, the military retreated in shame, back to barracks, or to prison, and the country returned to democracy with exuberance. By the time I returned to Buenos Aires in the late 1980s, it was to witness a country in chaos, but democracy in bloom. Sometimes the two went together. Hyperinflation had taken the country by the throat. I had only ever heard of hyper-inflation in the history books, mentioned in the same sentence as the Versailles Treaty, always warning that Germany's hyperinflation was one of the principle causes of the rise of Hitler. In Argentina, hyper-inflation was a lesson in frenzy. Every supermarket hired price punchers to keep sticking higher prices on every milk carton, can of beans and toilet roll. Shop in the morning because prices will rise by afternoon. Spend what you have now, immediately, because you know it will be worth less in an hour or two. Pray for *la estabilidad*, stability. The only happy people were those paying off fixed loans. That monthly car payment? No problem, it was now cheaper than the price of a dinner.

But with all the chaos of hyperinflation, there was no sign, none whatsoever, of the military making a move. Even as the President, a lawyer named Raúl Alfonsín, lost control, no one voiced the fear that the tanks might roll in. Once Mrs Thatcher had whipped the generals, the military concluded their role was no longer to rule the country, as they had felt entitled to do for half a century. They stayed in their barracks and let the civilians run the show.

# El Show

And what a showman they got. The man who came to power, via a noisy, no-holds-barred election in 1989, was one Carlos Menem. Señor Menem looked like a figure from gaucho central casting, jet-black sideburns, hair almost to pony-tail length, leather jackets, cowboy boots and heavy jewellery, with a reputation for womanizing and shady deals. But Menem exercised power with a street savvy and cunning that defied caricature. The first time I interviewed him, just as the election campaign started in late 1988, he took me aback by using the interview to make news, news I simply had not expected. He wanted to sit down with 'La Thatcher', as he called the British Prime Minister. He wanted a conversation with Madame Thatcher. And he wanted to talk to her face-to-face, not in some alternative arena such as the United Nations. This broke with Argentina's repudiation of Thatcher, and with Argentina's formal position that the Malvinas issue could only be settled at the United Nations. But the next President of Argentina knew what he was doing. He was signalling to the wider world that he would do business with everyone, even 'La Thatcher'. He was saying to Wall Street, and the World Bank, and investors: you have nothing to fear, much to gain, by listening to me. And he knew how to use my television network to achieve his goals.

I knew I was being used. It was always a curious ballet when a politician, particularly a president or prime minister, wanted to use your microphone. At one and the same time it was thrilling, worrying, challenging. I hated being used, yet I wanted to get the story, be the first to know what signal they wanted to send. The secret was to be clear with my questions, what I needed to have answered, yet always to listen closely, very closely.

A few weeks after Carlos Menem took power, I received a call from his chief of staff at the Casa Rosada, the pink Presidential Palace in Buenos Aires. President Menem sent his best wishes and would like to see me in Buenos Aires. If I could spare the time. I made the time, and sold my editors on the expense of sending me with the beautiful Argentine producer who had just joined the company.

My hunch? That Menem wanted to announce that he would go anywhere, any time, to meet Margaret Thatcher and negotiate the future of the Malvinas. That he would even name a date. That he would offer a neutral location. He had already instructed his foreign ministry to hold low-level talks in Buenos Aires and London later that week. My concern? It made Menem look good, but it represented an offer Madame Thatcher could instantly refuse because it did not mean an end to the state of war. It would be seen in London as largely posturing on his part, playing to the court of international opinion, little more. So for this adventure to work, President Menem of Argentina had to end the Malvinas War, irrefutably, undeniably, on my television camera. Only then would we avoid the trap of being seen to be used by a country still in conflict with Britain. On the long flight to Buenos Aires, the Argentine producer encouraged me to ask my questions, but clearly thought it seriously naïve of me to imagine her new President was going to oblige. 'Do you have any idea how we are all taught from the first day of primary school in Argentina that the Malvinas are ours!' she remarked, with a flush in her cheeks that spoke to pride laced with anger.

In his office at the Casa Rosada, President Menem could not have been more gracious as he ordered coffee, chatted with the producer about her Argentine roots, then sat down to swap football stories while the cameras were set up. We had seen him playing the game himself with the immortal Diego Maradona, and he delighted in telling us how Maradona had set up a goal for him to score in a charity match, both of them in the national team shirts of white and sky-blue. ITN had hired an immensely likeable Chilean named Ricardo Correa for this adventure. Ricardo had a bad hair day, losing his wallet the night before, looking like he had just woken up, hungover, confused, not even sure how he wanted to film this or where to put the cameras. Finally, *el Presidente* said he had another meeting shortly, and the Argentine producer, clearly exasperated, exclaimed: 'Let's just roll please. Now!'

And President Menem ended the war. On camera. For the record. Once and for all.

First came the bluster, the display of defiance that any politician in his position had to deliver to his own people, who would hear and read of this interview in the local media. 'We are going to insist and insist,'

Menem told me with a fixed glare that suggested Braveheart taking on the Anglos. 'One of man's great virtues is perseverance and Argentina is going to persevere as it has since 1833 when the Malvinas were taken away from us.' Did Argentina still claim sovereignty over the islands? 'Yes, yes, yes,' he replied, clearly loving that piece of theatre. I stayed silent, letting him fill the void. 'But it is a subject we can put under the umbrella of talks, as they say. I want talks to get relations restored between our two countries so that afterwards we can discuss sovereignty.' That note of compromise had opened the door to the question I wanted answered. Keep it simple, I remember thinking, don't leave too much wiggle-room for diplospeak that meant no one would be sure what he really was saying.

'Mr President . . . ' Rarely did I use a politician's title on-air, because to me it suggested deference. But I wanted to appeal to the man's sense of self-importance before I put him on the spot. 'Mr President, is the Malvinas, the Falklands war over?'

'*Sí.* It is definitely over. The war is over. There is absolutely no chance of another war.'

Make my day, Mr President. Thank you, and good-night. We had a lead story, headlines in the British newspapers. More importantly, the US Administration welcomed the end of war. The government led by 'La Thatcher' had been given the irrefutable cue to talk. And I got the biggest hug from the Argentine Producer, Sonia.

# War, Peace and Skirts

Margaret Thatcher towered over British politics, ruling with an iron handbag, and she and I had a curious history in our encounters.

At the beginning and end of her public life, I had chance meetings with Madame Thatcher. First, when she was the young, local Member of Parliament for Finchley, in the late 1960s. A hard-working MP, she made the effort to visit the local schools. My duty, as head boy of Finchley Catholic Grammar School, was to accompany Margaret Thatcher, MP, through the grounds. She stepped out of her slightly battered Ford Cortina, which she drove herself, and adjusted her hat, a quite ghastly concoction. Doing the tour, as we proudly showed her our library, a piece of masonry fell from the ceiling, missing us all by a matter of inches. 'Oh dear,' she remarked, 'that sort of thing makes such a mess.' She still had her original, high-pitched voice, nothing like the media-trained tenor of her Downing Street years.

But by the late 1960s Margaret Thatcher was a hard-working mother of twins, with a fairly well-off husband. She was of my mother's generation, truly the first of her kind. Only one generation of women before, my grandmother had been the first to enjoy the power to vote. Yet Margaret Thatcher, the daughter of a greengrocer, led that second generation, and won power. The feminists fumed that she was nothing more than an honorary man. But the fact was that Margaret Thatcher dispelled the myth, once and for all, that women could not lead their countries, in peace, in war and in skirts.

Almost forty years later, she came to Washington to bid farewell to her closest political ally, Ronald Reagan. The funeral, at the National Cathedral in Washington DC, was grand, sombre, and reinforced the myth that President Reagan had ended the Cold War single-handedly with a vivid moment in Berlin: 'Mr Gorbachev, tear down this wall.' Sick as she was, hollowed out by the onset of dementia, she made the ceremony. Poignantly, her tribute to 'Ronnie' had been recorded months earlier, while she was more lucid. It played, on a giant video screen, while she sat silently in the front pew that day. Waiting for my boss, the

Secretary-General of the United Nations, I met her leaving the service as she headed off to California with her daughter Carol, the only politician invited by Nancy Reagan to travel with the family, to the burial ground on the Reagan Estate at Santa Barbara. As she left, I shook her hand and asked her daughter to convey my best wishes, unsure if her fading memory would understand. But she still had the same proud, strong eyes.

In between those bookends, I had witnessed her skill, determination and bloody-mindedness, not as Prime Minister at home, but as a stateswoman abroad. Sometimes her obstinacy masked her genius, I concluded. She saw, before anyone else, that Mikhail Gorbachev was 'a man we can do business with', in her memorable phrase, a new kind of Soviet Communist party leader, capable of bringing the Cold War to an end. Spending an evening with her at the British Embassy in Moscow, as the Soviet Union collapsed, she refused to listen to any suggestion that her friend, Mikhail Gorbachev, was losing control of the revolution. 'You look sceptical, young man,' she scolded me on TV. 'I tell you that Mr Gorbachev will survive.' She was wrong about that.

But that stubbornness could be such an asset. On a visit to Israel and the Occupied Palestinian Territories, she single-handedly charmed the two sides, then bullied them both into finding new ways to talk to each other. At a cocktail party given in her honour by then Israeli Prime Minister Shimon Peres, she flattered her host like a woman in love, and Peres clearly reciprocated. One Israeli journalist called their chemistry 'a political lustfest'. Then, the following day, she summoned a meeting of Palestinian figures from the West Bank and Gaza, travelled across the line to East Jerusalem, and did exactly the same. The Palestinian leadership, such as newspaper editor Hannah Siniora and longtime negotiator Saeb Erakat, positively swooned over Thatcher's style and substance.

Characteristically, she gave both sides a telling-off when she left. At the press conference in the ballroom of the King David Hotel in Jerusalem, she challenged them equally, without fear or favour, to seek peace. 'Friends need to speak with candour,' she declared. 'And those of us who are your friends tell you candidly: it is enemies who make peace with each other. It is enemies who must find the arena in which to sit down, and talk.'

Next to me sat Denis, her husband. Throughout the press conference, she took his eyeline, focused on him as her audience, and spoke to him. 'Hear, hear,' Denis agreed more than once, as she hammered home her call for Palestinians and Israelis to negotiate. 'Hear, hear, Margaret,' he nodded, as she tried to jolt them, Israelis and Palestinians, to recognize the *realpolitik* of peace.

Denis was a likeable man, but often misunderstood as being merely buffoonish. Now, Denis did specialize in the hilarious. 'I've just opened the largest s—thouse in the world,' he once remarked within our hearing, after cutting the ribbon on a British-made sewer in Cairo. But Denis was loyal, to the point of giving me a tongue-lashing for a tough interview with his wife. 'Denis, he's just doing his job,' she scolded him. The man, so often mocked as a gin and tonic sidekick, was perhaps the secret of her strength, I judged, as far back as when she was a young MP for Finchley, driving that battered Ford Cortina, his wealth enabling her to pursue her dreams, and his unstinting support nurturing her extraordinary self-belief. Denis was the unseen key to her ascent, as she set out to charm and handbag the world.

# At First Sight

If Mrs Thatcher could make peace with Argentina, it was fair that I should also give it a chance. Even if I viewed with alarm my Argentine wife's eye for a leather handbag.

Mendoza was not for the faint-hearted. The highest mountains in the Americas dominated the western horizon. The sun had no mercy at midday. It was officially a desert, with rare rainfall, barely enough to keep grey scrawny bushes alive. When moisture did fall, it tended to be ice stones, *piedra*, large hail, that destroyed crops. It was an earthquake zone, living on the tectonic plates that so devastated Chile when I was a child and again in recent years. Other than that, it was paradise.

One by one, we toured the wine regions. Lunlunta, too close to the city. Tupungato, too remote. San Rafael, too far a drive. Agrelo, too many large wineries. But then, in the Valle de Uco, we discovered a small village, La Consulta, which seemed neither too big nor too small, neither too far nor too close. Just right.

La Consulta was a one-traffic-light village, with a few shops and restaurants, all of which closed for siesta time. Nothing stirred after 1 p.m. Even the stray dogs slept. But just outside La Consulta, driving out towards the Andes, was a plot of land for sale.

The road to get there was a track of pebbles, definitely the road less travelled. The field had five rows of poplars, and one gnarled splendid cedar pine. Except, except, except. From this small field, looking west, stood the Andes – so stark, so mighty, so monumental, God himself would be awed by his handiwork. A view so sublime, so tempting, it was priceless.

We saw it, and we knew. We knew. We took pictures of the land, the mountains, even the corn stalks. One image stood out, the two of us with our daughter Alegría, a baby in arms. We joked about calling the farm Finca Alegría. You see, we did know. This was it. If ever there was a wrong frame of mind in which to negotiate a good price, this was it. Love at first sight.

We fell in love with the view. And a field of onions, corn and tomatoes, with little else to recommend it.

But before you commit, you introduce your love to your friends, right? Just to make sure that you have not momentarily taken leave of your senses.

I decided I needed a seasoned Mendoza spirit whom I trusted. Meet Daniel, labour rights lawyer, aspiring politician, man-about-town. And in Mendoza, where who you knew counted for loyalty, he was, above all, the husband of Sonia's friend. That was what brought us together, in a friendship that would endure highs and lows, the low of their eventual divorce, the high of him winning a seat in Congress.

Daniel always gave me good advice. A *Mendocino* in both style and substance, he had the air of a man in charge. Tall, imposing, he had made his name winning compensation for workers injured in third-world industrial conditions. He was not easily frightened; if anything, he was intimidating. So it was Daniel who drove with me, alone, *hombre a hombre*, to vet this love of mine, this tomato field. Should I commit? He explained all his savings were in land, a plot here, a *finca* there. 'Never trust the banks,' he warned. I laughed at his distrust, and wondered at this lack of sophistication, the kind of thing I expected to hear from old ladies stuffing stashes under their mattress, not earning any interest, unlike sophisticated first-world me. But I was encouraged that he was favourably inclined towards my love, this field, a ninety-minute drive from his house in the city of Mendoza.

From my house in Washington DC, Mendoza was only a fourteen-hour plane journey, over three separate flights in the course of one long night. And this field, only another hour and a half from the airport. It was not that far really, I reasoned. Unless I missed a flight connection. But otherwise I could do it in a night and a morning, door to gate. Leave Washington after work at 5 p.m. and arrive on the land by noon the next day. Nothing really, I reasoned.

So there we were. Two men, one English, one Argentine, looking out at the mountains, walking along the onions, fingering clumps of earth as if we knew what we were looking for. Daniel sniffed a tomato, bit into it. Looked at the fields next door. The pig pen a hundred yards away. The towering mountains. He reached his verdict.

'*Inglés*,' he slapped my back, '*compre*.' – 'Englishman, buy.'

And that was how Daniel became our lawyer, the man who would sign the deal.

Back in Washington DC it was time to raise the money. Luckily, banks were offering home equity loans as eagerly as friendly neighbours handed out chocolates at Halloween. We would remortgage our house to pay for the land.

'Mamá is on the phone, from Buenos Aires.'

I nodded. I liked my wife's mother.

'She wants to talk to you.' Sonia gave me the look.

I picked up, based on years of training. Never cross an Argentine woman.

'David, can you hear me?' It was the voice of the matriarch. 'You can *not* do this. You will never see you money back. Listen to me. Never, ever, put your money in Argentina. You cannot trust this country, do you hear me?'

I murmured. It was always nice to know you could count on the support of family and the unwavering loyalty of Argentines for their own country.

'Loyalty, patriotism, that's for the World Cup, you idiot,' clarified my wife, 'not for money. That's why we have Switzerland.'

## 13 September

We owned a vineyard. Well, not exactly. It didn't have a single vine on it yet. But we could see them. It didn't have a house on it. But, in our mind's eye, it stood. It didn't produce a wine yet. But we knew it would.

But it had already made one huge difference in our lives. We had a hefty monthly payment to make, in solid US dollars. Our priceless view, we now knew, carried a price tag. The great Argentine experiment with stability had pegged every Argentine peso to the US dollar. One for one. Every dollar we earned was worth one peso. And now we had signed the deal, every dollar we earned would, for the foreseeable future, certainly become a peso. Every love affair had a price. 'For richer, for poorer . . . for as long as we both shall live.'

## 20 December

'Mamá is on the phone from Buenos Aires for you, David,' Sonia said after a chat with her parents. 'She sounds worried.'

I had only left my wife's mother two days before, in Buenos Aires.

'David, the country is collapsing.' She did sound frightened. 'The peso is collapsing. Everyone is out in the streets, banging pans.'

This became *el colapso*. Within hours, the peso went into free-fall. No more one-to-one with the US dollar. Banks froze all accounts. Overnight, millions lost their savings. Everyone lost what they had, all their bank savings, except the wise old ladies with mattresses of dollars. And my stout-hearted lawyer friend, 'never trust the banks', Daniel.

Our vineyard investment was collapsing with it. Our field plummeted in value; on paper it was almost worthless. At best, we overpaid royally.

'What do you think?' I asked my wife over the Christmas holiday that saw Argentina go through five presidents in thirteen days. After all, it was her country flushing down the toilet. 'No point in selling now, is there?'

The land, our dream vineyard-to-be, well, it was still ours. Not worth anything. But ours. Certainly not the smartest investment we ever made, but what could you do? No point in selling out then.

'It's not a real loss,' she murmured. 'It's just paper.'

I agreed. You see, I did not buy a view, I bought a dream. I might have been paying for it every day, but I was living it. Worthless on paper, but worthwhile to me.

We drank to that.

All our money in Argentina vaporized. The government froze all bank accounts, and we, like many others, never saw a cent again. But we did get a rose, a pink rose, three years later, courtesy of a Citibank teller, once we finally gave up on trying to get the money back, and closed the account.

So every day Argentina reminded us of our place in the universe. We were in the hands of economic forces beyond our control, as well as natural ones. Our destiny was not entirely our own. The government could snap its fingers and *adiós* our business. One hailstorm could destroy our harvest in five minutes. All of it. Gone. We could lose everything, any hour, every single day. This was living on the edge. And it was not in our control. A humbling experience for any control freak, as most journalists are. The only way to cope was to remind myself I had chosen this, and to remember why. It was more than an investment. More than a dream. In my mind, it was my one best way of staying alive.

And we might also win. If we were patient, those same forces of nature could gift us an extraordinary harvest. One day. When we had planted our vines. When the grapes were mature. When the country recovered. When we could make a wine. When we had the perfect harvest. A harvest so great, our wine would conquer the world, or if not, we prayed, at least win over the palate of one fine gentleman with a million-dollar nose living not far away from us, in the United States.

Hope, they said, was the last thing to go. Remember the joke? How do you make a small fortune out of wine? We did not find the punchline very funny any more.

\*

Daniel, lawyer, politician, friend:

The first time I saw this land with David, I just remember thinking two words: majestic and tranquil. There are so many ways to see the mountains when you live in Mendoza; in the course of a day you can glimpse the mountains from half a dozen different angles. And you don't have to be in the country, you can see those peaks from the city of Mendoza. But, listen, the view from their vineyard is captivating, it grabs you by the brain, and the heart, demands your attention. So I understood how David and Sonia felt. I felt it the minute I saw the place. That's why I said: '*Inglés, compre.*' It was a decision that took itself.

I learned very quickly, because I represented them, that these were serious people. David loves to make fun of everything, but this is a person of intent. The country was one foot in the grave when they first came here, the economy was already on a death spiral. But they saw the opportunity, and they never backed away when it got tough. There were hard negotiations with the owners of the land, there all sorts of problems over water rights, and tenants living on the land, and the banks letting us move dollars, let alone the price the people wanted. And all of it was complicated by the fact that the land is in a military zone: you're so close to the mountains there that it's part of the frontier region with Chile. There's a big military barracks not so far away, with the Regiment of the Mountains stationed there. You know, just in case the crazy

Chileans do something. David and Sonia told me to do what was right, negotiate the best deal possible, but be fair. And they made it clear going in: we are going to buy this land.

Has David told you the secret of the purchase? Across the road from their land was a huge vineyard, which had been bought and planted by the French company, Moët & Chandon. Before we agreed to a final price on his land, David kept wondering how much the French had paid for theirs. Then I remembered I had a friend who had worked for Moët in their management. I arranged for the two of them to have dinner, and so David asks him to find out how much they paid for the land, the price of a hectare. When we heard the number, we knew we would be paying a lot less than the big boys. So it was a sound negotiation, because we knew how much land in the Altamira zone could be worth.

David says that I've always given him important advice. I don't know about that; seems to me we laugh together more than we do business. I do remember he came to lunch at the Congress in Buenos Aires, when I was a *Diputado*, and I told him to plant the vines and build a house immediately. Now. Not tomorrow, or next month, or next year. Now. I could see from internal government memoranda we received at the Congress that inflation was taking off again, and that labour costs, for example, would be going through the roof. Particularly in Mendoza, because there was a boom building with all the wine investment, and foreign companies coming in. In the underlying economic numbers I could see how prices could explode in a matter of months. I know he acted on that. He did plant, he did build. I'm relieved that he did, because had he waited the costs would have been much higher. And, given the country's general direction, the risks would have seemed even greater.

I hope David is ready for risk for as long as he lives here. Sonia understands that in her blood, she grew up with it. But David will have to learn that risk is a hardy perennial in Argentina. It's just the way we are, and the way we live . . .

\*

# Cruel Winter

A few months later I returned to Buenos Aires to report on a country in freefall, an economy in meltdown and a government that proudly boasted the biggest default in history. Indeed, my friend Daniel was one of the parliamentarians who cheered from the rafters inside the Congress when the third of those five Presidents announced that Argentina would not pay its debts.

Yet almost everywhere you turned in the capital, in the depths of a July winter in the southern hemisphere, you saw stark, chilling reminders of the misery the country's collapse inflicted on its people. Argentines always celebrated the fact that at one period in their history, in the 1920s and 1930s, they were the richest people on earth, per capita. They invariably cited their natural wealth, everything from their mouth-watering meat to their oil wells. The country that had everything. The other America, so they said. Now, tragically, in the aftermath of that historic default, the unthinkable had struck Argentina.

Hunger: vividly personified by mothers and daughters begging on the streets of Buenos Aires, by fathers and sons scavenging in garbage dumps, by whole families setting up cardboard shacks on street corners. Before dawn, thousands gathered outside European embassies, waiting for days in bitter cold for the chance to emigrate. Such a poignant image: their ancestors had fled Italy, and Spain, and Holland because of poverty, now the descendants sought exile in Madrid, and Rome, and Amsterdam because of the very same. At night more crowds gathered outside the offices of the newspapers, men and women lining up for hours to get a free copy of the first edition with the classified ads for jobs.

Ironically, I arranged to see my old TV adversary, President Carlos Menem, once the darling gaucho of Wall Street and the World Bank for opening Argentina to dollarization in the 1990s. But not to talk about the economy. The former President's fall mirrored that of his country. He had gone from his cosy golf meetings with the US President, his speeding red Ferrari and his girlfriends, to the less accommodating life of an accused felon for illegal arms shipments. After days of secret negotiations, because the court specifically outlawed any press meetings or interviews with him, I was driven to the rendezvous by one of his oldest advisers, a small video camera buried under my baggy winter coat.

When we reached the house that had become prison, in the fashionable Buenos Aires suburb of Don Torcuato, two police guards at the gate asked me to step out to be frisked, then waved us on when Menem's adviser vouched for me. In the garden sat half a dozen armed agents, smoking and sipping coffee. We were ushered into a rather humble reception room, where Menem was waiting. The greeting as warm as ever, he wanted to know how Sonia was, how many children we had, how my Argentine in-laws were faring in the crisis. I wondered about his spirits. 'OK, I'm OK,' he replied, but there was a sadness in his eyes, a touch of humility I had never seen in him before. He had aged dramatically, and apologized for the absence of his Chilean wife Cecilia, a former Miss Universe, half his age. 'She's having a massage.'

Obviously prison had its comforts. But he was furious the judge would not let him out to play golf. 'There's no basis for these charges, no basis,' he said. 'I'm a prisoner, for what? And I can't even play golf.' In his final years as President, Menem had been known to take his golf coach along with him when he travelled abroad as head of state.

What followed was classic Menem, and classic Argentine politics. I asked whether I could take a few pictures of our meeting, to broadcast and to show the world his situation, as I put it, even though I was thinking all it really showed was how far he had fallen. He agreed. The minute the hand-held camera rolled, Dr Menem seized the opportunity, street-wise as ever. 'I'm innocent of all these baseless charges,' he declared, knowing that I understood how he was using me, and I was using him. 'And my people must know: I will return to power, I will be a candidate again. I will return.' I was no expert on Argentine history, but even I knew this was the phrase immortalized by General Perón when he was forced into exile: '*Vuelvo. Volvere.* I will return.'

As I drove back to Buenos Aires, my celebration of a minor scoop was tempered by a call from an assistant to Dr Nicolás, my friend in the world of wine. 'I'm waiting at your hotel, and Dr Nicolás is waiting for you at his favourite restaurant.' I could not afford to keep Nicolás Catena waiting.

# Revolution in a Bottle

Hard to imagine a more unlikely revolutionary. Thin, somewhat shy, instinctively understated, always gracious and forever humble, Nicolás Catena eschewed any notion of having changed the world around him.

But my friend was the man who revolutionized Argentine wine. The pioneer who led the industry out of its high-volume, low-quality past to a seat at high table in the new world of the global wine business. The risk-taker who bet the future on a grape called Malbec and made it a worldwide star. The scientist who brought research and development to an old-style business that had lain dormant for so long. 'The Sleeping Giant' the wine buffs had, with perennial disdain, called Argentina. Dr Catena, the economist who studied not just production charts and revenue streams when time came to decide on a vineyard, but altitude and latitude, the temperature at midnight and midday. The Ph.D thinker who taught everyone lucky enough to work with him that Argentina was a serious player capable of change and challenge.

We had met Nicolás through his daughter Laura, a vivacious livewire, a doctor of medicine who made the rest of us recognize that we lived life in the slow lane. Intensely intelligent, yet always ready for a laugh and a salsa on the dance-floor, Laura Catena balanced one life as an emergency-room doctor in San Francisco with another as wife and adoring mother, and with yet another as lead player in the family business, shuttling between California and Mendoza, her devotion to the movement her father started absolute and unswerving. 'People thought my dad was crazy,' she told us on the day we met, both she and Sonia carrying babes in arms as she led us on a tour of family vineyards in Mendoza. 'Even his friends told him he was mad to think he could make Argentina compete with the best in the world.' She paused. 'But you know what? My dad had a dream, a vision, and the courage to make it happen.'

They had something special, this father and daughter. Forged, they both recalled, in her days as a student at medical school, first Harvard in Cambridge, Massachusetts, then Stanford in California. 'My dad was not the kind of parent to let you have a credit card, but he gave me one only to buy and taste wines, to learn, and help him learn too,' said Laura, clearly savouring the memory of their time together, and reminding us that she shared her father's careful ways. 'When he visited, we would sit down and try some of the world's great wines.'

The turning-point came when Nicolás had a break from the family business in the early 1980s, to take up a professorship at the University of California at Berkeley. 'I saw what the new world of American wine was achieving, in Napa and Sonoma, just a ride from us in Berkeley, wines as good as any in the world,' he recalled. 'I believed that we could do likewise in Argentina. But we had to change. And we had to accept the challenge of change.'

He went home to Mendoza, a man on a mission. He transformed the family's business first, planting new vineyards higher and higher in the Andean mountain range, bringing stainless-steel tanks and French oak barrels to the wineries, building laboratories to monitor grape throughout the growing season, employing the best and the brightest from the Old World, and training the brightest talents in Mendoza. Their ratings zoomed upwards, so too the price of his wines. The prizes followed, and the praise flowed for the man himself. He ended the millennium creating a joint venture with France's venerable Rothschild dynasty, producing a sublime blend of Argentine Malbec and Cabernet Sauvignon that the French sold proudly in old Europe. 'Nicolás has been instrumental in changing Argentine wine, more than anyone else,' judged Baron Eric de Rothschild.

To see Nicolás in his humble office on the top floor of company headquarters outside Mendoza, an awe-inspiring pyramid based on the design of a Mayan temple – 'I didn't want a French château or an Italian palazzo, we must honour our own heritage in Latin America' – was to watch a maestro at work, in complete command of an orchestra he had assembled, the businessman, the economist and the scientist all rolled into one.

'What we did was study, listen and learn, then apply,' Nicolás explained one afternoon when I visited with a well-known photographer keen to take his portrait. 'It's not about me. It's about Mendoza. It's about having vineyards among the highest in the world, with sunlight markedly more intense, a singular combination of temperature, altitude and latitude. And it's about being lucky enough to work with great people, from the bottom to the top.'

I wrote a note to him in those early days, entitled 'Revolution in a Bottle', a mini-essay designed to capture the sea-change in Argentine wine under his leadership. He chuckled, breaking into one of his warm, generous smiles. He read the first few lines, detailing Argentina's emergence from its sleep, then asked me: 'Who is the revolutionary?'

# A Life-changing Moment

So a man with Nicolás Catena's perspective was exactly what I needed to ground me after secretly filming an indicted former President. However, I was late arriving at the private dining club in the heart of Recoleta, the most elegant of neighbourhoods, *barrios*, in Buenos Aires. A rendezvous as discreet as the man. Nicolás made light of me being late. Sighing about the country's crisis, he was ever thoughtful, welcoming me with a glass of his latest award-winning red wine, named after his late mother, Angélica. We sat in a quiet corner, ordering steak. His delightful wife Elena, a successful businesswoman in her own right, helped me order my *bife*, cooked just the way I liked it. Argentines are unfailingly proud of their country's meat, and always want to make sure heathens like me enjoy it to perfection. As if anything less would not educate me on the failings of British beef.

Because I had just come from seeing the former President under house arrest, I was in my worst, most garrulous form, recalling every detail of my secret encounter, Menem's declaration to the world, his determination to return to power. I advanced the idea that Menem's arrest showed how far the country had come: democracy alive and well when you could prosecute the last President, democracy healthy when the country lived through chaos without a murmur from the military. Dr Nicolás listened patiently, but eventually cut me off, not with words but with a brown envelope which he pushed across the table.

'I hope you don't mind me interrupting, but there is great news for you in this envelope,' he said, topping up my glass. 'It is news that could change your life.'

Inside the envelope sat one sheet of paper covered in numbers. Of course, I had no idea how to interpret them, but I studied them seriously, groping for what to say. Dr Nicolás, cutting-edge thinker in full flow, explained that these were the findings of the most sophisticated and serious study he had ever made of the microclimate in Mendoza. 'The joy is in the detail, not the devil,' he laughed. By having his Research & Development team study temperature, day and night, for years in the various wine zones in the region, he had reached his conclusion.

'Your zone, Altamira, is in my view among the best in the world for growing Malbec,' he said with no emotion. 'If not the best.' It was the certitude of an analyst who delighted in raw numbers, then absolute judgement. 'You should plant vine on your land, and I can help you. I even have clones of Malbec in mind for your land.'

I could not say 'Yes', given the state of the Argentine economy, not to mention our own semi-disastrous investment, an onion field worth by then a fraction of what we paid for it. But equally I could not say 'No', certainly not to the man who had inspired and led that revolution in a bottle.

'Think about it,' Nicolás said. 'Talk to your wife.' He looked at his Elena with obvious concern. 'I'm not sure this is good business on my part, it's not something I ever do. But I could have my people plant vine on your land, you pay me for their work, then you sell me your grape. It's good for you, and for me, I hope. And it's good for Mendoza that people like you come to Mendoza, to invest, to build, to create, to bring your world to us.'

He paused, looking me squarely in the eye over the top of his glasses with an intensity I had never seen before, or since for that matter. 'Remember, crisis creates opportunity,' he said. 'You may never have another chance to fulfil your dream.'

I didn't digest the importance of that meal together at the time. Only years later, when we had planted a vineyard with his blessing, patience and help. When we had paid all the bills for vine, irrigation pipes, tractors, water reservoir. When we had suffered scything hail-storms, sought his advice about netting to protect our grape, then invested even more. When we had built a house, and seen Nicolás, Elena and Laura share our joy. When we had watched early harvests sold to his wineries, his winemakers delighted with the quality of the grape we produced for their wines. Only then did I appreciate, fully, the extraordinary partnership we had with Dr Catena and Laura, who had undoubtedly encouraged her father on this. With Nicolás and Laura on our side, everything was possible. Without them, nothing was possible. A debt that went beyond business. A debt that could never be repaid. A debt that represented a dream, after all.

Ever the astute businessman, Nicolás finished that life-changing evening in Recoleta with a simple question. 'Why did you buy that land, why there?' In other words, how had I, the complete amateur, found the pot of gold at the end of the rainbow? I ducked out of answering, first time around, with some banality about the Irish in me.

He insisted. 'What was it that made you buy that land?' he asked again as I took a final sip of his glorious wine.

The moment deserved nothing less than the truth. *In vino veritas.* 'It was the view.'

# Performance Anxiety

The first harvest for our own wine loomed rather like the first big story, a thrilling mixture of uncharted territory and performance anxiety.

Or that first encounter with the love of your life, a sublime cocktail of hope, fear, longing and yes, performance anxiety.

For me, that harvest was tied to another first. Meeting the President of the United States in the Oval Office. On the hierarchy of importance, the Washington establishment was clear: there was meeting the President; meeting the President in the rope line at a White House event; and the *summa cum laude*, meeting the President in the Oval Office. The first two were mere photo opportunities, not worth mentioning, but the Oval Office, that was worth a quiet namedrop to impress your friends. The question on my mind as I accompanied the Secretary-General of the United Nations into the West Wing, down through the Roosevelt Room, into the sunlit chamber of the Oval Office, was, 'What on earth am I doing here?'

For me, watching George Bush through a rare lens, first as a White House correspondent, then as a United Nations officer working with his administration, the lesson was never to underestimate that President. As a journalist, I did. As a diplomat, I could not.

I first saw him in action, as a candidate, raising a million dollars in an hour in a ballroom in the Washington suburbs. 'I love America and I love Americans,' he told the businessmen and women with chequebooks, back in 1999. I underestimated him, struck by the banality, missing the fact that the fellow represented a remarkably effective over-achiever, focused on the goal of the moment, raising money for his campaign. George W. Bush, the leader of my generation who truly changed our world. George W. Bush, such an achiever when you sensed how little he brought to the table.

Seeing him at work in the West Wing years later offered glimpses of his ability, his charm, his ruthlessness. Far from being slow, or stupid, or clueless, as the caricature had it, Bush focused on agenda, policy direction, his goals, and the quickest way to reach them. So, in my time, he effectively told the UN to put up and shut up over Iraq; he demanded action against Iran; he declared genocide in Darfur, then handed the crisis to the UN without offering a single peacekeeper; and he allowed attack politicians in his party to come very close to bringing down one UN Secretary-General, in defiance of the wishes of the rest of the world. He brooked little argument; he tolerated little dissent. His style was to tell you where he stood, but offer no follow-up, no further exposition of his reasons, and scant discussion.

For President Bush, politics was personal. Meetings at the Oval Office tended to cover carefully pre-agreed agendas, particularly when the UN was involved. It so happened that I was accompanying the UN Secretary-General to meet with President Bush not long after President Hugo Chávez of Venezuela had used the podium at the UN to denounce Bush as 'the devil incarnate'. 'You can smell the sulphur,' Chávez told the General Assembly. Now Bush sat in the Oval Office. He complained to Secretary-General Kofi Annan that Chávez had publicly accused him of having an affair with some Venezuelan beauty, a critic of Chávez. The Secretary-General looked at the ceiling, saying softly that he had no way of stopping the leader of a member state behaving any way he chose to behave, or words to that effect. The President returned to the subject. Chávez had given a speech suggesting Secretary of State Condi Rice had fantasies about the Venezuelan leader. Now it was not just the Secretary-General looking away, but Dr Rice as well. It was hard to escape the impression of a President who saw all politics as personal, and criticism as grounds for reprisal.

The meeting ended awkwardly. As a courtesy, we had informed the White House staff in our pre-meeting agenda sessions that Kofi Annan had undergone surgery on a shoulder a few weeks before. As he prepared to end the meeting, the President clapped him on the same shoulder.

'So, *Kofe*, who's going to get your job?' None of us could believe that our Secretary-General had just had his name mangled that way.

Diplomatic protocol prevented Kofi Annan discussing his successor.

'How's about a Moslem woman, *Kofe*?' the President persisted.

Secretary Rice intervened: 'Mr President, we have a team at the State Department looking at possible candidates.'

And so we left the Oval Office.

Whatever his critics said close up, George W. Bush represented a force of nature. As a politician, he cared little for policy, details, debating the nuances. But he changed what America stood for, arguably for ever. A President who de-limited freedom at home and legalized torture abroad. The President who re-defined world leadership as the superpower's agenda. The leader who promised the fiscal prudence of the CEO, yet spent the country into virtual bankruptcy. The man who preached less government, yet built the biggest American government in history. The President who undermined international institutions and multilateral alliances in so many arenas.

At moments like that, it fell to me to defend the UN, and Kofi Annan, in Washington DC. Put in the dock by a Congressman, or a Deputy Secretary of State, or a member of the cable news commentariat, the line of defence was simple: 'When it comes to war, or threat of war, the Secretary-General knows where he stands: on the side of peace. If he's not on that side of the argument, he shouldn't be in the job. Correct? My boss's job is to speak for peace.'

The fact remained that Kofi Annan was the first world leader to call George Bush's war in Iraq illegal and wrong. Others voiced doubts, but only after no evidence of weapons of mass destruction had surfaced from the rubble. With hindsight, others concluded that the bloodshed on the ground in Baghdad, Basra and Baqubah proved the flaws of the superpower. Others later found diplomatic channels to separate themselves from the Bush administration and its ever-shrinking coalition of the willing.

But the record showed that Kofi Annan was the only world statesman to challenge the superpower's self-styled right to go to war over Iraq and its supposed weapons arsenal. Whatever else he did, Kofi Annan changed the game between the superpower and the global community.

# Speaking Truth to Power

A complex man, far more prone to the blues than his calm public manner betrayed, Kofi Annan, more than any Secretary-General before him, recognized instinctively where his power lay. 'How many divisions does the Pope have?' he remarked in the back of the car after that meeting at the White House, seizing on Joseph Stalin's line during the Second World War: 'How many divisions do I have?' He answered his own question, forming a zero with his thumb and forefinger. The power, he understood, lay in his voice – and how he used it.

In old Europe, or Africa, certainly Asia and Latin America, most people gave the UN the benefit of the doubt. It was mother's milk to trust the UN to do the right thing. Not so in Washington DC, and not so in the years I represented the Secretary-General to the US Congress, and the State Department, and the broader body politic of the nation's capital.

There was intrigue, missing billions from a programme that was created to allow Saddam Hussein to sell oil in return for food to feed his people. There was scandal, never more so than when UN peacekeepers in Africa were accused of sexually exploiting under-age girls, and then the head of a major UN agency was accused by a female staffer of sexual harassment. There were investigations. At one point, I was dealing with six committees from the US Congress, on a mission to pursue every lead, every file, every audit, every e-mail. What did the Secretary-General know, and when did he know it? What did the Secretary-General do, when did he do it, and who profited? Ultimately, when would the Secretary-General resign?

The Secretary-General was my friend, and my boss. I had known Kofi Annan for years, turning to him during the days of war in the Balkans, genocide in Rwanda, the end of the nation state in Somalia. I had watched him closely as he rose through the ranks of the United Nations to become the first-ever leader chosen from within. I had been the first journalist to interview him after he was appointed Secretary-General, in December 1996. An intensely private man, who almost

48

always shied away from the intimate conversation, Kofi Annan had by his own standards been effusive that day, flushed with pride for his country, his continent and his family. 'The job is not about one man, or one country, or one vision,' he confided when the camera switched off. 'It's about humanity, and the voice of humanity; it's about speaking truth to all who have power, in the name of humanity.'

'I will keep you to your word, Mr Secretary-General,' I replied.

'Please do, you must.' He lingered as he shook my hand.

And so, years later, I went to work for Kofi Annan. Little did I know that, within weeks of taking over his small office in Washington DC, I would be presented with a scandal that almost cost him the job. Little did I know that I would be ringside at the not-so-diplomatic battle that followed. Little did I know how the fall-out would become personal, even vicious.

My boss was accused, chiefly by a right-wing columnist of the *New York Times* and Rupert Murdoch's TV and newspaper empire, of overseeing the biggest rip-off in the history of mankind, as the *Times* put it baldly. The operation in question was one authorized by the UN Security Council, which meant the United States, China, Britain and Russia among others. It was called the 'oil-for-food' programme, and its intent was to facilitate a way for Saddam Hussein to sell Iraq's oil, then buy food, medicine and basic materials for his people to survive the UN sanctions the world had imposed on the country. No matter that, for years, the United States had monitored the programme closely, daily at times, signing off on every transaction along with all the other major powers on the UN Security Council. No matter that the operation had ensured millions of Iraqis were fed, received medicine, had X-ray machines, fertilizers for farms and the like. No matter that the United Nations had no experience of oil trading. In the eyes of critics, the UN, and the Secretary-General personally, were to blame when fraud, corruption and kickbacks were uncovered in the aftermath of George Bush's invasion of Iraq in 2003.

I advised the Secretary-General to fight back, to come off the ropes and counter-punch aggressively against the false notion that somehow he had sole responsibility for the operation, when members of the Security Council, such as the United States and Britain, had approved the thousands of transactions the investigation unearthed. I urged him to put the programme in the context of a war being fought for Iraq, and to remind everyone of the role the UN had to play in the creation of a future Iraq. 'Every day we wait to answer the charges, sir, we lose another precious piece of our credibility, and integrity,' I messaged him at one point. 'It will take years to recover from the damage done if we wait much longer.'

At first Annan tried to defend himself. Bravely, he accepted my idea of coming down to Washington to appear live on *Meet the Press*, the Sunday-morning politics show that set the pace for everyone else in mainstream US media. I helped him prepare, spending a long Saturday night and early Sunday morning going over details of the way the oil-for-food operation worked, but I could see my friend in pain. By then allegations had surfaced suggesting that his son had profited from the Iraq programme. A friend from journalism days, the late Tim Russert, the host of *Meet the Press*, called me as I rode with the Secretary-General back to the airport after the show. Tim always turned to his beloved father as the barometer on a guest's appearance. 'My dad says your boss came across as a wise man,' Tim told me, 'not as a crook.' I spared telling the Secretary-General that last remark, fearing that it might send him even deeper into depression.

The UN's independent inquiry, led by an unimpeachable, towering figure, Paul Volcker, former chairman of the US Federal Reserve Board, showed UN malfeasance, naïvety and sparse oversight, but did not conclude massive corruption. But by then the damage had been done. That warning about credibility lost and integrity destroyed came back to haunt all of us.

And by then Kofi Annan had spoken truth to power one time too many for some in Washington DC. In the final lap of the presidential campaign that saw George W. Bush re-elected over Democrat John Kerry, my boss took to the airwaves one Friday night and called the Iraq war illegal. To be more precise, he was persuaded by a persistent BBC interviewer to agree with the premise that the war was illegal, at the third time of asking, on the basis that the United States and Britain did not have the explicit support of the UN Security Council for military action. My phone rang off the hook that weekend. One Republican Congressman, a fellow from the heartland of Indiana who spoke of the UN with barely concealed disgust, was less than diplomatic. 'Your man is done,' he told me. 'First the oil-for-food scandal, now this outrageous statement about Iraq. He's toast.' A Republican Senator, who led the charge by calling publicly for Kofi Annan's head, sought a resolution in both houses of Congress demanding his resignation. It fell to me to report to UN Headquarters that, if it came to it, such resolutions would pass easily in the poisoned atmosphere, with the Secretary-General being accused by many of having meddled in a US election. It was hard to mistake the silence on the other end of the conference line on the top floor of the UN. The Secretary-General of the United Nations was unlikely to carry on if he had a vote of no-confidence in the capital that paid most of the UN's bills.

And so I did retail politics. I went to those in power I had known in my journalism years, among them the chairman of the Rules Committee in the House of Representatives, a key figure in the chain that brought any such resolution from a member to the floor of the chamber. A friend of the UN, the chairman showed no enthusiasm for the United States removing Kofi Annan and he promised to make that known, dampening down the appetite for a quick move to dethrone my boss.

But the US Senate presented the greater danger. A Senator from Minnesota, one Norm Coleman, a pugilist in both looks and temperament, had led the investigation of the UN Iraq operation, and had staked his future on bringing Kofi Annan down. We did everything we could, in terms of providing materials, witnesses, documentation. We held background sessions for him and his staff, laying out the detailed operating practices of the Iraq programme, warts and all. We went to lunch, and Norm Coleman accepted that there was no evidence whatsoever of wrongdoing on the part of the Secretary-General. But the man was not for turning. 'Kofi Annan has to resign for the good of the organization, to open the way to changing the way you do business, and I consider it my duty to seek his resignation.'

And so, one wet autumn morning in the weeks that followed the re-election of George W. Bush, I waited in the rather dank, musty corridors of the Russell building in the US Senate. There was one Republican voice I wanted on our side above all others. The irrepressible, indomitable John McCain. He wasn't always liked by his colleagues, famously he had a temper and a short fuse. He wasn't always a fan of the UN. Once he berated me for what he called the UN's abject failure in Africa. Above all, he was a staunch supporter of the decision to go to war in Iraq, and he had lent his voice powerfully for George W. Bush in a close presidential race. But I was banking on a personal bond that had formed years before, when he was a maverick outsider running for President and I was one of the few Washington reporters to take his candidacy seriously, climb aboard his bus and ride through long, lonely days in New Hampshire, Iowa and South Carolina.

When the man arrived, fresh from the airport, he looked at me with a beaming smile. 'Mr Smith, I presume, from British television,' he remarked, grasping my hand, not shaking it, a mannerism born out of years as a prisoner of war and unspeakable torture that made a formal handshake painful. 'Time for a cup of fine, English tea?'

I reminded him that I worked for the UN now. He nodded, somewhat amused. 'Oh, yes, Mr Smith, a huckster for the United Nations.'

We asked about each other's families. I wondered how his son, a boy when I first knew him on board the campaign bus, had fared. On his way to college, the Senator replied, time for wine, women and song, he added, chuckling to himself. I was reminded of the party animal the Senator had been, by his own admission, in his younger days. The look on his face said it all. I had a few moments, no more, no time for tea. What did I want?

I knew better than to ask for him to support Kofi Annan. The scandal had taken its toll. The comments over the Iraq war surely left a bitter taste. The Senator didn't know the man I knew Kofi Annan to be.

So I made it about the position. I argued that it made no sense for the United States to be trying to bring down a UN Secretary-General at such a delicate moment, with the world so divided over the Iraq war and the obvious failure to dislodge al-Qaeda and the Taliban from Afghanistan. I advanced the belief that old Europe, already disenchanted by what had happened in Baghdad and Kabul, would see any move against the UN Secretary-General as hostile takeover. Briefly, but with a strong look in the eye, I gave him my word that there was no evidence whatsoever that the Secretary-General had done anything more than love a child too much.

'Heck, we've all done that,' the Senator said. He paused, telling an aide that he was coming. 'I'll see what I can do.'

Over the next few days, Senator John McCain let his colleagues know that it was not the moment for the United States to seek the removal of the man who led the UN. He, and others of like mind in the US Congress, stemmed the tide running against my boss.

A few weeks later, at Christmas 2004, Boxing Day to be precise, the tsunami struck South Asia. The Secretary-General broke his holiday out west in the Grand Tetons, took control of the crisis, flying to the region and leading the relief efforts, calling in two former Presidents, Bill Clinton and George Bush senior, to help him. As always, my boss shone at a moment of greatest need. He spoke powerfully for humanity, that voice of his ringing across our world, striking a chord with all of those who wanted someone to lead humanity at a moment of such catastrophe for the world's poorest. The tsunami recovery operation represented a singular success in that period of our history, the UN and the world at large pulling together, working together, across political, religious and ethnic divide, to bring help to tens of millions of people in dire need. The best of humanity confronting the worst nature could do.

Still, the tag of 'secular Pope' led some inside the conservative American establishment to scorn Kofi Annan's tenure at the United Nations. After the scandal attached itself to his family in his final years, those critics went to work, blaming him for whatever went wrong on the global radar screen, from the tragedy in Darfur to the tyranny in Zimbabwe, to the nuclear-weapons programme in Iran and the inability of the UN Security Council to act on such flashpoints.

Yet, when he acted, it had to be quietly, by persuasion. In his final few months, he worked overtime, moving a peacekeeping force into southern Lebanon to prevent a replay of history when the Israelis and Hezbollah started lobbing missiles at each other across the border. It fell to him to warn the Americans to hold off any thoughts of attacking Iran. Right to the end I saw him working the phone to persuade those who might have gone to war, typically the leaders of Ethiopia and Eritrea, to heed his plea for peace. I watched a leader of sure instincts, who understood when and how to use his power of the pulpit, and the microphone, and how to voice the moral authority that went uniquely with his job. In the face of George W. Bush, the over-achiever who so changed our world, Kofi Annan stood up to be counted.

# No Surrender

War was a world away from my dusty grapes bulging with promise. One overnight journey away, three flights, sixteen hours, and the pebbles crunched under my boots, the Andes loomed large and the sky gleamed ominous. The power games of Washington DC *realpolitik* seemed abstract compared to our next challenge.

For me the stakes were higher. It was love all over again. But, for the first time, romance met reality. My dream of a great wine hinged on picking the right moment to bring in the grape, and somehow using my power to make the workers, and the trucks, and the winery align. My hope of making a fine vintage squared off with my complete ignorance of how to make it all happen. 'What on earth am I doing here?' I felt as humbled as I had in the Oval Office.

Sonia woke me. 5 a.m. The look on her face did not suggest play. Instantly, I could hear and see the problem. We built a house on this land, on two floors, with huge windows, to lie in bed and look at the mountains. Instead, we were sitting up, pillows as cushions, with no mountains in sight. Only storm clouds.

Our slender, young trees bent and twisted; the air whistled. I suggested it was *el Zonda*, the warm wind that comes from the north, part of the folklore of these parts. Our friends and neighbours were always forecasting when it would come, how long it would last, what it would do. Sonia gave me a stare, don't be an idiot. '*Mi amor*, this is a rainstorm, not a dry *Zonda*.'

We both clambered out of bed. Raindrops hung on leaf and grape; puddles glinted below the black pipe of drip irrigation. I had paid all that money for a sophisticated water system, from the best irrigation engineers in Israel, and now nature did it the old-fashioned way? Our Malbec, so plump and full, had made us feel rich when we went to bed the night before. Now it glistened out of our reach. Sonia took my hand. Down below, even our dogs were taking cover. Poncho, our collie, was heading for the covered galleries of the house. Bruno, a hyperactive Dalmatian, had already made it to the garage.

What was I thinking, all those years ago? That I would trade away daily stress for bucolic sunrises? Who would want to be a farmer? We were not smiling as we threw on work clothes and headed downstairs, hoping that we could get out there with our harvesters and save the vintage. From what? From a threat as banal as the weather.

Weather was a British obsession, the filler of every non-conversation, and yet weather in Great Britain was remarkably predictable, and generally benign. Cloudy, with occasional showers, and patches of sunshine. Showers, with occasional sunshine, and patches of clouds. Sunshine, with occasional clouds, and a chance of showers. What was there to talk about?

Weather in the rest of the world deserved more respect, a killer in waiting. A storm over a war zone in Ethiopia, flying in a one-engine plane during Africa days. Floods in Florence, at one point the Michelangelos threatened, an indelible memory from my time in Italy. The frozen tundra over the oilfields of Siberia, a forgettable highlight of my Moscow years. And then drought, the worst killer of all.

At the beginning of my television days in the late 1970s, I put my less-than-stellar career on the line to report a drought in East Africa. First, I was in Uganda to cover the return of one despot, former President Milton Obote, to replace another, the murderous tyrant known as Idi Amin, or, as he called himself, 'His Excellency, President for Life, Field Marshal Al Hadji Doctor Idi Amin Dada, vc, Conqueror of the British Empire in Africa in General and Uganda in Particular, and the Most Ubiquitous of All King of Scotland'. What no one understood, my aid worker friends told me, was that Idi Amin had so destroyed the 'Pearl of Africa', as Uganda was fondly described, that famine now stalked a land of plenty that had always fed itself. They predicted human catastrophe in the northern part of the country, in the land of the Karamoja.

It would not be easy to get there to see if this was true. Back in London, my reports raising questions about Obote and his style of leadership had not been well received, falling foul of the invisible link that tied national media to national government, to the so-called national interest. The British government worked in subtle ways. No one from the new Thatcher government openly suggested I had the story wrong. Quietly, my editors were told by the Foreign Office that it was fanciful to suggest Obote was another tyrant in the making. The British government saw Obote as the answer after Idi Amin. After all, he could hardly be worse. Amin was known to feed, yes feed, his political opponents to crocodiles on Lake Victoria. I reminded my editors that this was the same Foreign Office which years earlier had quietly supported the coup that installed Idi Amin.

Still, much as my bosses had minds of their own, I was not flavour of the month in the newsroom when I tried to raise support for a trip to the Karamoja in northern Uganda. We needed a camera crew costing a thousand pounds a day, we needed a charter plane costing thousands more, and we needed at least ten days to reach the hunger zone. It was a close call, but finally they approved the trip.

From the air, you could see the land was parched. On the ground the endless army checkpoints, and the fear on the face of the young soldiers, hinted at the story, because the food supply lines had been cut by bandits, army deserters and armed gangs using rape as a weapon. The people of the Karamoja were literally starving to death in front of us when we got through to them after some hair-raising days in the air and on the road.

Nothing prepared me for the sight of children dying from starvation. The cameraman, a tall, gentle giant of a Sikh named Mohinder Dhillon, explained to me what I was witnessing. One-year-olds weighing just a percentage of what they had at birth, the protein deficiency marasmus showing in lifeless eyes, sagging skin and voracious hunger. I could not understand. These kids were starving, but so few cried. 'No energy, no energy to cry, David,' Mohinder told me, gently. Then there was kwashiorkor, the terrifying spectacle of a child with a bulging belly, born of starvation, not food, the lack of nutrients leading to the bloated stomach, the bloated face and the loss of appetite.

At one beleaguered feeding station, run by the brave souls who worked for Save the Children, Mohinder took me aside to explain something blindingly obvious to him but incomprehensible to me. They were weighing little ones and separating them into groups. 'Those who can make it and those who cannot,' he explained. In an instant my mind went to tales of the Holocaust: those who could perform *Arbeit* work, those who could not sent to the gas chambers. The key factor at the feeding station was the age mothers, or siblings, or grandparents, attributed to a child as the little one was weighed. Now Mohinder had told me, I could not bear to watch mothers selecting their babies, unknowingly, for one line or another, by the age they gave to the child.

Nothing prepares you to watch someone die. Nothing. This was the first time I had to look death in the face. We heard that a German journalist was heading back to Nairobi with a charter plane. Mohinder and I took the decision that we had to send our film to London, any which way. Now. Not tomorrow, not the next day. Now. So we drove furiously from the feeding station, Mohinder switching our old-fashioned film from camera magazine to can in a black sack to prevent exposure, to the nearest airstrip. I was groping for words to write a commentary to match his pictures when I glimpsed a body in the reeds by the side of the road. I told the driver to stop. Mohinder looked at me speechless, the pained look on his face saying we have no time to waste. The body was that of a girl, not quite a teenager, probably ten to twelve years old, her breathing barely audible, her legs and arms skeletal, her face showing few signs of emaciation but no movement either. Behind me, Mohinder had put his hand on my shoulder, trying to comfort me. I was inconsolable. 'We have come for the last moments,' declared a French nun, who had hitched a ride with us, standing over a child about to die. The nun performed the last rites.

We decided we should bury her. I became passionate that we had to show on film what had happened; how we found her; how we picked her up; how we dug a grave, and prayed over it, each enacting final rites in his or her own faith. There was no right option here. I had no monopoly on right and wrong. I did not have the answers. But I did not want that child dying in vain.

We sent our film to London. In those days before satellite and video, we entrusted the only copy of our film to a passenger flying to London, a human pigeon, and we hoped the bird landed.

The film editor who carefully turned Mohinder's film into television mosaic was a Holocaust survivor named Leo Rosenberg. He cried while he worked, he told me, as he brought the images to life in his edit-room at ITN.

Thanks to Leo and Mohinder, she did not die in vain. The news of a killer famine in northern Uganda launched a worldwide appeal for aid to the Karamajong tribe. Tens of millions of dollars were raised in emergency aid. Other news organizations ordered their reporters to head to the Karamoja, raising more awareness and more action. I consoled myself with the thought that the girl's death in front of us and our camera had been a catalyst for action. But, in truth, there was no right way to handle what we had seen. Ultimately, we had watched the end of a precious life, helpless to help.

Just as the huge relief operation started, it rained, and rained, and rained. Nature so cruel. Where once the land was baked dry, now it was soaked, making it harder for relief trucks to reach the stricken. We were also stuck in the Karamoja as the floods cut off the roads. Finally, relief trucks moved in, and soon Mohinder and I left for the capital Kampala. Our work was done. In the world of news it was time for the next story.

The herograms from my office in London told me my career was back on track. 'Your stock has never been higher,' the foreign editor wrote to me. 'You were brilliant, not mawkish or maudlin, just telling the story with compassion and grace.' In truth, I was a wreck, shell-shocked, depressed, certainly drinking too heavily.

On the morning we left Kampala, I went to see a young political rebel at his home in a leafy, green, semi-idyllic part of the city. Uganda the source of so much wealth, despite its tragedy. His name was Yoweri Museveni. He told me I was right about the new leader Obote, that he would become Idi Amin in another guise. He felt he had no option but to declare, to Mohinder's camera, that he was leaving the capital, heading for the bush, to form a resistance army opposed to Obote.

It was Museveni's first, and last, television interview before he disappeared into the bush to launch war against the new Obote government. Many years later I met him again, at the White House, being fêted by Bill Clinton, as President of Uganda. 'I'm glad to see you again,' he remarked, assuring me that he remembered that Saturday morning in Kampala so many years before. I was not so convinced about his powers of recollection, but I congratulated him on his presidency, then stuck a not-so-gentle reminder of the democracy he once favoured.

'When's the next election, Mr President?' I asked.

'When the people ask for one,' he replied.

# Rot

The memory of the tragedy in Uganda proved sobering on our harvest morning, as we put on our ponchos and boots for a quick look at the vineyard. We needed perspective. Weather had done far worse things than merely destroy our harvest. 'Not the end of the world, darling, *no es el fin del mundo, mi amor,* we'll just have to wait a day or two.' But still. This was my harvest. My first harvest for a wine. This was personal. However hard my brain tried to tell my heart to put it in context, get a grip, it was just grape. And I knew about waiting.

Journalists, and diplomats, spend half their lives waiting for something to happen. The press conference. The vote. The verdict. The war. The peace. I waited fifty-five days for the dictator in Spain to die. I can remember every one of them, the Franco death-watch. The same number of days for a Prime Minister of Italy to be returned to his people by his kidnappers. I could still sense the national trauma as Prime Minister Aldo Moro's body was dumped in the back of a car in the centre of Rome, a bullet through his head. But now I was fifty-five years old and this wait was personally unbearable, because every hour my grape, my harvest, my hopes were suffering. There was no way of knowing whether we could save it. So much for the dream, as the rain stopped for a couple of hours, resumed as night fell.

By mid morning, the decision was made. There would be no work in our vineyard today, nor tomorrow either if the weather forecast was right. Luis, the manager of the farm, the man who built the vineyard so lovingly, and a winemaker himself, stopped by to spell it out for us in his usual calm, relaxed manner. 'This will be fine, don't worry, a couple of days of rain, it's not a problem, we will be ready,' he said, pausing to add in more sombre tone, 'We must just hope the sun doesn't come out too strong and quick.' I was confused. With the skyline decidedly black and clouds looking full of rain, I would love to see the sun come out. 'Don't be worried, this weather will pass, but we want it to stay cool.'

Luis had lived all his thirty-odd years with vine. His family owned a

59

winery in Mendoza that made crisp, sparkling wine that the French would be proud to call their own. He grew up in La Consulta, the pueblo closest to our Altamira. I cherished the thought that young Luis would sell candy at the Cinema Paradiso owned by his grandfather. The building was still there, an empty shell, abandoned. On our better days we talked about re-opening, maybe revive it as a big-screen movie bar for La Consulta, open Friday through Sunday night with a selection of local wines and Sonia's tapas. Luis was our guide, our guru, our genie. Without him we would not have built a vineyard. Without him we would never have dared to think of making a wine. Without Luis, quite simply, we did not know what we were doing.

He swept away from his brow a mop of blond, curly hair. 'What we should watch out for is a fast sun, the sun that follows rain with intense heat,' he said as the dogs splashed in the puddles on the edge of the Malbec vines. 'That is a worry for me . . . only a small worry because it is now quite cold,' he added, his fine features creased by a soft smile. I tried to tell Luis he was then the most eligible bachelor in the area. He laughed it off, typical of a spirit who was so talented yet so humble, determined yet never pushy, a high achiever with an inner peace. If Luis had his way, he would have painted for a living. His passion was his easel. If he talked about our land as his baby, and he did, then he discussed an afternoon with his paint brush as true love. But he was now immersed in the new age of wine, managing half a dozen vineyards, all of them much bigger than ours; also travelling abroad to the United States and Europe to help sell the wines that came from those vineyards. 'The only problem will be if the sun comes out strong, the grape wet from two, three days of this rain, then humidity setting in if the sun is cooking hot.' He paused. 'And we can get botrytis.'

Botrytis. Now there was a word to cause a heart attack if you owned a vineyard. There is good botrytis, the 'noble rot' as it is called, which gives the classic sweet wines of Europe, such as Sauternes, their special, highly concentrated flavour, the grape rotting in time-honoured fashion to make those wines so special, and so expensive.

But I knew we were talking about Rot with a capital R, which was the only botrytis in Mendoza. *Botrytis cinerea* is the botanical term for the fungus. Luis talked of 'getting botrytis' like a patient might get pneumonia, or worse. Its trademark was a malevolent rot that spread rapidly through a bunch of grapes, then a whole row of vines, and in short order an entire vineyard, the mould eating away at skins, then clusters of grape berries, destroying a harvest, surviving on dead plant tissue to do even more damage.

Sonia had read her 'wine bible'. She knew what botrytis would do to us. 'We work for eight years to get to this point, and now it rains. On this day of all days. It can't be happening,' she declared, her voice much louder than usual. For years my wife anchored TV news for a global leader, CNN. She had a formidable reputation for being the coolest person in a crisis, the go-to presenter when the live shot did not work, or the interview collapsed, or the leader of a country was shot and war broke out. 'We live in a desert,' she glared, 'it is not supposed to rain. Ever.'

Our foreman, Gabriel, took a call. Botrytis rot had been discovered on a neighbouring property. Sonia walked out.

I found her walking through puddles between the rows of muddy vines, tasting grape, talking to herself. 'It is perfect,' she kept saying as she cradled wet grape in her hand. 'This grape is so ready.' Rain, too much rain; just perfect, so ready, so ready, what was the desert doing to us . . . ?

My lovely wife, I feared, was one rainy day away from a muttering bag lady.

# Honorary Mendocino

Fortunately two of our favourite people came to lunch, precisely because they could not work in this weather. Pepe, as he was known affectionately, was then the chief winemaker for the powerhouse winery that had changed the face of Argentine wine in the previous twenty years, producing quality where once the only goal was quantity, making Malbec a star on the world stage, the man probably immortalized in local wine history by telling his boss one year that there could be no vintage because the harvest lacked the quality people had come to expect from their wines.

'It's not about producing a great wine one year,' Pepe once told me, the man's inner steel showing out from underneath such a quiet, gentle demeanour. 'It's about producing great wines year after year. It's about consistency.'

His colleague, and successor, could hardly have been more different. Alejandro was larger than life, a gregarious spirit running high on caffeine and alcohol from constant tasting, in your face with a mischievous sense of humour and sheer love for the job he did seven days a week, twenty-four hours a day. 'We have to be the best we can be, and then more than that,' he said, and you knew it was his mantra, 'because there's all these others trying to catch up with us now.'

To watch the two of them at our table, to bring out the best of our cellar, and to wind them up ever so gently by serving wines made by their rivals, this was a treat. And it was a lesson from the best teachers.

Wine, after all, is nothing more than fermented grape juice. But anyone who has found three-week-old grape juice in their fridge knows it can be pretty disgusting, and should not be served that evening, no matter how desperate, not even if candlelight hides the fuzzy grey blobs floating around the glasses.

So winemakers deserve our respect. They take grapes, squeeze out the juice, and spend the next days, months, even years testing for acidity, testing for sweetness, testing for alcohol, testing for balance. They are chemists at heart, happiest debating polyphenols, malolactic fermentation and Ph levels.

They know how long to leave the juice sitting on the debris of skins and pips, to soak up flavours and colours. They know what temperature is ideal to ferment gently. They know when to punch the juice around, to extract even more flavour, squeezing out the skins. And they know when it is time to leave well alone, pour the fermented juice into oak barrels and let it be. They know how many months to leave the barrels resting, and when each barrel needs topping up. Their enemy is the air, oxygen. Every barrel needs to be full, and sealed, just like a wine bottle. If it is half-empty, it will turn as sour as yesterday's leftover plonk. To avoid this disaster, every barrel must be constantly topped up, to make up for the natural evaporation of alcohol, and the natural need of the winemaker to keep testing, tasting, testing, tasting, just to make sure the wine is evolving nicely.

Listening to Pepe and Alejandro, I realized how little I knew, yet how much they had already taught me.

Red wine, it turns out, does come from red grapes. White wine, usually from white ones. But it is possible to make white wine from red grapes as long as you squeeze the juice out and never let it touch the grapeskins again. You see, all the colour comes from the skins. When I thought about it, all grapes are greenish inside, not deep purple. And rosé? Not a mixture of both wines, it turns out, but a very, very weak red wine, made by leaving the juice on red skins for only a few hours, instead of three weeks. Just enough to tinge the juice and give it that taste of lazy, summery afternoons.

But did they know how the wine would turn out? 'Of course,' said Alejandro.

'No, never completely,' corrected Pepe. 'It is alive, it matures.'

But could they take any grape, and make it into a great wine, with enough of their know-how? Did they just need a few expensive oak barrels to give it some finesse?

Clearly, I was a buffoon to ask this. 'David, we can make a terrible wine from good grapes like yours,' Alejandro explained, 'but no one can make a good wine from terrible grapes. No one. Garbage in, garbage out.'

So, it was all down to the grapes, to the vineyard. 'Oh no, *mi amigo*,' he corrected, 'we need to understand the grape, and coax it just right, for a great wine.'

This was not good news. As we stared at the muddy vineyard, it did all come down to the sodden grapes.

Alejandro launched on. A wine was truly made in the vineyard. But not in the mysterious ways hinted at by generations of French connoisseurs. '*C'est le terroir.*' *Terroir*, French for exactly what made my piece of land unique. Soil, climate, weather, landscape. The French loved the geology of wine, all that talk of gravel, schist, limestone. It was the old school of vineyard snobbery. The new school was predictably brasher, the child of Crocodile Dundee meets California Girl. Between them, the Australians and the Americans decided to upstage the French, and they staked their success, not on the dirt they planted in, but on the actual plants. Where the French loved their stones, the Californians loved their clones. Every type of wine plant was categorized, selected, Chardonnay clone 221, Cabernet Sauvignon clone 84. More and more clonal selections, narrowing down which specific Cabernet plants produced the most delectable wine, or the most aristocratic, or, just plain, the most.

Why, exactly, did different grapes produce different kinds of wine, with Cabernet Sauvignon always so solid and upright, and Beaujolais Nouveau so thin?

Clearly, this was another stupid question, the equivalent of why is a Granny Smith always green and sour, and a Red Delicious red and rarely delicious. I was wearing out my guests' patience, and patience was something winemakers needed to cultivate. After all, they received grapes once every year, and waited months, sometimes years, two or even three, before knowing if they had succeeded. No batch of grapes was the same, no vintage exactly alike. It was as if Tiger Woods had only one chance a year to play golf, and that one time was the British Open.

I had also learned that, much as I wanted to hear about the business, the last thing Pepe and Alejandro wanted today, well . . . was another conversation about wine.

It was time for a siesta. But not before we discussed what men do best in Argentina: talk football, shift effortlessly to politics, with a dose of sex thrown in, and naturally end with more football by the time coffee arrives.

Outside it was still raining, but it hit me, I was one of them. I had become a *Mendocino.* Or at least an honorary *Mendocino.*

# Hail Mary

Luis called that night. He would wait no longer. The team of harvesters would be with us in the morning with rain gear, ready to work no matter what. 'We have to. Botrytis is stalking Altamira.'

By 7 a.m. the team moved out, in driving rain, covered from head to foot in bright yellow ponchos, and leggings, and mariners' hats, totally out of place so far from the sea, the women giggling at their menfolk, the men telling their women how ridiculous they looked. I joined them, draped in my thickest anorak and dirtiest baseball cap. Boots sinking into mud, struggling to grasp scissors properly with wet gloves. I knew, in a matter of seconds, this was not going to work. '*Podrido*,' said the man working down the line from me. 'Putrid.' I knew what he meant. On the vine at least the grape had healthy leaves offering some protection from the rain. In the bucket, on the truck, on the road, it would be soaked, squashed and ruined before we could get it to the winery.

We cut our losses, and called off the harvest. Day Two ended with no return. No luck, no sign of a break in the clouds. We seemed doomed. My wife, normally demure, was becoming a melodrama queen, so much so I fled the house to drown sorrows with a friend who owned a nearby winery.

On the evening of Day Three, Luis called a crisis meeting, even though his message was reassurance itself. The forecast looked fine for Friday, bright, sunny, but not so warm that we had to worry about humidity and rot. He was sure we could bring it all in; the grape was still healthy.

But just in case, he wanted to agree priorities, which grape came first, how much of each grape we would take on the first run, what we wanted for our wine, what would simply be sold to the winery. Because? He stopped, clearly pondering how to say what came next. Because? 'Because it's Palm Sunday, and at most people will work Saturday morning, giving us a day and a half when we need three full days.'

Jesus, Mary and Joseph, and me a Catholic altar-boy in my youth, the harvest was out there dying on the vine, everyone in this community depended on the harvest, and we didn't work on Palm Sunday weekend? Luis doubted that we could, Sonia nodded in silent agreement, giving me one of those you-don't-understand-my-country looks. And Luis wanted us to understand something else. Across our valley, across Altamira, everyone had lost three days this week. There were only so many harvesters, and now so much grape the winery would only be able to handle a certain amount on any one day, with capacity stretched to the limit, and so on.

I understood the subtext. Luis was telling us that, much as he did not want to lose our grape, he had six other vineyards to handle, he needed the team of harvesters elsewhere by Monday, and the winery would be handling other grape next week.

Nobody said it. Nobody needed to. It was that weekend or bust.

# Making the Ask

Fortunately, before I took us all to a bad place by spelling all this out, and analysing options, Luis headed home. Our wine was out there, our dream was withering on the vine, and I could not see how to bring it to harvest.

The control freak did not sleep well. How could I win this, and persuade them all to bring my grape in? Once again, I needed to work on the ask. I had always considered myself brilliant at making things happen, juggling several different balls in the air at once, a TV story here, a newspaper story there, a child in kindergarten, another at university, a deadline tomorrow, a deadline next week, a speech that day, a lecture another. But this one kept me up all night.

I had always considered it a valuable skill, the ability and the know-how to make the ask. For years, I parachuted into capitals to cover a breaking story, knowing that I had to deliver the President or the Prime Minister, or the rebel leader, or the Ayatollah, or the exclusive visit to the front lines, or the daring foray up country to the danger zone. That was what I was paid for, that was the challenge. It all came down to the ask, the ability to clinch the interview with the leader, or seal the deal with the colonel that put you aboard the convoy.

There was nothing quite like that thrill, of setting up the trip that told the story, or finding the way across the battle line, or of getting the exclusive interview. In Moscow, as power began to disintegrate within the Kremlin establishment, I discovered the value of ignoring the official rules. It was a question of opening the forbidden door, with confidence, a camera and my execrable Russian. I would wander by the meeting-rooms, the private offices, even the cafeterias reserved for the Politburo and senior members of the Communist Party. One day, we found Mikhail Gorbachev, then at the height of his powers and on the cusp of the revolution that brought an end to the Soviet Empire and the Cold war. What was the future of Perestroika, I challenged him? The first answer took him twenty-two minutes to finish. Not Mr Soundbite, but with his open access and easy smile, it was easy to see why he was a hero to the West, to Mrs Thatcher and Ronald Reagan. Yet, as a reporter, it was just as easy to understand why his own people thought him a windbag who delivered only words, words, words.

Another day, we found Boris Yeltsin. I learned that if I played to his vanity, he was always ready with a controversial soundbite. Often half-sober, with his boxer's jaw and billowing forelock, he could be irascible and temperamental, depending on his mood.

Another stalwart of the cafeteria was one of the last of the Communist hard-liners, a Politburo heavyweight named Yegor Ligachev. Comrade Ligachev liked his coffee and his vodka, so I knew I could find him, usually alone, mid morning in the cafeteria. There had to be a revolution underway, I believed, when a man such as Ligachev, who probably in his heart believed that Gorbachev, Yeltsin and all foreign correspondents should be shot, took questions.

Looking back, I could be shameless, I could be manipulative, I could be cheeky. When I arrived in Washington from the free-wheeling chaos of democratizing Moscow, I learned the rules were different. In my first week, at the height of Gulf War I in January 1991, a well-known Democratic Senator took four attempts to answer whether he supported the war, asking us to turn the camera off three times, so he could practise again. Take four, and he had delivered his multi-layered answer to the question, did he support the war?

Enough already. I chose another route. I broke the rules, just by acting as if I were at the Kremlin.

It meant lurking in corridors with a camera team, to waylay a Senator or a Congressman on their way into work, or en route to a committee hearing, or maybe a Senator heading to a tryst. A British accent helped: 'So, Senator, what did you do to deserve bumping into me this morning?' Or: 'What's a good man like you doing in a place like this?' They would hear the accent, and invariably stop. After a while, they came to expect me, the eccentric Brit who hung around corridors, with a big, burly American cameraman. Senator John McCain said I brought him good luck. Joe Lieberman called me his Englishman. Senator John Warner, formerly one of Elizabeth Taylor's husbands, liked to talk life and love once the camera switched off, recalling how her favourite line was: 'To thine own self be true.'

The trick was to avoid expulsion by the Sergeant-at-Arms. Before the camera switched on, it was critical to ask whether the Senator or the Representative wanted to talk, had the time and so on. That way I could always tell the Sergeant-at-Arms, whenever he threatened to arrest me, that I had the agreement of the politician in question to interview then and there. Did the Sergeant-at-Arms really want to prevent the Senator speaking of his own accord? As it happened, not many politicians said no in Washington. One who did was the late Senator Ted Kennedy, a man so scarred by scandal he refused to believe a British correspondent would just want to talk to him about Northern Ireland. Another was Vice-President Dick Cheney, who thought of the media as 'filth'. Robert Byrd, a renowned Senator from West Virginia since the 1950s, who made it evident I should not just be arrested, but gaoled for contempt of the institution. Other than those rare exceptions, most Washington politicians never met a camera they did not love, or believed they could make love to. I simply offered them the opportunity.

But there had been 'asks' to remember. About a year before I gave up journalism for the United Nations, I went to Caracas to interview that firebrand of Latin American life, Venezuela's President Hugo Chávez, shortly after he had survived a *coup d'état* against him. My network in London sent me, insistent that all was arranged by a middleman who claimed to have great contacts in Caracas. I arrived to find the presidency knew nothing about me, my network, or this supposed arrangement, and Chávez's voluble press team made it clear I would not even be added to the long list, suggesting instead they could take me dancing and introduce me to beautiful *Chavistas* if I had a spare evening.

My one shot at this ask came on Sunday morning, when the President anchored a television hour from the courtyard of the Palace, taking phone calls from around the country and dispensing largesse, such as homes, and cars, and schools, live on the air. I bluffed my way in along with local TV, insisting the President himself knew of my presence in Caracas. Fortunately, his press folks must have still been out dancing. When the show went to commercial break, I simply marched over, waved insanely to get to his attention, shouting in my best Spanish: 'Why are you trying so hard to avoid me, Mr President? When I've come here to tell the world your story!'

Chávez gave me a truly filthy look, with his extraordinary gene pool, Afro, Indian, Spanish. Then he broke into one of his huge grins, no doubt remembering the camera was on, took one look at my business card, and with a wave of the presidential hand I was in, escorted by a beautiful *Chavista* dressed in paramilitary fatigues to a seat of some honour in the presidential courtyard-cum-TV studio, looking on as the leader chatted live with the nation. At one point, he seemed to give a woman caller a hospital, yes, a hospital, for her apparently poor community. At the end he came across to shake hands, beaming a broad smile, telling me expansively how much he appreciated me wanting to see him, he being a humble footsoldier in the march of history, that was his phrase.

I spent the afternoon with Hugo Chávez at his home, after a dash across the city in a heavily armed motorcade that made me realize the *Chavistas* did as they pleased. The man himself was clearly a cauldron of emotions, his brain working faster than his mouth, his views, judgements and opinions spewing out in a manner that suggested the spirit itself was hyper. He made no secret of his ambitions: to build a Pan-American front based on the egalitarian goals of the Liberator, Simón Bolívar: 'Latin America has been divided and ruled for too long by mother America.' He did not disguise his contempt for the then President of the United States, George W. Bush: 'Bush is an evil force, but Bush does not speak for the American people.' He diagnosed common cause with European Socialists, and seemed less than pleased when I told him the days of Socialism in Europe had passed. 'It is a mistake to think Socialism lost because the Soviet Union lost,' he declared.

Sitting down for the interview, in a living room dominated by a mini-altar to the Virgin Mary, Chávez the showman made news across the world. The allegations poured out. Of the Bush administration and the CIA being behind the *coup*. Of the American navy being in Venezuelan waters at the time. Of a US-registered plane sitting on the tarmac while he was held at the Orchila Island military base. 'What Washington had in mind was for me to go quietly into exile on board one of their planes.' He laughed out loud, giving Washington the finger without having to say it.

Sometimes, of course, 'the ask' sent you where you did not want to go. I travelled to Colombia regularly during my Washington days. Dangerous as it was, incomprehensible as its endless war seemed, I always found myself coming back to the statistics that told us that most of the world's cocaine came from Colombia, and that no country on earth had a war like theirs.

The damage could be measured in the millions of lives destroyed across the world, typically in the 'crack' ghettoes that scarred every major city in the United States. But every time I heard of another drug bust, police capturing x pounds of cocaine with a street value of y million dollars, I would chafe at the dirty little secret of the drug war: namely, that the drug was only worth so much on the street if it was being used by people on my street, in my neighbourhood, with my level of income.

The drug war was based on the lie that the issue lay with the producer, not the consumer. We all knew otherwise if we looked around us. Several TV colleagues had lost virtually everything because of cocaine addiction. My own company, and the BBC and CNN, had sent some well-known faces into rehab. I had watched one star correspondent build his TV persona at an American network going live, high on cocaine, then self-destruct because of the habit. But the lie made a country like Colombia the front line for the war. Better to fight it in Bogotá, Bucaramanga or Baranquilla, than in Chicago, Cincinnati or Carlsbad, California.

So I took myself to Colombia on a regular basis, being shot at by rebel groups while flying with American crop-sprayers as they sought to eradicate coca fields; taking helicopter rides with Colombian generals to see the army fight the rebels in the rain forest; riding shotgun with the country's politicians as some of them declared war on the narco-traffickers, and made themselves instant targets for assassination.

After the birth of our second child, in 2000, Sonia put her foot down. 'Forget about this story,' she lectured me. 'What about your commitment to staying alive for us? Nobody cares about Colombia, believe me. Nobody cares.'

So I came up with a compromise, to get around my wife's ultimatum. Seeing that the President of Colombia had just gone to the jungle to meet the rebels, I rang the presidential palace in Bogotá and made the ask for an interview. When the message came back positive, I assuaged Sonia's anger by promising I would stay in the capital, see the President and come home. That was enough, I assured her, because we had plenty of pictures of the meetings in the jungle with the leaders of the Revolutionary Armed Forces of Colombia, known by the acronym that was a nightmare for any broadcaster, FARC. Try saying it in English, repeatedly, and you will see what I mean.

I had always enjoyed Bogotá, a city of rare bookstores, of gold museums, a culture of elegant, striking, thoughtful men and women, speaking to my ear the most elegant Spanish on earth. I went straight to the Palace to see Andrés Pastrana, President, Amero-phile and former TV journalist himself. At the end of an excellent interview, in which he revealed the raw emotions that went with travelling to the bush to see those trying to overthrow him, the President suddenly leaned forward.

'Why are you not going to see the rebels?'

'Pardon, sir, not sure I heard you correctly.'

'I said, you must go and see the rebels. You have to see for yourself how this process is moving.'

He picked up a red phone and gave orders.

'There's a flight we can get you on this afternoon. You must go and see the FARC, I insist.'

As we flew on a rickety, two-propeller transport plane south to the war zone, I reasoned that the journalist in Sonia would understand how rare this was, how no self-respecting correspondent could possibly say 'No'. The President of a country fighting a civil war had just insisted that you go sip coffee with his enemies, and he found you seats on a flight to make it happen; indeed, he ordered his military to escort you to the point where you were handed over to the rebels. I did not tell Sonia, of course, until we returned. The former journalist turned Ur-mama was not amused.

And so we spent a few days with the FARC, memorably guarded by silent, statuesque women armed with AK-47s in a military camp close to main town they controlled, San Vicente del Caguán. We glimpsed life under the FARC across a stretch of the Amazon basin the size of Wales, the streets dominated by young soldiers in battle fatigues, the shops operated by the FARC, their control of a local economy absolute and fuelled largely by drug money, and their revolutionary creed reinforced on every corner by a banner, or a slogan, or a mural espousing the Bolivarian revolution along the lines of Hugo Chávez. What intrigued me was their embrace of modern technology, specifically use of the internet. We found a highly trained unit working at a computer HQ, sending a steady stream of news, images and propaganda to 'fraternal' websites around the world that raised money for the cause, presenting young fighters as young lovers, girls in uniform as calendar models, albeit armed with machine-gun bullets as neckwear, and the movement's leaders as thinkers writing speeches on their personal computers. Che Guevara meets Bill Gates. And a far cry from receiving the latest statement from the Red Brigades on a carbon-copy of a typewritten folio, as we had in Rome in the 1970s.

I had imagined I would have to tread carefully on the issue of drug money. The FARC made tens of millions of dollars a year out of drug trafficking. That was the source of their military might over the years, the reason why no government could defeat them, not even with American support. 'Yes, we levy a tax on the drug trade, just as we tax any commercial activity in the land we control,' I was told by Carlos Losada, the smooth-talking head of the FARC's public-relations department. 'Yes, we make money out of drugs.'

This was an organization with a business plan, a PR department and single-minded leaders with a strategy. We were presented with one Simón Trinidad, real name Juvenal Ovidio Ricardo Palmera, son of a wealthy Colombian landowner, formerly a banker and economist, who joined the FARC in the 1980s and became its lead negotiator with the government of Andrés Pastrana. He was a natural-born wheeler-dealer, dressed up as guerrilla leader, a man who would trade anything, war or peace, guns or drugs, people or political movements. 'Why should we make concessions?' he asked. 'Because he's the President and we are the rebels? Forget it. What we want is power, plain and simple. Power in Colombia.'

Years later, when another government decided to confront the FARC with massive military aid from the United States, Simón Trinidad was captured, extradited to Washington and put on trial for drug trafficking and terrorism, specifically the kidnapping of foreign citizens. I went to his trial one day, when one of the more attractive calendar-girl guerrilla fighters told the court Simón Trinidad had commanded Front 41 in the Sierra Nevada de Santa Marta. 'The instruction he gave us was that any gringo, tourist, civilian or whatever had to be kidnapped,' she testified. 'No one should be able to escape. They were very important for a prisoner exchange, or because they could be used for a big ransom.'

Another lucky escape, then.

But faced with Palm Sunday, a reluctant vineyard crew and an over-booked winery, I knew I would need all my luck. None of my manipulative journalism skills would be any use. It was a long, sleepless night. By 4 a.m. I knew I had no leverage except goodwill. By 5 a.m., begging seemed to be the sound strategy.

# First Harvest, 2007

Dawn. Not another grey day, we prayed. We saw a sliver of sun rise, piercing the vine with shafts of light, then dance across the creases of the *cordillera*, touching snow caps with paint-brush delicacy.

There is a God.

A tractor appeared at the entrance to the property, carrying two families, grandparents down to small children. Mothers and fathers led strapping teenage sons and more delicate daughters, sleep still heavy on reluctant eyes. I raised my palms to give thanks.

Gabriel, the foreman on our land, stood ready to greet them. He planted a red flag, hand-stitched with 'Finca Alegría', at the first row of vines to be picked.

It was back-breaking work, cutting grape at knee-height with secateurs, cleaning away, between loose leaves, row after row of hanging fruit. The challenge was speed, without slicing the plant, or worse a finger. Grape bunches landed in a metal *tacho*, or bucket. Filled, it weighed 20 kilos, or 44 pounds, before it was carried on shoulders to be emptied into tubs headed for the winery. Every *tacho* earned a stub, a *ficha*, stamped with 'Finca Alegría', to be presented on pay-day.

Avoiding *tacho* number 13, which I noticed no one wanted, I grabbed secateurs and headed off down the first row to join Gabriel's wife Marta and his son Jonathan who were now working in tandem deep in the Malbec grove. Marta, only her eyes visible as she masked her entire face against the sun, patiently explained how to clear leaf from vine and grape, then to seek out the new, young stem that will lead me to cut at the apex and so dispatch a stunning cluster of my grape cleanly into my *tacho* below. She moved effortlessly along the line, the rhythm of one seamless movement – leaf, stem, grape – punctured only by the sound of the decisive snip that deposited Malbec in bin with an echo all of its own. The first thing I noticed was that my back could not take much of this. I knelt down on both knees to engineer bearable access to the line of grape. Then I struggled to locate that key cutting-point, leading me to snip, snip away at smaller bunches. Marta came to help, sympathetically applying skilled surgery to the kind of clusters that filled a bin. Jonathan sped past, a *tacho* every twelve to fifteen minutes. I was still lining my bin. It took me forty-five minutes to fill my first *tacho*, and secure my *ficha*. I managed three in two hours. Worse, with my clumsy fingers I lost grape aplenty, the juice running down to my wrists, staining my clothes, and my face as I mopped my brow.

Jonathan returned with a knowing glint in his eye. Apparently I had been talking to myself, trying to coax grape off the vine with words. Judging by the tone, they knew I had been cursing. Jonathan was a smart, assertive young man. I am not sure he believed me, but I told him I was the second person in my family to go to university, after my older brother. He and I talked about his dream of going to college. So I felt comfortable seeking his advice. How was I going to persuade the harvest crew to come in all day Saturday, and the day after, Palm Sunday? He looked at me sceptically. 'You can always ask, I suppose,' he replied. I suggested Sonia as the plaintiff. He shook his head. 'Argentines find it very easy to say no to an Argentine; more difficult with an outsider.' Not exactly encouraging, and while I understood, I did not sense Jonathan would be with me for the ask.

There was nothing else for it. Work on them, one by one. The next three hours, my bin in tow, working rhythmically alongside one harvester after another, focused on the men. These were strong people, proud, resourceful, dignified and determined. Alfredo, all sombrero and Zapata moustache, the foreman at a nearby vineyard who had brought his family, knowing that we in turn would send our workers to help there, Alfredo reassured me about the grape he was cutting and nibbling: 'This is fabulous Malbec, and it will make the best wine.' His son, Nelson, a lean, handsome twenty-something, who had a girlfriend working at his side and an infant at his feet, could barely stop to talk as he produced one bin after another with factory-style efficiency: 'This weather is cool, we have to make the most of it now, not tomorrow when it may change.' Lorenzo, a thin, middle-aged fellow who picked up each *tacho* as if it was a mere paperweight, told me how lucky we were that the weather had eased: 'On the farm next to my house, they have botrytis.' Roberto, a tall, gangly teenager, clearly the champion *ficha*-gatherer, working in tandem with his sister, carrying her bins down the line, Roberto was thinking Saturday night: 'I go dancing, always, till early Sunday morning.'

All those tired one-liners I had used down the years to make the ask, to break the ice, to clinch the deal. 'So, *Señor Presidente*, what did you do to deserve bumping into me this morning?' 'So, Senator, what's a nice guy like you doing in a place like this?' But a harvester in Mendoza? Why would he or she give up Palm Sunday just to save my dream, or, to be blunt, my bank account? I was a Brit; this was Argentina, God's own country, where the Almighty himself gave a hand to help the national team score in the World Cup.

I was still on my knees squashing grape rather than cutting it, looking like a very unhappy gaucho. Alfredo, the elder in this group and natural leader of the crew, was agnostic, twiddling one fierce moustache: 'We normally work till the siesta on Saturday, no more.' His son Nelson, an influence with the younger crowd, was openly indifferent: 'I have a baptism; it's Palm Sunday.' Roberto, the disco-king, could not take it seriously as he marched down the line with yet another *tacho*: 'I sleep Sundays.' Only Lorenzo, working patiently alongside his wife, offered hope: 'If my *compañeros* work, I will work.'

And then something happened, sight unseen, almost invisible. A whisper here, a glance there, a nod between partners, a brief exchange as harvesters crossed paths with their *tachos*. Sonia stopped by, telling everyone that all the children were happily playing at the house, Alegría in charge of the crèche. Sonia had brought water, juices, Cokes. Timing is everything, my darling.

Gabriel announced that we had now filled twenty grape containers, a cracking pace. Gabriel, please don't give the impression that we're going to get this done in twenty-four hours. Marta told me everyone would go home for lunch in about an hour. Marta, I heard myself saying under my breath, I don't need to hear that we will lose three hours of harvesting to the lunchtime siesta.

All these thoughts were racing unspoken when Alfredo's formidable wife, a grandmother with the complexion of a girl, announced the verdict: 'If we don't get all the grape in on Saturday, we can be here on Sunday.' Nelson's girlfriend, the mother of Alfredo's grandson, chimed in brightly: 'We can always go to mass on Sunday evening.' Roberto's sister, who was a study in serious contrast to the disco-dancer, remarked shyly: 'I will try to bring him too.' Lorenzo's wife looked at her husband, nodding: 'We know how much this means to you and your *señora*.'

Not for the first time, Argentina surprised me, and reminded me how much I still had to learn about my adopted country. It's the women.

The harvest came in, peacefully, rhythmically, happily. The weather stayed on-side, hot but never oppressive. I played harvester. Sonia played provider, with constant rounds of liquid. Our children played mum and dad to the little ones who had such a raucous time playing in our yard. There was lots of laughter in the vineyard, especially at the sight of the Englishman on his knees, still swearing in Spanglish. There was unbridled joy as one couple announced a pregnancy, and everyone gathered round to congratulate the mother with kisses, the father with hearty backslaps. And a few tears back at the house as the children had to leave Alegría's play-camp at the end of the day. Sonia and I packed our kids in the car and followed our grape to the winery, excited to see it sorted, pulped and filtered into stainless-steel tank. The first harvest for a wine, and even the industrial side of winemaking seemed inspiring.

We still had a third of the Malbec to bring in. Luis suggested we pay all those who came to work on Sunday five *fichas* for showing up. I thought about doubling it. He shook his head. Twenty of our original crew of twenty-two appeared early on Palm Sunday, most of them riding in aboard Alfredo's tractor-trailer, a few women a little sleepy, some of the men slightly hung over, but all ready to work. Even Roberto, who told us all with great pride that he had come straight from the *boliche*, the disco, in La Consulta. For once, his sister seemed to be doing the heavy lifting as we poured grape into those buckets with the air of those celebrating a job well done.

The goal was to finish by Sunday lunchtime, and we did. As the final buckets were loaded, Sonia and our kids drove up on our tractor with our small offering. Baskets loaded with *choripán*, chorizo sausage in fresh bread, a speciality, washed down with beer, wine and soda. I served, Sonia served, the kids served, and I heard the women giggling about never before having met the *dueño*, the boss, let alone been served by him. We talked, about expecting babies, about inflation, about our soccer team in Mendoza, about this year compared to last year, about *choripán* with beer and its effect on the spirit.

The first harvest ended with a team photo of everyone, taken from the back of the harvest truck. However the wine turned out, we had a portrait for the ages.

*

Luis, vineyard manager, winemaker:

Sometimes your body talks to you, you get sick with a flu or a pneumonia, and you have to stop everything, sleep, rest, live wisely, so the body recovers. I think the planet is talking to us right now, I see this illness in the mountains, I see it down below in the valley, I see the change in the vineyards. And the planet is telling us we have to change, if we want to keep our climate as good as it is for our vineyards.

So for me this year's rain at the harvest was not a surprise. I almost expect a difficult harvest now. I try to plan for it, thinking of every possibility. I lost a vineyard in 2001, to a terrible hailstorm, big stones of hail. And every time I go back to that vineyard I feel the loss. I see it in the spirit of the people who work there. I try to rebuild their *animo*, as we say in Spanish, but I can't. It's very sad.

And then there was the harvest of 1998. It rained for twelve days straight, just as we were going to harvest. Botrytis reached almost every vineyard in every region of Mendoza. It was like going to a funeral. I was working with my father then, and I remember thinking it was like going in black, visiting the vineyards where we had grape, or where we bought grape. What made it even worse was that, of course, we tried to save the grape, even as it was dying before our eyes. The workers would be deep in mud, and water, the soil was just mud, and the grape was rotten already. And when we reached the winery, it was like a death smell. All you could see was a cloud of spores from the fungus, a grey cloud I remember, and the smell was so strong, the smell of dirt and death. We say in Spanish *podrido*. 'Putrid.'

This year I was worried, but I wasn't frightened. We brought in some of the grape early so that we wouldn't be gambling everything on the weather. What worried me most was that we had so much good grape, I mean high-quality grape that should go to the best wine, and I didn't see how we would bring it all in when we lost those days to rain. I feared we would have to choose what grape to save, and what to lose.

What saved us was the new kind of planting. These days we plant, as I did in David and Sonia's vineyard, so that you never have clusters of grape that close together; we have good distribution. So when the rain stopped, the sunshine and the fresh air dried the grape quickly without rot. And it helps that the soil in Finca Alegría is sandy, with stones, the water goes right through, not clay as we have elsewhere in Mendoza. It dries so much faster in their vineyard.

I remember David and Sonia in their kitchen on one of those days when it was raining. We were all looking out of the window at the vineyard, and the water, and the grey sky, the puddles forming. Sonia's face was just *angustiada*, angst-ridden, that is so unlike her, she is always such a calm spirit. Sonia's face always says peace, but not now.

And David was listening to me, but he wasn't hearing me. He has so much experience, of so many things, but I could see he had no experience of this, the balance between nature and the farm. I understood why he was so nervous, but I wished he would listen to me. In the same week, my father and I were waiting to harvest land near by, with grape worth probably 100,000 dollars. When it's yours, you know the fear that comes with the rain.

I'm very happy with the harvest. Our berries took in a little water, just a little, so some of the grape is diluted, but not so that you would notice. We made our priorities, and that meant the Malbec came first, and the Malbec is excellent. I'm at peace with what we did in Finca Alegría. The way David and Sonia are, working in the vines, bringing food to the workers and showing them a human side, that was something special, the way they talked to the people as equals. It is very charismatic, and it will help us in years to come when we need the help of those people.

So I'm at peace. I'm just worried about how we're living as a planet, and where we will be in ten, twenty, thirty years' time. Because I think of the Alegría vineyard like a son, and I want it to have a long life . . .

\*

# Reality Check

Slowly, for three weeks, our grapes fermented into wine. Then it was time for waiting, months and months in barrels. There was nothing to do.

Except, except. We could start thinking how we could promote the wine. In the real world, marketing, advertising and public-relations departments were paid to plan these million-dollar campaigns. We were two people, with four kids, two jobs, and not a lot of spare time or money. Surely there was a television series to be made here, we thought. And what better place than my old network, Channel 4 of London, known for its cutting-edge productions and its formidable commissioning editors.

Humorist Clive James once entertained the television industry with his assessment of talent:

' . . . If you can't write, then you direct.

'If you can't direct, then you present.

'If you can't present, then you shoot.

'And if you can do NONE of the above, then you become a commissioning editor at the BBC or Channel 4 . . . '

I flew into London for a warm meeting with a commissioning editor at Channel 4. I had submitted a two-page proposal for a TV series, *Bottling the Dream.*

It began:

Sonia and David, experienced broadcasters for CNN and ITN, mum and dad to four kids, part-time wine buffs, have a dream. To build a vineyard from scratch. To plant their own vine. And to make a wine that will pit them against the best in the world . . .

My friend, the commissioning editor, appeared positive. 'I can see this on our screen, and we should do it, because you were a face of this channel for so long,' she told me, beaming. 'There's just one issue.'

I waited.

'We don't make television ourselves. It's all outsourced these days.'

So a day later I found myself stepping out of the London Underground at Tottenham Court Road, the stop for the old Odeon Cinema. As a child, I had blurry memories of my father taking me to the afternoon cartoons at the Odeon, in the days when everything was black and white and London invariably grey. Mickey, and Donald, and Bambi. Except Bambi was in colour, very vivid. My father less so.

Now I was back on Tottenham Court Road to visit the production company selected by the Channel 4 network to be the makers of *Bottling the Dream*. It was one of the dozens of start-ups to emerge in the years after the British government mandated entrepreneurial flair. Widespread outsourcing gave work to supposedly creative spirits rather than network apparatchiks. In fact, many network apparatchiks had left to start their own companies, and exchange their BBC pension plans for much larger personal wealth. A cursory look at the history of this company told me they specialized in 'Reality TV':

*Interior Rivalry* – the show that takes no prisoners in the search to find Britain's best home stager . . . The stakes are high, for each week contestants face a new challenge . . . working round the clock to transform living rooms, kitchens, gardens and finally whole houses on tight budgets.

What was a home stager, I wondered.

Grow your own drugs – whether you've got haemorrhoids, nits, eczema, depression, or even a dog with fleas, this show has a cure for you . . . Our ethnobotanist can show you how to make creams, cough sweets, teas, insecticides, bath bombs . . . from the stuff growing in a window box or a corner of the back garden.

What was an ethnobotanist? What was a bath bomb? And who on earth wanted to make insecticides at home?

*Better Off Wed!* The show that asks couples to stop and honestly evaluate whether they are compatible enough to make a lifelong commitment to each other . . . Our couples will watch their relationship play out in front of their wedding congregation, before they are asked to make the biggest decision of their lives . . . Do they really think they are better off wed?

That one, at least, I pictured clearly. Emotional striptease meets divorce court.

Debbie greeted me, an engaging, wide-eyed spirit at the company. After all, the commissioning editor had sent me. She sat me down with a cup of tea on an orange couch and glanced over my proposal before we watched the ten-minute pilot I had made, featuring the landscape, the locals, the challenge of making great wine. Debbie recoiled, visibly, as I cut grape, picked up my bucket and walked through the vineyard, talking straight, as if I still worked for network news. 'Done a few things in my life, but nothing quite as challenging as trying to make wine,' I concluded pompously as I walked past the camera with a forty-pound bucket of grape on my shoulder.

'I hate that, that straight-to-camera stuff, so unreal.' She shook her head. 'I don't get news, the way it's done, the style, the takeaway. Unreal. Don't get it, never have.'

OK, Debbie didn't get news.

'I gather you were one of the people in at the beginning of the channel.' She took a sip from her mug. 'It's hard for me to imagine what television was like back then.'

Back then . . . I offered the thought that, down the years, I had something of a following with certain viewers, after more than two decades reporting from across the world, and after so many years working on a programme seen night after night on the same channel. I recalled personal messages from so many TV watchers after my final broadcast.

Debbie cut me off. 'How long ago?'

Debbie wondered whether I had thought seriously about the amount of work involved in making a TV series. I thought I knew about the hard work that went with making TV, I ventured. Eight weeks in the African bush, producing television on the Ethiopian famine. Ten days in the frozen Siberian oilfields, making a mini-documentary on the collapse of the Soviet political-industrial complex. Fear in the highlands of Peru, pursuing the merciless war being waged by Maoist rebels against the central government.

Debbie shook her head. 'It's just that a concept like yours needs a totally different approach. For example, we would want to shoot you and your wife – she's lovely, by the way – we would want to shoot you together all the time, round the clock, you know, feeling the tension, and the stress, and the emotions that arise.' She paused. 'The image would be a constant two-shot, the two of you reacting to each other, angry at times, worried at times, not happy, happy.'

I joked that I hoped we would be allowed to sleep without a camera on us. Silence.

'And then there's the people who are working with you, the vineyard manager, the winemaker, the accountant, even the bank manager. We need all of them to show us the stresses and strains of this,' she declared, standing up to pace the room. 'And I'm thinking that we need to be there when you disagree with what those people are doing.'

I said that we relied on such people rather than disagreed with them. One of the joys of the venture so far had been the friends we had made among the people we worked with, and the basis of many relationships lay in mutual respect.

'And finally, there's the children,' she continued. 'They would be at the local school, right? Dealing with culture shock?'

I replied that our youngest children lived in Washington DC, attended a bilingual school that prided itself on giving kids personal attention, and that we had no intention of moving them full-time to the Andes.

'That's a problem right away,' she interjected. 'This needs family tension, tension across the family, including the kids, and for that the family should be there, to create the drama of living in a remote place, new environment, new friends, and so on. It can't just be stress among you two, you and Sonia, it's got to have a generational fall-out. The kids should be living through this challenge.'

I reminded Debbie that the proposal was entitled *Bottling the Dream*, stressing the D-word.

'Not a good title,' she frowned. 'There's no takeaway in that title.'

We agreed to talk again, knowing that we would not. Debbie, ready to produce 'reality'. And me, faced with the new reality of television. What happened there? Did my old network leave me? Or did I leave them?

A savvy cameraman from ITN days, a wine-lover himself, messaged us: 'Don't worry. If the channel's producers had their way, the show would end with Sonia leaving David in the Andes for a polo player; David drinking himself to death alone in the château. That's the formula of "Reality TV". But the wine itself would triumph, to give us all a feel-good element . . . '

# Hacks

Did mainstream media lose the plot? When did 'reality' become such prefabricated artifice? And, I suppose: was journalism dying? The question I heard time and again in the years after I left the business. The question I always met with categoric response.

No, journalism was not dying. Rather, journalism faced the kind of challenge that the Industrial Revolution presented to our forebears. The kind of clash that came only once in a hundred years, when technology first collided with long-established working practice, then outpaced and overtook the craft. The kind of revolution that handed the power of the pen and the printing press, suddenly and dramatically, to the reader, the punter, the citizen, certainly in the developed world, via the chatroom, and the blogosphere, and Twitter, and the flip-camera. The kind of challenge that had an established industry scatter in countless directions, embracing and offering online product for free, only to realize that it was committing financial suicide. The kind of stampede to the future that made speed the number-one goal, forgetting that content had also been a prerequisite for success ever since the Gutenberg Press.

For that generation of journalist one ahead of me, this industrial revolution proved painful to watch. Many of them had carved out the media landscape in the years after the Second World War, during the birth of TV and the shift from the written word to spoken narrative. They had been pioneers in their own right, making truth-telling, picture, tone and style essential elements of broadcasting that had a purpose, indeed a mission to explain. If you watched, and listened, and read new media from their perspective, the changing landscape represented journalism lost.

Journalism that was obsessed with speed, rather than getting the story right.

Journalism that focused on the dramatic, not the important.

Journalism that fretted about profit margins, not narrative.

Journalism that turned mainstream media into slugfest, shouting matches, losing all sense of the mission to inform and explain.

Journalism that turned some anchors, and columnists, and bloggers, into demi-gods in their own minds, who believed they had the right, the self-proclaimed duty, to tell the audience what to think and how to think.

Journalism that propagated half-truths, even proven lies, in pursuit of ratings and audience share, or political agenda.

Journalism that served as Greek chorus for the government of the day, cheerleading as politicians took nations to war, not questioning why.

Journalism that seized on populist issues, and fed the majority populace with what they wanted, demonizing others in the process.

Journalism that made the narrative us versus them.

Journalism that screamed conflict, not compromise.

Journalism based on doing whatever it took to generate an audience.

Journalism that flouted just about every rule in the handbook.

How did that happen? And why?

From where I sat, as a member of a middle generation of journalist, positioned between the post-war pioneers and the millennium mavericks, a number of lessons emerged.

*Lesson number one:* Technology ruled, OK? I entered the business waiting in line for a coin-box phone. I left journalism with a personal phone that could transmit my image and voice across continents, direct to TV or mobile phone.

I did start journalistic life waiting with coins to feed a phone box, specifically to phone in the score of a soccer game, for which I was paid the handsome sum of four old British shillings, sent to me through the mail in a postal order by London's evening newspapers, of which there were two: hence double the money for one piece of information, minus the phone charges. A gentleman at the paper in Fleet Street, with an audible typewriter, asked me to identify myself, give him my password, which he checked from a long written list, so proving I was a trusted source. Then I intoned the result: 'Boreham Wood 2, St Albans 1.' Usually the news ended up stamped on the back page of the Saturday-evening football edition, in coarse, grubby black ink, entitled 'Late Scores'.

In my Reuter days, in the big-time for the first time as a foreign correspondent, I graduated to a telex that enabled me to report direct to my bosses, after I had punched a tape that required ten to fifteen minutes to prepare a typical 800-word story, then fed it through the machine without interruption. You allocated five to seven minutes for that, and you did it only twice a day, the Nightlead early in the afternoon, the Daylead before you went to bed, the world divided into two twelve-hour news cycles. Unless there was big, and truly big, breaking news. Europe's last fascist Dictator died, the final link to Hitler and Mussolini, and we fed out the carefully prepared tape breathlessly, saying simply:

> Madrid, Nov 20, Reuter –
> General Franco dead – official.

But others beat us to the story in those days of ticker-tape and steady hands.

And head office in Fleet Street noticed immediately, sending us this message marked 'Urgent'. Part Latin, part English, but that was the way back then.

> ProMadrid exLondon, grateful explain how Associated Press had Franco dead at 0510, UPI 0511, Reuters 0512.

No answer to that. History had been written, and obviously others were quicker to the tape, or others received the call before us. Until then the office joke was 'UPI – first with the story, and first with the correction.'

By the time two Popes died within fifty-three days of each other in Rome, I worked from the first generation of VDU, visual display units, the early computers, and the time-delay was considerably reduced. However, the old rules on truth and sourcing still applied. Woken at 3 a.m. by a phone call from London, informing me that Pope John Paul I had died according to Vatican Radio, I laughed and replied: 'Don't be ridiculous, the Pope died a few weeks ago.' I was ordered to get to the office immediately. Reuters reported what Vatican Radio was saying, but they waited on their own correspondent to confirm it.

TV proved a shock. I had film, and soundtrack, and a camera crew to manage. But the delivery system remained a minefield. Journalism was not just about finding the story, and filming it, and writing it; it was crucially about delivering it. So Mohinder Dhillon and I led the world in reporting that dreadful famine in the Karamoja, in northern Uganda. But everything hinged on finding a way out for our unprocessed film and commentary track, the only copy we had of a week's worth of dangerous, at times excruciating, work. We gave it, in a sealed can wrapped up tight in an ITN bag, to a pilot on an airstrip in Uganda. He gave it to a friend in Nairobi, Kenya, who met his plane at Wilson airfield. That friend went to Jomo Kenyatta Airport, and there waited to select a human pigeon taking British Airways to London. The pigeon was prepped to hand the can of film to a driver, who met him or her at Heathrow Airport. Usually it worked, and thank God it worked on the Karamoja famine. Occasionally it didn't. I once entrusted film to an Italian aid worker, a former girlfriend, leaving Mogadishu, Somalia, in the middle of a war. She reached London, the new boyfriend found her first as she came through customs. Need I say more? They disappeared for three days, then she remembered the film and called my office.

In the Middle East, in the mid 1980s, I began to see the technology kick in. On the better days in Beirut I dispatched a driver with an edited story for the nightly news, and we made it via satellite. It cost a packet. Hence the most important conversation of the day centred on whether I had material that justified the cost of a satellite that night. I looked back on those conversations as being the last chapters in the age-old ballet between journalist and editor, the conversation that tied us to our forebears at the Crimea, or Gettysburg, or Khartoum, or Gallipoli, or Iwo Jima and Saigon. 'Do I hold the front page for you?' they asked a century before, I imagined. In my time the conversation sounded a mite more prosaic. 'Am I telling the editor of *News at Ten* that you have a lead story worth three to four minutes, worth paying thousands of dollars for? Is that what we have here?'

But at last we had reached the defining moment. 'The news' meant 'the news' that day, not news filmed last week. When we delivered that, and we succeeded, it was a new frontier. I thought of the day in Beirut when we broke through the front lines to a hospital for children mentally ill, and starving, filming them under bombardment, exultant when the images reached London that night and stunned those who watched. I remembered the night in Israel when I was able to report live back to London – how exciting it seemed at the time – that a man of peace had won an election. I recalled the day I reached Pakistan and persuaded my Oxford classmate Benazir Bhutto to give me an exclusive interview in the hours that followed the assassination of the country's President, handing my tape to an engineer who fed it to London from a portable satellite dish.

Going live, from Jerusalem, or Moscow, or Washington DC, followed inevitably; so too the hand-held machine to deliver such journalism; and the issue became not when, how and how much. But how often. The treadmill of 24/7 had arrived, with journalists expected to file repeatedly and endlessly in the course of a working day, broadcasters often obliged to stand at a live camera location and offer one live shot after another for different outlets, thereby being denied time to research and report first-hand what they ended up saying.

And the cornucopia of media meant that you competed with a vast array of rivals for valuable time and space. The technology made the world a densely populated village of journalists, some experienced practitioners, many more novices learning on the job, and millions who became instant citizen journalists capable of taking a picture, or researching an issue, writing their own account for a personal blog.

In that environment, speed became the driving force. Looking back, it was understandable, if a shade comical, that my bosses at Reuters fretted about being two minutes behind a competitor on the death of General Franco: history, after all, was being written as dawn broke over Madrid that November morning. But to watch the titans of millennium journalism wrestle over who was first with O. J. Simpson's car chase, or Britney Spears going into rehab, or Oprah Winfrey's latest make-over, or how many cocktail waitresses Tiger Woods bedded . . . well, the technology giveth and the technology taketh away.

*Lesson number two:* The profit margin ruled, OK?

Such were the days of penury, and job cuts, and downsizing after I left the business that it was hard to recall how protected the journalism industry had been in a bygone age.

My generation of journalist was taught not to worry about the cost of a story, but to make damn sure the story justified the cost.

We could set off for Beirut, or Belfast, or Beijing, concentrate on fact-finding, eyewitness research, scrupulous attention to detail, as high a percentage of the truth as we could assemble, then add compelling narrative. Money was only a factor if you did not deliver product.

Once I was stuck in Amman, Jordan, waiting for an exclusive interview with King Hussein. Monarchs, as you might imagine, act of their own volition, and His Majesty flew out on his personal jet just as he should have been sitting down with us, leaving no word as to when he might return, the buzz being that he had left to see a mistress in Europe. I admitted defeat. In the Byzantine world of an Arab Kingdom, you relied on having someone inside the court to convey your message. I decided to call my contact and tell him I was leaving, seeing as the King had flown out that morning. 'We do understand,' the King's man told me. 'And His Majesty will, of course, be covering your hotel costs. Just let the hotel manager know.'

As I put down the phone, my editor at ITN, David Nicholas, rang. 'I worry about the cost, you worry about the story. I want the interview.' He paused, hearing me sigh. 'And forget about them paying our costs. Whether we get the interview or not, we don't let governments or kings pay for us. Call the Palace back, and tell them you're staying.'

The following day, King Hussein returned. We were summoned to the Palace within an hour. 'My dear sir, I do apologize for your long wait,' said the Hashemite monarch in the disarming manner of an erstwhile Sandhurst army officer, the only time a king addressed me as 'sir'. He delivered a cracking interview, lambasting the Americans and the British in unusually strong language, suggesting that the United States and Britain were sowing the seeds of further conflict in the Middle East. My boss, David Nicholas, was happy with the interview, particularly at the way the White House picked up on our story and Downing Street felt obliged to respond.

'Just remember, boyo,' he said, mocking his own Welsh tones, 'I worry about the cost, you worry about the story.'

Those days did not last. The networks lost their monopoly on television advertising as Cable TV exploded with dozens of channels, and by the mid 1990s I was both journalist and line manager, under orders to control, enforce and maximize budgets as well as research, report and present. I weighed every trip we made, balanced story against cost, budget against narrative, research against time-sheet. Decisions were no longer based on the relative merits or importance of one story versus another. In the same period, I watched countless news outlets, including my own, spend liberally on developing websites that offered product for free.

Something was wrong with that picture.

From across the spectrum, the tell-tale signs were of an industry at the crossroads. Even the wealthiest television news networks cut back. At *ABC News*, a dear friend, the late Peter Jennings, lead anchorman, talked of his dismay at cutbacks ordered by his corporate owners. Worse still were the stories placed on his nightly news programme because of their appeal to certain demographics. 'We have to draw more middle-aged women, hence stories about women in their forties, looking after both their mothers and their daughters,' Peter said.

My brother-in-war, the photographer Don McCullin, explained he was having trouble getting work, at least the kind of work that had made him a legend worthy of museum exhibitions. 'The pictures that Sunday magazines want these days are of wealthy, fat bastards sitting by their swimming pools,' he said with his trademark disdain for the frivolous.

I made him smile, sharing with him how, after my days with the FARC in Colombia, I had written a lengthy report for the *Observer*, a respected Sunday newspaper in London. 'I can pay you a hundred pounds,' said the *Observer*'s foreign editor, noting that the sum did not reflect the minimum wage, let alone the rarity of working in a war zone. 'Sorry about that, David. If you were a celebrity chef, and you did six easy ways to cook pasta for the weekend section, the fee would be in the thousands.'

The money was gone. News and information were free. Yet tens of millions of new readers had discovered the *Guardian*, and the *New York Times*, and the *News of the World* via the IT revolution. It was a dramatic expansion of market, not a contraction. If the new world was prepared to pay ten dollars a book, served wirelessly via a Kindle, then was the consumer so opposed to paying a few cents or pennies for a reliable, trustworthy, content-rich news source?

As ever Rupert Murdoch, machiavellian genius, led the way in demanding that the news industry draw the line and make the client pay for on-line service, beginning with the *Wall Street Journal.* Where Rupert led, others followed. But this time even the liberal media wished him success.

Murdoch's legacy, and it was lasting, lay in the politicization of mainstream media on both sides of the Atlantic. He bought newspapers, and supported them strongly, in pursuit of influence allied to his agenda.

He created TV networks, and made them formidable operations, in pursuit of profit linked to his ambition. He made prime ministers and presidents, he dumped them when it suited him. And he succeeded. By the time I left journalism and joined the United Nations, Murdoch's empire represented the cutting-edge of American journalism, forcing virtually all others to follow in his jetstream. Much as old colleagues scoffed at Murdoch's product, particularly the ultra-conservative Fox News channel in the United States and the *Sun* newspaper in Britain, the knock-on effects were felt throughout the news business, with others in mainstream media tilting left, or right, or populist, in search of a response to the Murdoch effect.

I had a couple of run-ins with Mr Murdoch down the years. First, he tried to hire me for *The Times* in London in the late 1980s. I declined. Then, his publishing company paid Newt Gingrich, conservative Speaker of the US House of Representatives, an outsize sum of money for his memoirs. Coincidentally, at that very moment, the Murdoch empire was seeking changes in US law to enable its expansion. In the corridors of Congress, I waited for Mr Murdoch with one of my lines that worked so well with politicians. He barely stopped. 'I don't have to speak to you, and I'm not going to.'

Whatever fear and loathing the man engendered, Murdoch's chutzpah and savvy were a force to admire. In my Washington years, he went from near-death experience, certainly near-bankruptcy in the late 1980s, to market leader and driving force of the new journalism. If you ever wondered why America went to war in Iraq without question, then part of the answer lay in the power of Murdoch's Fox News channel. Rupert Murdoch's subalterns led American media via the 24/7 cable news cycle in that period, hammering home the Bush administration's claims that Saddam Hussein had weapons that threatened New York, Washington DC and Los Angeles, spreading the spin that Iraq had a hand in 9/11, even suggesting that Saddam could go nuclear.

Yet they were not alone. Where Rupert led, others followed. No serious journalist forgot the moment when the venerable *New York Times* apologized for how it misrepresented Saddam Hussein's weapons arsenal before the war. There were no WMD (weapons of mass destruction). The question, in fact, was whether the media had become a weapon of mass deception.

There lay the most important lesson. An Iraq war did not happen without government seizing the opportunity to enlist the mainstream media to its cause. Without government working its favourite journalists to plant its version of events. Without government seeding the idea, via national media, that war, not peace, was inevitable. And mainstream media could not blame Rupert Murdoch for that. The fault, dear Brutus, lay in themselves and no one else.

The media, to put it bluntly, was suborned over Iraq by carefully calibrated government campaigns on both sides of the Atlantic. Trust us, the campaign's spin doctors said, we have the goods on Saddam. Trust us, they maintained, once we have removed Saddam we can put Iraq back on its feet in a matter of months. Trust us, they added, then we will launch a diplomatic offensive on the wider crisis in the Middle East, starting with the Arab-Israeli conflict. Trust us, this will be the beginning of a new age of freedom and democracy in the Middle East.

Those who dared to question this spin heard from the enforcers on either side of the Atlantic: Karl Rove at the White House in Washington, Alastair Campbell in Downing Street. Both had a habit of threatening to cut off your access, if not your balls. Before long the White House media saved its questions for another time. Without access, without the White House briefing, the Prime Minister's interview or the live shot from the White House lawn, there was no job.

The spin machine in the West Wing and Downing Street ruled. And why did that matter, beyond the obvious concern about how democracy functioned in the age of quiescent media? Governments in Washington and London became obsessed about controlling the news cycle, feeding it constantly with a speech, an interview, a soundbite, a line. The truth was that government played 24/7 news at its own game, inventing the latest, breaking news for the never-ending drama cycle. Locked together in a relationship of mutual convenience, both government and media sought to control the news cycle as if it really mattered, as if policy was made on breakfast radio, then implemented on nightly news. The result? Both became addicted to short-term thinking, feeding the 24/7 beast. Ultimately, if controlling the media machine forced governments into short-term thinking, the price was good governance. Serious indeed.

# In Vino Veritas

The world of wine journalism is a rarified one, where the opinions of a few respected writers move an industry. It is a privileged world, insulated from the mainstream industry. The wine world represents a niche, followed by two key audiences. First, the wine investors looking to invest in icon wines at auction, and secondly, the connoisseurs willing to learn about a drink they enjoyed. With so much choice, with such an unpredictable product year after year, people turn for advice to certain critics above all others. Among them, a very learned lady who writes for the *Financial Times*, one Jancis Robinson.

I was looking forward to dinner. In the world of wine, I could hardly have been in better company. I was going to sit across the table from Jancis, arguably the world's most respected wine writer, enjoying a splendid meal at one of the oldest *bodegas* in the city of Mendoza, 1844 the year of its construction. All around us the best and the brightest of British wine writers on an all-expenses-paid trip.

'What do you think of this, Jancis?' I asked as we sipped a delicious Mendoza Chardonnay, more than a decade old; 1997 to be precise. Silence. And the conversation returned to university days, Jancis telling us about life at Oxford in the late 1960s. I took another mouthful of the Chardonnay, swallowed carefully, waiting to return to the question on my mind. 'Forgive me, Jancis, but what do you make of this wine?'

Ms Robinson paused a moment, took the smallest of sips, then looked at me over her trademark spectacles and replied: 'It's better than anything I've tasted from Burgundy of the same year, same age. Excellent.' She confided that she would put it on her shopping list, alongside a South African Chardonnay she loved and bought for herself.

When Jancis excused herself early, pleading jet lag at the end of her first day in Argentina, my dinner companions gave me a pat on the back. 'You know, nobody asks Jancis what she thinks of a wine, it's just not done,' explained Marisel, master chef and food writer from New York. 'You wait for her to write a wine up. I can't believe you asked that question. Well done.' The owner of the vineyard, and the winery that

94

produced the Chardonnay, our friend Laura Catena, exulted: 'Thank you, thank you for that. Wow! That quote is priceless. We are better than Burgundy! We age better than Burgundy!'

Welcome to the world of wine journalism. Elsewhere the working journalist had been taken down a peg, or two, or three, by the technology revolution which shared so much information with so many people, diluting the influence of the professional. Yet wine writers represented a species apart. They reminded me of a press corps from a bygone age. Privileged, courted, sought after by those in power, they oozed influence. Their opinions mattered; they made and broke reputations. Yet the best of them showed how to defend their independence at all costs, how to avoid politicization, and a few proved you could make money online.

Travelling with wine writers for a week in Mendoza, I sensed the *modus operandi* of the press corps from my younger days, in Madrid, and Rome, and Beirut. A gaggle of journalists in contact with each other regularly, often on the road together, so aware of each other's foibles, predilections and pressure points. A press corps where everyone abided by some clear rules designed to foster a measure of unity, keep everyone on the same page and preserve a hierarchical pecking order.

In Rome, so long ago, it had meant a tightly knit crew that gathered at the Foreign Press Club, in Via dell'Umilta (ironic that, because the last thing a press corps boasted was humility), just off the splendid Plaza de España, a true legacy of the Mussolini period with its bar subsidized by the government. So too phone calls and telex messages, and even airline tickets were available at a special price to *la stampa*, the press. You chewed over stories of the day, compared versions, and determined where the Italian narrative was heading. The leader of the pack was a flamboyant, passionate Brit named Peter Nichols, correspondent for the London *Times* for decades. At critical moments, such as the collapse of yet another Italian government (in my time the country had three governments in eighteen months), Peter gave the lead, advising us when the Prime Minister was about to declare *crisi aperto*, the open crisis that signalled the end for that particular administration. Reuters usually carried the story first, being the lead round-the-clock outlet in those days, setting the table for colleagues. Then Peter wrote at length for *The Times*, Leslie for the *Daily Telegraph*, John for the *Guardian*, Marlise for the *New York Times*, Sari for the *Washington Post*, and so on. I learned to expect the call from Peter, steering me to the story with endearing finesse, telling me what to do while making me believe that I knew what to do. And it was an honour, positively so, to spend a weekend with him and his adorable wife, Paola, up at their villa on Lake Bracciano. Sadly, the Murdoch organization replaced him, in Peter's words, as if he were a pair of old boots. He died not long after.

Occasionally, of course, came a gate-crasher to the club. In Rome he presented himself in the form of one R. W. Apple of the *New York Times*, 'Johnny' Apple, as he was known, a bear of a man, triple-chinned, rumpled, with a raucous voice and a spirit to boot. Johnny Apple was then in his forties; he had yet to make his name as an iconic journalist, political seer, confidant of the powerful and, later, superb writer on food and wine. Sent to Italy from his base in London, at the height of the national trauma over the terrorism of the Red Brigades, and the kidnapping of Italian Premier Aldo Moro, Johnny appeared at my side one morning as I elbowed my way into the Turin courtroom where the leaders of the guerrilla group stood trial, pushing my way to the cage where I talked to them on first-name terms. Behind me, every step of the way, I felt my new friend Johnny pushing me forward. 'I heard how you pull this off most days, and get to these guys,' he told me. 'I wanted to see it for myself.'

Without a word of Italian, he watched me chat with the founder of the Red Brigades, a bearded, rather intimidating figure named Renato Curcio, who was fond of calling me *stronso*, an affectionate way of saying 'turd', and equally fond of making such declarations as: 'The kidnapping of Aldo Moro represents the highest form of proletarian justice in a class-ridden society.' I wondered aloud to my new American friend: 'So what would proletarian justice look like in a classless society?' Johnny laughed, then promptly hurried me outside for a debrief of everything I had obtained, pumping me for information before I had found the phone box to file my report to Rome.

When I saw Johnny's version in the *New York Times*, my initial reaction was less than enamoured. My new friend – Johnny had bought me a wonderful dinner, washed down with a bottle or two of lush Barolo, a stellar Italian wine – gave the impression somewhat that he had fought his way alone into the courtroom and spoken to the men behind the kidnapping of an Italian Prime Minister. But then he had real talent.

The man wrote like a maestro, he wove texture, nuance, balance into compelling narrative, like some fine wine. Every self-respecting press corps needed a gate-crasher. I had helped him. And he had taught me something priceless, how to write and explain in one seamless voice. He had the power of story-telling, dynamic, analytical and thoughtful at one and the same moment. We remained friends, and years later came payback. Before Johnny died, *bon vivant* to the end, I encouraged him to visit Mendoza, specifically to try the wineries and the restaurant of a dear friend, my mentor, Nicolás Catena. Johnny, always ready to enjoy magnificent wines with a good meal, was impressed and wrote a terrific review in the 'Food and Wine' pages of the *New York Times*.

Now, as I criss-crossed the province of Mendoza, riding the bus with the wine press corps, tasting at one *bodega*, lunch at another, then early-evening drinks followed by a vineyard dinner that had all the elements of a feast, I detected the same rules at work, certainly the same hierarchy in the coterie of journalists alongside me.

The leader of this pack, clearly, was my dinner companion Jancis Robinson, long-time writer for the *Financial Times*, author of the *Oxford Companion to Wine*, famously the first MW, 'Master of Wine', from the wine-writing class, not the wine trade. From appearances tenacious, a little brusque, tightly focused, thoroughly professional, the girl who read philosophy at Oxford had become the woman who put it all together in the world of wine. Others wrote more elegantly, perhaps. Some had more adventurous palates. But Jancis tasted, judged and wrote with a clarity and direction that was uniquely hers. And she had built a formidable following of devotees, particularly online, prepared to pay for her views and her adventures on jancisrobinson.com. Eat your heart out, Rupert Murdoch.

From our conversation I sensed a rather more shy spirit, humble in recognizing both her weaknesses and strengths. No one had such an encyclopaedic, universal, non-parochial view of the wine world, and the knowledge to go with it. Yet she was disarmingly honest about her own limitations. 'I could never do what you and your wife are doing, too much of a risk,' she made clear. 'The idea of a hailstorm, for example, destroying everything you have built, too much for me. Get very good help. Listen, be humble, and be patient.'

I wondered how she viewed the extraordinary influence she had, the ability to make or break a wine venture, rather like Robert Parker, the inventor of points, in the United States. She looked a trifle dismayed, her eyes a little sad behind her academic spectacles. 'No British writer, no British critic has the massive clout that certain Americans do,' she replied. 'I say what I think, but I don't have a massive idea of my own importance. Really I don't.'

Parker she generously described as 'the world's most experienced and trustworthy taster'. 'The last thing I would want is the power to taste this wine and declare it destined for greatness or consigned to the bin of rejection,' she explained. 'People like me, on the other side of the Atlantic, we just don't have the power to decide in an instant what your wine, for example, will do. And we don't want that power.'

But, of course, Jancis did wield that power, only without the clinical brutality of points. Her verdicts were more elegant, but just as steely.

Those travelling with her did not disagree. From more than one of the boys on the bus I heard what an honour, yes, honour, this was to be included on a trip with Jancis. Respect laced with admiration abounded, remarkably free of envy, and there was little doubt whose voice carried most weight and authority when it came to tasting. Even if everyone knew, no one was supposed to ask Jancis what she thought.

Close to her in the pecking order came the endearing, semi-rakish, somewhat picaresque figure of Oz Clarke, one-time Shakespearean actor turned wine writer. Every press corps needed an Oz; it was the Johnny Apple factor. Irreverent, but never offensive. Opinionated, but never pompous. Hard-working, diligent, painstaking in preparation for a presentation he made in Mendoza, while making it look easy. Behind the warm smile, and the fine features of a man who had once played General Juan Perón in *Evita* on the London stage, Oz had a palate to die for, I learned, and a palate that could recall a wine tasted years before, a formidable memory bank on which to draw when it came to defining what he liked. That was the key, so they said, to Oz winning the World Wine Tasting Championship back in the 1980s; which launched the West End actor into a new life as a wine writer and critic.

'Give me a sense of place in your wine, give me individuality, give me what you think people want, give me drinkability,' Oz told me one afternoon as we rode the bus to a magnificent winery and restaurant created by a friend, Carlos Pulenta, on the outskirts of Mendoza. 'Don't give me blandness, and conformity, and imitation. And please don't forget. It's not about having people like me write you up. It's about making the drinker want a second glass of what you make.'

Even if you hit the magic formula, Oz proved disarmingly blunt about the prospects for financial success. 'Making wine seems to me to be an extremely easy way to lose a lot of money,' he declared, adopting the tone of a friend telling you what you did not want to hear. 'The world has more than enough wine already, but I suppose you always think it's going to be the other bloke, not you, who goes to the wall. Anyway, you're an old journalist, and you can't put an old journalist down. You never take no for an answer, people like you. You will probably drop a bottle of yours on my front door, right?'

Oz, and a next-generation writer called Joe Fattorini, took the view that the real challenge of wine criticism lay in finding the gems at a price the average drinker could afford. 'It's easy to go to a lavish event celebrating Krug champagne, in the Krug room of the Dorchester Hotel, and drink vintage Krug while the master chef serves you a meal to match,' concluded Joe, a bald, brash thirty-something of a Yorkshireman who specialized in instant YouTube videos and sharp new-age commentary. Memorably, he filmed himself taking a bath in Malbec on our trip, his bald head purple with wine, then dispatched the video to his website. Equally memorable, I gathered from his colleagues, who viewed him as the talent to watch, was that he had dared to pan a new wine from a major Californian producer with this soubriquet: 'A complete car-crash of a wine, you can taste the under-carriage coming apart on the first sip.'

That was vintage Joe. 'The hard work, and Oz has taught me this, is finding great wines that nobody knows about, wines that many people can afford,' replied Joe, wrinkling a truly expressive nose. 'The hard work is cutting through the bullshit about wine.' How did the California wine maker react to that review of a car crash? 'You've dealt as a journalist with the masters of spin enforcement, Karl Rove at the White House and Alistair Campbell in London. Well, I had a PR agent for California who ripped my head off verbally for the "car crash", I lost count of the times the F-word was used. That's the challenge of staying independent.'

Maybe, but I had another thought riding the bus with the wine press corps in Mendoza. The thing that set this press corps apart for me was the central dilemma of its existence. Here you had some of the most respected wine writers in our world, celebrated for their independence of thought and judgement, fêted for their objectivity and freedom of expression. Yet they were being fêted and celebrated by wine producers who paid for business-class travel, five-star hotels and more memorable meals that I cared to think about. Surely, some compromise here?

'Obviously, we need them, and they need us,' said Joe as we headed out together, early one evening, to a sumptuous gala event hosted by the large Terrazas winery, a subsidiary of the French giant Moët & Chandon. 'But then you work in a media world which everyone knows has been deeply politicized, where journalists are intimate almost with those in power, where every story is measured by how much it costs to get it.'

He gave me a knowing smile, suggesting wisdom beyond his years. 'I look at that dilemma with a simple set of questions. How else are we going to taste for ourselves hundreds of new wines in a new place like Mendoza? How else are we going to see for ourselves how the vine is planted, and harvested, and treated? How else do I understand Argentina, because no magazine, or TV network, is going to pay my way? There are only a couple of people riding this bus, David, who make serious money out of wine writing.' There was no need to name them.

Sitting as I did on board, but an outsider looking in, I concluded that this press corps had more independence than the White House crowd I knew so well, or the Downing Street crowd I worked with. Certainly they were more aware of the dangers of intimacy with those who fed you, more conscious of the imperative not to be politicized, and were paid to be so, in their case into supporting one producer against another, one region against another, one style of wine-making against another. They cherished their freedom, and their own voices, just as they treasured their palates. Survival depended on it.

Anyway, as a glorious, rather drunken evening ended in the early hours with Jancis making notes of wines she had tasted and Oz trying to sing an Argentine bolero, I wondered to myself: who, in their right mind, in this press corps, challenged a professional as disciplined as Ms Robinson? Or a charismatic leader with such a formidable nose for the fake as Oz Clarke? In their hands, that press corps stayed reasonably true to itself and its mandate. As so often in life, leadership proved the vital variable.

I left them all with one nagging question. How on earth did they stay sober?

# Schmoozefest

The White House press corps ranked among the least alcoholic, yet the most drunk on power. On a Saturday evening in late spring every year, more than a thousand hacks plus their celebrity guests gathered at the Washington Hilton to schmooze with those in power, chief among them the President, First Lady, the Cabinet, US Senators, all the way down to the Governors of those fifty states, with stars of other constellations sprinkled across the ballroom. The zoology proved spellbinding on occasion. Angelina Jolie and Brad Pitt meet the chairman of the Joint Chiefs of Staff, the head of the US military. Bill Clinton meets Muhammad Ali. The President meets Cindy Crawford.

Forget about the material I taught at journalism school, all those high-minded dilemmas about the intimacy between press and government, about the compromise of supping with those in power, about the ethics of schmoozing with those you covered as journalists. What was there not to like about mixing with the good and the great: a cocktail with the President, a glass of wine with the head of Operation Iraqi Freedom, dinner with Jane Fonda, once married to Ted Turner of CNN fame, the mogul who gave the United Nations a billion dollars?

'Thanks for persuading Ted to do that,' I remarked at one point during my evening with la Fonda, groping for a conversation gambit after my fairly feeble and star-struck attempts to entice her to tell me her favourite movie roles, a question she clearly heard oh, so often. 'His decision, not mine, no sir, not mine,' she replied tartly, reminding me that she and Ted had divorced. 'I let him take the credit for that.' That Saturday evening in Washington did indeed represent a ticket that Hollywood stars accepted, that Fortune 50 companies tried to buy, that even Bill Gates accepted.

And who could say no to the chance to watch the world's most powerful politician humiliate himself in front of those who wrote the narrative of his presidency? The tradition, dating back a century, called for the President of the day to make fun of the press corps, and himself, laugh a little at the hacks, and with the hacks. But, above all, laugh at himself.

In the early 1990s, when newspapers and TV stations still had licences to print money, George Bush Senior, the original Mr Malaprop in the Bush family, made the evening look as painful as a tooth extraction, trying to get us to chuckle at his capacity for non sequitur, reminding us all how he invented Bushspeak with such gems as: 'We are blessed, so don't cry for me Argentina, the message is I care . . . it's no exaggeration to say the undecideds could go either way . . . when I want a little advice about Saddam Hussein, I turn to country music.'

Through the boom years, when the internet was such a dazzling new theatre that wealthy TV networks lined up to join forces with Microsoft, giving product away to have the Microsoft label attached to them, Bill Clinton was apt to use the evening to score points with a press corps that investigated him endlessly, pursued him relentlessly and second-guessed his every move in the early days of 24/7. After he was impeached, for oral sex in the Oval Office, his riffs to the White House correspondents reeked of self-pity. 'You know, during the Hundred Years War, the European press corps didn't even start second-guessing until 1370,' Clinton told us one Saturday evening late in his tenure, the finger wagging as he warmed to his theme. 'And just imagine the headlines if today's press corps covered yesterday's wars. "Lincoln speaks at Gettysburg – fails to articulate exit strategy."' The President paused, the timing of a comedian waiting for laughter. 'Or General MacArthur to Philippines: "I shall return – refuses to specify timetable." '

George Bush Junior patently disliked the evening, even though no modern-day leader enjoyed an easier ride from the media than 'W.', but then he always preferred an early night in bed with a baseball game on TV. And when his relationship with the media turned sour, as the wars in Afghanistan and Iraq shifted from mission accomplished to mission disaster, and journalists at last asked questions about his decision-making, his wife Laura took the microphone to tell us about life at the White House under Dubya. 'Nine p.m., and Mr Excitement here is sound asleep, and I'm watching *Desperate Housewives*,' she reported as she spoke to us, her husband silently at her side. We all laughed.

It was left to a successor President to speak truth to that gathering, striking chords never heard before in that arena, and there was no laughter as the following warning echoed across the Fourth Estate.

'Like so many other businesses in this global age, you've seen sweeping changes and technology and communications that lead to a sense of uncertainty and anxiety about what the future will hold . . .

'Across the country, there are extraordinary, hardworking journalists who have lost their jobs in recent days . . . and I know that each newspaper and media outlet is wrestling with how to respond to these changes, and some are struggling simply to stay open.

'Your ultimate success is essential to the success of our democracy. It's what makes this thing work. You know, Thomas Jefferson once said that if he had the choice between a government without newspapers, or newspapers without a government, he would not hesitate to choose the latter.'

Grand words, but for the men and women listening, the question was not whether government would survive without newspapers, but whether newspapers would survive at all.

*

Joe, wine writer:

David was being impertinent when I first saw him. He was doing something that nobody else in the room dared. He was asking – demanding might be closer to the truth – that Jancis Robinson, MW, the Snow Queen of wine writing, give her opinion on a glass of Argentine Chardonnay. I recognized him immediately across the table at the Argentine Wine Awards in Mendoza, even though we hadn't yet met. I used to mimic his *Channel 4 News* broadcasting technique, specifically his handover to the anchorman Jon Snow back in London: 'You know, Jon, there must be an air of quiet panic at the White House today.' I used to ape that when speaking to Radio Scotland: 'You know, Fred, the town of Dornoch has never seen anything like this wine festival.'

I repaid the favour a few years later at the White House correspondents dinner in Washington DC, when David took me along for a truly remarkable ride. David saw me ask – well, demand might be closer – that a heavily medalled admiral come out wine-tasting with me the next time he was in London. 'And what do you do, admiral?' I asked as he tried to get out of this impertinent invitation. 'I'm chairman of the Joint Chiefs of Staff,' said the executor of two controversial wars. 'I advise the President on military matters. And I gotta confess, I'm kind a busy now.'

David and Sonia haven't just built a vineyard from scratch. They aren't just making wine. What they've done is to climb into a mysterious wardrobe in a strange house and then walk out into a peculiar, parallel world. But instead of fauns and talking lions and beavers they've met a cast of characters no less strange – squiffy wine writers, ratings-obsessed collectors, venal retailers and wine makers ranging from the haughtily aristocratic to the plump and mercantile, to the hollow-eyed and destitute. David wasn't actually being impertinent when he grilled the regal Jancis. He was just being normal. But in a very abnormal world.

If Sonia and David had known that this bizarre reality awaited them, I suspect they would never have jumped in. Especially not with hearty dollops of their own cash. Those of us on the inside are in awe of Jancis Robinson. And it seems perfectly normal to us to spend a hundred pounds or five hundred dollars on a single bottle of wine, just because one man said 'it scores 96/100'.

The first time I sat and talked with David, riding along in the press bus through Mendoza, the conversation was electric two-way fascination. I was fascinated by his world, diplomacy, politics at the highest level, then broadcasting, again on a global stage. And he was fascinated by my world. Over the years I've tried to help them both find a way through the tortuous path, from planting their vines all the way to watching someone walk out of a store with your bottle asking aloud whether they should have 'the rib-eye or the sirloin'. They've taken care of me in their magnificent vineyard – believe me it's in the very shadows of the Andes, yes literally – then in the shadow of the Vice-President's house in Washington DC. Over dinner I've tried to help them understand why Americans get fine Argentine wine in a way the British don't. Or the science behind barrels and in-oak malolactic fermentation. They indulged my fascination with their world, with its equally bizarre cast of oddities.

When David took me to the correspondents dinner, he slipped on to the red carpet like a pro, swiftly moving through. I lingered amateurishly behind a posing Pamela Anderson. 'Get out of the way, bald arsehole,' shouted the photographers as David returned to chivvy me along. I entered the reception with the same Tiggerish enthusiasm that I'd seen in David at wine events. (Sonia, by the way, is the Christopher Robin of the partnership. Later on, she even went off to school in Bordeaux, of all places.) 'Hi, I'm Joe Fattorini,' I announced. 'Nice to meet you, Joe,' replied an elderly statesman. 'I'm Charlie Wilson.'

'That's funny, they made a film about a guy named Charlie Wils . . .' I blurted out. Impertinently. David introduced me to General Colin Powell. He politely declined to come wine-tasting with me. The British Ambassador said yes, thank goodness. Larry King, whom David teased, then introduced, said he 'luuurved Luundun' but needed to check with his agent.

If David and Sonia knew what they 'ought' to know, they'd have given up on the project before it ever began. If I knew how I 'ought' to behave among Washington's movers and shakers, I'd have missed some of the most enjoyable moments of my life. 'When I was a child . . . I reasoned like a child . . . when I became a man, I put childish ways behind me.' Maybe. But sometimes it's a good idea to step through the wardrobe.

*

# What's the Point?

A slightly unnerving sensation it was, riding along in Mendoza, with a bunch of people who could make or break my dream. With the 'Reality TV' venture gone, the next step was to meet the actual people who made it their business to buy and sell wine.

My travelling companions are wine buyers for major stores in New York, Los Angeles and Seattle. Restaurateurs from foodie markets, like San Francisco and Boston. Distributors who can reach more potential buyers than I can imagine. As we board the bus, one chunky, middle-aged character says, 'I have the Eastern seaboard,' meaning, every state in the Eastern United States, from Maine to Florida.

I avoid him, Big Al, and sit down next to a well-built, affable Frenchman.

So here we were, bumping along together, higher and higher into the Andes, in the land known as Mendoza. On our way to do some hard physical labour, to prune vines at 5,000 feet, with frost waiting to burn our fingers. City slickers meet secateurs. Thank God it took three hours to reach this vineyard, because we all counted on coffee to clear the 6 a.m. blur in our eyes and the alcoholic haze from last night.

Eric did not carry a gun, but he did have the power to shoot me down. I surmised my new friend ran the operation without which I had not even a prayer of bringing our wine home to Washington DC, specifically the city's largest wine store, just around the corner from my house. Not that I had to get along with him or vice versa. But it sure helped.

I had a little experience of 'ride-alongs' with those you needed to cultivate. It was the camaraderie of getting along with the man with the gun. Where had I felt this before? Beirut, Bulawayo, Beijing, journalism days, and in the world's drug gateway, driving with the homicide squad of Miami-Dade. 'You be cool with me, and I'll be cool with you,' drawled the detective in Key Biscayne, one night in the cocaine nineties, as our patrol car swerved at some speed through a neighbourhood which oozed menace, hunting a killer from the drug cartels. We never found the hit man. But I found my motto: 'You be cool with me, and I'll be cool with you.'

So I wanted to be cool with my new friends from the wine cartels, and hoped it worked the other way. Eric, it turned out quite quickly, was not the Frenchman I imagined, ready to strike at a moment's notice to defend his daily baguette or his Grand Cru.

'The French have become so lazy about their product,' he said, punching his fingers together. 'The French wine industry is not dead yet, but it is walking to its own funeral.'

Great news, I thought, Europe's loss represented Mendoza's gain – specifically, my gain. Eric looked askance. 'I have a 900-acre farm in my family, generations of wine. In Bergerac, the Dordogne, east of Bordeaux.' Ah. Maybe not such good news after all.

This was the kind of Frenchman I needed to sell my wine, a man who knew the business: the middleman, standing between me, my wine and the great American consumer. The middlemen, as Eric described them, seemed a halfway house between the Neapolitan and Sicilian mafias. He explained the process patiently, making sure I understood every payoff, marking it with a knowing Gallic eyebrow and a what-do-you-expect shrug.

'You already pay the distributor to place and move your wine, but you have to accept deep discounting if you really want to encourage him. Then you pay the distributor's representatives – they like gift certificates, to a store or a restaurant or spa or something, rather than money, that way it's definitely tax free – and then there are the retailers . . .'

We were interrupted. 'I get offered money on a regular basis, despite the fact that everyone knows I won't be bought and I won't do it,' confirmed Leandra, a striking, curly-haired wine buyer for a high-end store in New England sitting behind us. 'Just as people pay to get their book in the front of the bookstore, some wine folks pay serious money for their shelf space up front.' She had a wicked smile, winking: 'You know, all my family is from Sicily, so I know Sicilian when I see it.'

The temperature dropped as we entered the charming pueblo of Tupungato, last stop before our final ascent to the high-altitude vineyards of this region. I once scoured this area for land, only to realize I was too late. The household names of global wine had already bought it up: the Antinoris from Italy, the Kendall-Jacksons from California, Concha y Toro from Chile. That put the Tupungato valley beyond my reach, a source of occasional pangs. The town itself was a delight. No shortage of good restaurants, coffee shops, even a wine bar, with the well-heeled flying doctors of wine from France, or America, or Australia sitting next to you, cutting a deal, reading the wine press, making you feel you sat at the epicentre of the new global wine trade. Time had taught me, however, that I liked to visit Tupungato, sit in the sun and sip a coffee, but not as a place to live or put down roots. Too many foreigners.

As I was explaining this to my new friends, Eric interrupted with the impatience of a man who had heard enough, after a genealogy of wine-making and too many hours hustling wine. 'Don't worry about payoffs, or bribes, to get your wine to market,' he said, waving his hand as if to dismiss the thought. 'It all comes down to your points. Trust me. It's all about the points. I am French, I know, but I love those points.'

Leandra leaned over the back of my seat with a Sicilian glare. 'I hate points, do you hear me?' Her voice was now attracting attention. 'I hate the goddam system that says points, points, points. Points don't mean anything, everyone gets 90 these days.' Others stopped conversation mid sentence to listen. 'You know what? I've started taking down the points wrappers in my store and I'm not going to stop till I've got rid of them all, every one of them.'

Once again, I found myself riding along with the crowd I needed to befriend. I needed them more than they needed me as they talked me through the Sicilian future ahead to get my wine into their shelves. More would soon be heard about this points system.

# Along for the Ride

I was glad that wine crowd was more restrained than my very first bus companions, a local football team. 'We don't have any money for travel,' decreed my first editor, a cigar-smoking, heavy-drinking character called Roger Norman. 'So you'll go on the team bus, with the players and the manager and all.' This was access at its best. 'Just try not to get too close to them.' The journalist's dilemma: drink with them to get the story, but stop before you thought you forgot that your job was to tell it.

Every Saturday, in the winter of 1970-71, I rode along, the cub reporter for a local paper in suburban North London who covered the town's supposedly amateur, in reality semi-professional, football team, ignoring what I knew happened on the bus. In journalism the best stories remained untold. The team boasted a star goalscorer who, on the ride out to a match, would offer his teammates betting odds on how many goals he would score. Invariably, on the way home, he collected his winnings, triggering memories of opportunities he missed. One defender was not a betting man. He preferred oral sex at the back of the bus with a female fan. Occasionally the team won. Then we could count on beer: one stalwart midfielder grew so drunk after those rare victories that they had to carry him off the bus.

Years later, in wars, I learned the same trade-off between access and stories. You needed access to get the story. But, to keep access, you could not always tell it. It was a trade-off the Pentagon understood, as well as every military dictator in the developing world, and every working reporter.

Much as so many came to deride George W. Bush, Dick Cheney and Donald Rumsfeld, that troika conducted a master-class in using the media to their ends during the invasion of Iraq. 'Forget the bald truth – it ain't going to happen,' said David Bloom, a dear colleague from one of the American TV networks. He died riding along, 'embedded' with the Third Infantry, towards Baghdad in 2003. Painfully, he died not of war wounds but natural causes, triggered partly by sitting in tanks for hours on end. 'I'm joined to these guys at the hip, or wherever they carry the weaponry,' he told me over a satellite phone, as I watched images of him broadcasting from a tank convoy, his own seat behind the barrel of a gun, a resourceful pioneering spirit covering his first war.

The problem with being embedded was that you owed them. For me, it was nothing less than life itself. Every time gunfire broke out, I relied on the soldier next to me, my life in his hands, his machine gun. Fear, and gratitude. In Beirut, with large pieces of metal flying through the air, I flinched, terrified. The US Marines at the airport perimeter stood uncowed. Weeks later, in October 1983, I walked through what was left of their marine barracks, blown up, in central Beirut. I cried. My guys, my comrades-in-war, were there, died there. In Rhodesia, about to become Zimbabwe, I sought protection from the Irish Guards. A hungry crowd at the feeding centre turned on us once the food rations ran out. It was not the story I wanted to tell, the ugliness of a desperate crowd turned violent. Nor how those soldiers knew how to beat back a crowd and, yes, save us. And how grateful we were.

The man who saved us in Beijing, in the razor-tense days after the Tiananmen Square massacre, was neither American nor European. He was a colonel from the People's Liberation Army. I would never learn his name. Some twenty young conscripts stopped us at a roadblock, pulled their weapons, rifles at our faces, their eyes strung out. A moment away: a volley at point-blank range. At the sound of an order, the men in green uniforms wheeled to take aim at another young man, Chinese, on a bicycle. In broken English, he offered to help us. But with the rifle out of my face, I caught the attention of a more senior man in uniform who looked in charge. Earlier that morning, as we left the hotel, an American colleague had given me a bumper sticker, just in case, he suggested. It said, in Mandarin, 'Foreign Press'. The colonel read the note, walked up and down the line pushing the gun barrels downwards. He turned, and gestured for us to join him into an armoured personnel carrier, loaded with more men and *matériel*. Inside there were laughs, jokes we did not understand, but also fear. I knew the colonel could shoot us if he wanted to, just as, in my gut, I feared he would find a way to shoot that student.

Instead, he was trying to save us. He returned us to the Great Wall Sheraton before heading back to duty. We left him at the foyer of the hotel, thankful he had spared us. Or simply had orders not to shoot 'Foreign Press'.

Vice-President Dick Cheney might have wanted to shoot the press, along with ducks and his hunting friends. But much as he froze out a few reporters covering the White House, many more stayed inside the tent. For some, the best part of the job was joining the presidential trips. It was a privilege, riding along on Air Force One. This was first-class travel and a whole lot more. The champagne flowed, the menu was worth eating and governments hosting the President were apt to give the press a gift or two: a Rolex from the Sultan of Brunei, a fine leather bag from the President of Peru, a beautiful Mayan rug from the leader of Mexico, a rare perfume as you left old Europe. Best of all, what distinguished the ride on Air Force One was that there was nothing to do: no passport control, visa checks, hotel arrangements, wake-up calls; all breakfast, lunch, dinner and tea sorted; all of it in the hands of the White House travel office, and all of it executed with absolute regime.

In the summer of 2003, the entire White House press circus travelled with President Bush to the Middle East. Only a few days before, the man himself had declared 'Mission Accomplished' aboard an aircraft carrier in the Pacific. Now he was flying to the region to launch a new phase in the diplomatic process known as peace. First, in the Egyptian coastal playground of Sharm el-Sheikh, the potentates of the Arab world waited, from the King of Saudi Arabia on down. The White House handlers led us to believe that the President did serious business with the kings, and regents, and presidents of the Arab world assembled in Sharm el-Sheikh, twisting their arms to accept the reality of Israel in a man-to-man gathering over coffee.

The question was, what had been achieved with the Arab leadership in Sharm el-Sheikh, the day of this much-vaunted diplomatic break-through, over that coffee klatsch the President had held? A feisty reporter from the *Financial Times*, James Harding, who later became editor of *The Times*, joined me in pestering the President's spokesman about the substance, any concrete step, any exchange that belied intent. He was interrupted by a journalist from the *New York Times*, whose speciality was the so-called 'colour piece'. 'Can we get back to the atmospherics of the coffee session?' she asked. 'Give us a sense of the décor; you know, the drapes, the furnishings.' The spokesman approved. He knew his sofa fabrics, Arabic coffee cups and the colour of the curtains.

From there we all went to Aqaba, on Jordan's Red Sea, where the leaders of Israel and the Palestinians were summoned. This was the next step, we were told, in building the new Middle East. But first the White House handlers built (yes, they built) a 'bridge to peace' outside the King's palace in Aqaba. Ever aware of the television news images, the President was to guide the Israeli, Palestinian and Jordanian leaders across the bridge over Red Sea. 'Remember Moses?' one White House PR specialist hinted.

We waited. For a few seconds, the gang of four hesitated. The then Israeli Prime Minister, Ariel Sharon, was a shade hefty. 'Oh, shit,' inhaled the same PR man. Would they all fit in one line across the bridge? Who would be left out, the image ruined? But they managed. George Bush, on a fake bridge in Aqaba, parted the waves.

The language that flowed from the press room that day was seismic. The balance had shifted on Middle East Peace. The President had gone further than any US President before him in calling for two states, Israel and Palestine, living side by side. George Bush, the warrior, had defined himself for ever as a man of peace. The Bush legacy would be a road map to a solution of a conflict as old as Jesus, Joseph and Mary. The war in Iraq was barely mentioned.

What no one reported, myself included, was one small, perhaps insignificant, secret of the historic Israeli-Palestinian summit in Aqaba, one of those off-the-record nuggets that said something about the priorities of the man. President Bush had deliberately cut back his time that day with the leaders of Israel and the Palestinians. He reduced his man-to-man conversations to just a few minutes. The reason? Not a negotiating tactic. We learned George Bush had wanted his usual ninety-minute workout.

But why did I do that, why did I delete the paragraph that would have undercut some of the myth-making of the day? It was called self-censorship. It thrived whenever there was such intimacy between rulers and the press. Quite simply, I did not want to cut off my own access to the Bush White House. Nor did anyone else.

At the end of that trip Air Force One, with the President and the entire press corps, landed in Kuwait, to watch and salute the men and women of the US army, marching for their Commander-in-Chief. How he strutted. His war had been executed almost without bloodshed on the American side at that stage. Saddam Hussein had fallen with scarcely a fight. Whatever the misgivings of the French, or the Germans, or the Russians, those were heady days for that President. And the media stood at his side, cheerleading, celebrating, actively complicit in the brazen marketing of George Bush.

A few months later, I decided to leave the job of covering Washington. It had been my dream, my addiction, for thirty years. I gave up journalism. Life was too short to drink bad wine.

# Counterpoint

Little did I know then that I had traded a world of words for a world ruled by numbers, the points system. I had imagined the wine world was savoured not measured. After all, it was a business that made good living its business. In that, at least, I was not entirely wrong.

'Welcome to the great stand-off in the world of wine,' said Eric, the Frenchman, as we settled down to a hearty lunch, a fine Argentine steak, *bife*, washed down by a magnificent blend of Malbec and Cabernet Sauvignon that our hosts had selected. 'This is communism versus capitalism, England versus Germany in the World Cup, how do they say in America, the Yankees against the Red Sox?' Ready to ward off any challenge, he lifted his voice to speak to the table at large. 'In the world of wine-making and wine-tasting it's all about the points.'

Points? Could pleasure be measured in points? Eric had not let go of his single-track message to me. From a distributor's angle nothing worked as well as points to move bottles off the shelves. He was clear about how severe the ratings were.

An élite group of wine connoisseurs sat in judgement, sniffing, sipping, spitting. They sent one wine to stardom (90 points plus), another to oblivion (less than 80 points). It was Olympic figure skating in the wine world. Whatever the judges were thinking, or however suspect their motives, no one wanted to see their wine land with a humiliating thud on its rear.

One judge towered above all others, I learned. A lawyer with a fine nose named Robert Parker. And what a nose. A nose insured for a million dollars. This was the nose that launched a thousand wines, including many we had drunk. So even if I managed to get past all the middlemen in their Sicilian suits, I still did not have a prayer unless Robert Parker spat my wine and enjoyed the expectoration. I savoured my *bife* steak, sipped the wonderful Malbec blend and resolved to learn as much as I could about this man.

Legend had it that Mr Parker's colleagues thought he was mad back in the 1980s. 'Friends and family advised that his career in law should be given top priority, and that wine writing was a romantic, unprofitable profession,' said the million-dollar nostril's website. But he tore himself away from being an assistant general counsel for the Farm Credit banks of Baltimore, to become arguably the single most influential figure in the global wine revolution of the past half-century. Robert Parker had it all: 'The man with the paragon palate' (*Time* magazine); 'The high moral purpose of a reformer' (*Newsweek*); 'The most influential wine writer in the world today' (*Los Angeles Times*). Parker himself, I was told, was understandably proud that an American had rewritten the rules of the semi-religious relationship between man and wine, but he never made any secret of the fact that he put in the hours to achieve his primacy, studying, tasting, learning, listening for years before he sat in judgement. If he had the world's best nose, it was because he worked at it, and because he got more calls right than wrong.

Thousands of wines came to market every year: from Australia, France, Italy, Spain, Argentina, Chile, the United States, New Zealand. The list went on, a bacchanalian menu. A hard life, but someone had to drink it all. By the dawn of the millennium Mr Parker and his team had already judged 200,000 plus wines. They had been hard at work ever since, averaging 10,000 a year, we're told. By all accounts, it seemed a very sober process, his hand-picked acolytes, versed in his ways, spending hour after hour rhythmically quaffing vintages that producers were desperate to offer for the ritual. 'It usually takes a morning, the palate is always better in the morning. Three to four hours, fifty to sixty wines at a time, usually from the same region. Judgement is instant,' explained one of my new friends on the bus, an American distributor who asked not to be named, just in case he upset the Parker team. 'It's nothing personal, just business, his people know exactly what they're looking for. When they smell it on the nose, feel it on the mouth, it's magic. Bull's-eye,' he added with a real glint in his eye. He recalled a session when one of his lead wines scored 93, to the surprise of many in the room, given its relatively low price. 'A wine is going up, or going down. There's a curious sense of finality about it all. Someone spends a few seconds with a wine that has taken years to make, and decides whether or not it has a future.'

So that was where my life, and that dream of ours, was heading. Hanging on the spittings of one man. After all the grief we had been through. It might be damned, condemned to a dunce's 70s or remedial 80s. Read the language of Mr Parker's points system and you get the point:

*70–79 points*
'An average wine with little distinction except that it is soundly made; in essence a straightforward, innocuous wine.' Faint praise. Who wants to buy an average, innocuous wine?

*80–89 points*
'A barely above average to very good wine displaying various degrees of finesse and flavour as well as character with no noticeable flaws.' I was not sure, reading that, that even a score in the 80s helped us. Barely above average? No noticeable flaws?

*90–95 points*
'An outstanding wine of exceptional complexity and character.' In short, terrific wines.

*96–100 points*
'An extraordinary wine of profound and complex character displaying all the attributes expected of a classic . . . wines of this calibre are worth a special effort to find, purchase and consume.' The Holy Grail. Now we're talking, sir.

So, listening to Eric, close to the mountain top in the Andes, as he expounded on the points system, I thought quietly to myself: 90 points or die. Yet how disarmingly American to ensure the scale began at 70, so no one had the humiliation of scoring zero, even if the verdict condemned your bank balance to something close to it.

It seemed so arbitrary: 80 dead, 90 alive. Yet the points system was so clear, so efficient, I could not resist learning more. Personal admission. I loved ratings. Points. The Final Four. The Top Ten. The Top Fifty. Those lists that told you the best hotels, the best restaurants, the thousand places to see before you died. From the world's most beautiful women or best-dressed men, to the planet's best universities, I could never have enough of ratings.

# Number 32

Clearly I was never going to show up in *People* magazine's 'Sexiest Men Alive', nor even the 'Worst-Dressed List'. But when a serious British newspaper, the *Daily Telegraph*, listed me as number 32 in the '50 most important Brits in the United States', I laughed. Lists were ridiculous. But then, when your name was there in the rankings, what was not to celebrate? Just seventeen places behind David Beckham! Twenty-four behind Nobel prize-winner Paul Nurse, the 'David Beckham of Science' according to the newspaper. One place behind cancer-research pioneer Frank McCormick. Three ahead of comedian Sacha Baron Cohen, 'Ali G', 'Borat'. More influential than Borat? Me? Suddenly I could not get enough of my ratings. And all this importance based on my second career representing the United Nations in Washington DC.

Rankings, arbitrary as they are, bestowed approval, a validation I craved.

The need for recognition may be primal, but to me it was forged with seeking to understand why I never had a father, why he left. In my mind's eye, I have a few blurred images of the man who married my mother. I remember a walk once with him to a funfair, a ride on the London Underground to a soccer game with him, or sitting in the back of a taxi on our way to a cartoon cinema, the Empire, in Leicester Square. Years later, I scoured the family archives for photographs of me with him. There were none. The only photographs I had ever seen showed a lanky man with an unreadable smile, dark eyes, dark hair and a jaunty turn to his head. In one photograph he held my elder brother, a chubby, happy baby. But none with me, even though he left when I was two. So in my mind I was the child of a single mother, even though my Catholic parents never divorced. I never tasted real, die-hard poverty. But I did know what it was to wait for child-support payments that never came. For most of my school years I did have two shirts to my name, the one on my back and the one in the wash, plus one pair of trousers. I did grow up as a member of the first generation of latch-key kids. I brought myself home from school at the age of six. I bought the groceries by age eight, working from a mother's carefully budgeted list. By nine, I took myself regularly to Highbury Stadium to see my beloved Arsenal. Before my tenth birthday, I crossed London alone to see them lose 1–0 at Fulham, finding my way to a stadium by the River Thames simply by following the crowds, dressed in Arsenal red and white. I did see birthdays come and go without any contact from my father. And, much as our mother celebrated our achievements, there was always the void of not knowing, vividly, daily, instinctively, from where I came. And not knowing why he did not come home to see me, ever.

In later years it became clear I was not the only one. We represented a needy bunch of baby-boomers, children of single parents from the 1950s and 1960s on both sides of the Atlantic. Independent, yes. Needy, craving acceptance, desperate to be liked and fearful of not being loved. Always seeking approval. Invariably unhappy unless approval came with ladled-up cream on the top. Usually insecure without that thumbs up, or that high mark, or that pat on the head. In short, addicted to approval ratings.

I recognized this only in my fortieth year, by which time I had been married and divorced myself, with two sons living hundreds of miles away from me and my life revolving around seeing them as often as I could, determined not to replay family history. To me this was a decision that took itself. Every other week I fled Washington DC on Friday evening for a weekend in the Midwest with my boys, Mark and Matthew, taking up residence for forty-eight hours in a hotel near their mother's house, to stay in their lives, to pick them up when they fell, to celebrate when they succeeded, to cry with them when the tears flowed. Mark, the elder, a loveable character always trying to keep everyone happy, even when he was sad. Matt, a sensitive child who needed help to overcome his fears, and thrived when he did. My friends feared for my sanity, seeing the stress that accompanied such journeys, but for once I trusted my own feelings. I loved being Dad. And I was staying in the con-versation with my children, against the odds maybe, whatever the cost maybe, in a way my own father had not. Every time I picked up the boys on a Friday evening, cooked them dinner at a motel that offered a kitchen, played ball with them and put them to bed, I felt the same odd yet reassuring emotion. My own DNA, a source of such weakness, had grown to be my greatest strength. I came to experience a certain sadness for my father. I wished he had savoured the pride I felt seeing two boys become men, each in their own way coming home to me as they reached adulthood, each in their own way pursuing the conversation with me as the torch passed. Therein lay an award I cherished.

And the commitment paid off. Wherever else I failed, I succeeded perhaps in making all my children believe in one family. By the time the second set arrived with Sonia, a measure of wisdom had kicked in, primarily because, second time around, Sonia educated me to recognize what was at stake. In Alegría, our only daughter, came a personality as large as any I had met, vivacious, challenging, indomitable, even at just a few years old. Joy was her name in Spanish, and joy she brought in buckets. In Nelson, the last-born and without doubt the most relaxed child of all, came the spirit who could wipe away tears, dispel the blues, smiling that there's no such thing as a bad day. By then I was hooked on being Dad. I wanted to be the one to watch the school play, to attend sports day, to take them to the dentist. And nothing gave me as much pleasure as watching my older children live, and play, and laugh, alongside their young siblings, the laughter invariably reserved for the medieval thinking of their father. If ever I felt thumbs up, a pat on the head, it lay in watching all my children act as one family. Approval indeed.

Bizarrely, I recognized my own addiction to approval by meeting a man who lived, and died, by his approval ratings. One Bill Clinton, then Governor of Arkansas, a figure of both admiration and disdain, long-shot candidate for President of the United States.

Clinton was the most professionally charming man. Professionally charming: that was the thought I had on first meeting. It came back to me every time I met him, even years later when we worked together, as Clinton led the UN campaign to help Asia recover from the tsunami of Christmas 2004. It was well known that truly successful politicians knew how to make every person they met feel like the most important person on the planet, for the five, or ten, or maybe fifteen seconds they were shaking your hand, or touching your arm, or posing for a picture with you. Translate those people skills into the business of government, where you worked people all the time to make things happen, and it was a priceless attribute in a politician. Ronald Reagan, on my one acquaintance, had it. Margaret Thatcher, through the years I interviewed her, had it. Not so Tony Blair. Certainly not Gordon Brown. Boris Yeltsin had it on the road to power, when he was sober and talking to foreign correspondents like me. In contrast, Mikhail Gorbachev did not. Nor George Bush Senior. But his son, Dubya or W., did.

But the maestro of our generation was Bill Clinton, a presence face-to-face so seductive that it was hard not to be charmed by the people skills of a born schmoozer. What I found intriguing was that Clinton yearned for you to give him the same in equal measure, to flatter him, to thank him, to approve of him. Clinton sought that, literally, from the last person he met or spoke to. His need was constant.

Spool back to one of my early interviews with him, in the living room of a supporter's home in Manchester, New Hampshire, during the snowy November of 1991. He wanted to swap stories about student life at Oxford, asking me which college I attended while regaling me with exploits of his own along the River Cherwell. He went out of his way to dazzle intellectually, taking a question about health care in America and turning into a mini-thesis about what was right with the British National Health Service, wrong with America's privatized system. Learning I had moved to Washington from Moscow, he waxed lyrically about the end of the Cold War and the peace dividend that awaited all of us, Russians as well as Americans. At the end, with the cameraman looking at me as if to say already enough, the next President of the United States asked me if I was happy with the interview. I told him it was terrific, quite exceptional in the way it spoke to Brits back home. 'Especially as there are no votes in me, or my network,' I added. Those larger-than-life features creased with a broad smile. 'I'm happy that you're happy,' he said, then gave me a trademark armrub-cum-handshake.

I had interviewed the man several times more, memorably on the night he called himself 'the comeback kid', when I was ushered backstage by Hillary Clinton like some long-lost friend, before I met his mother Virginia in Arkansas, for a segment I was preparing on Clinton's life, specifically his complicated childhood as the son of a natural father who died before his birth, then stepson of a violent drunk. Virginia was more than just a character who sported a bleached white streak in jet-black hair, she was a force of nature. Understandably proud, she was also unmistakably determined, and fiercely demanding of her son, telling me what he needed to do to win the White House: 'My Bill should look the Bush family in the eye, and show them up for what they are, people who know nothing about main-street America, absolutely nothing,' she told me, adding quietly off-camera: 'Problem is Bill doesn't like con-frontation, never has, he likes being nice to everyone, and likes being liked by everyone.'

The light bulb came on for me during that day with his mother in Arkansas, a jumble of personal memories and conflicting impressions of an emerging politician somehow forming a familiar picture. The son of a single mother, the product of a home that had seen conflict and hard times, growing up hand-to-mouth, adored by one parent, no knowledge of the other. Yet, at the same time, a high-achiever, highly ambitious, ready to go anywhere, any time, to fulfil hopes placed in him by the single parent. And, above all, desperate for approval, needy, yearning to be liked, in constant fear of rejection.

As the Clinton years unfolded, somehow it was no surprise that Clinton could smoke, but not inhale, in his own inimitable phrase. That he sounded like a born-again socialist one day, a new-age conservative the next. That he admitted guilt over Monica Lewinsky while insisting he was innocent. That the smartest politician of our generation never delivered, truly, on his exceptional promise. I watched him some days and felt that I understood his every move to the core. Invited to the White House signing ceremony for a congressional Bill that effectively outlawed welfare payments for poor mothers, because a close friend in the White House had been its author, I remembered thinking to myself: how could you do this, Mr President, when our mothers needed all the help they could get to bring us up? Yet that action represented a master-stroke in political terms, because it deprived his opponents of the one issue that might have defeated him in an election year. In that moment, Bill Clinton was both the boy in need of approval and the master politician giving everyone a reason to like him. In his case, liking him translated later that year into landslide re-election.

Yet Bill Clinton did not deliver a legacy that matched his talent, or a legacy that endured. Stand back from the spin of a White House that cast the President as a victim of a right-wing conspiracy. Look back at the high hopes and the broad agenda for change that brought Bill Clinton to power in 1992. Despite a booming America in the Clinton years, the lost opportunity remained, the failure to use great national wealth to meet real needs.

# The Hustler

One of the real joys of my new wine chapter in life was not having to talk about Bill Clinton or George Bush any more. I was a man trying to get wine to stores, to tables, to homes and restaurants. Business was business, and I realized that I was now in the business of points.

So no politics, no future of the planet, no superpower agenda. Just my new French friend Eric dismissing my fears about scoring points with my wine as the bus reached destination, groaning at this altitude on rocky road, and we prepared for hard labour. Eric warmed to his theme and held forth.

'I love my points. I do. Parker gives a wine 90 points, and all I have to do is wait for the phone to ring, for my wine stores to be fighting each other to get it, ' he told me. 'Sometimes they don't even wait for Parker to publish his numbers. The rumour mill has such a wine getting such a score, and folks who run their wine stores steam in, saying give me as much as you can.'

Leandra did not contain her dismay, her language becoming more robust as the argument was joined. 'Parker is out of control. He has destroyed Italy because no Italian wine is ever good enough for him. For a while he made Australia with his high scores, now we all know Australia is producing way too much bad wine and way too little good stuff. He has his favourites. Just watch his scores closely. The whole points system is a bad joke. Bad for consumers. Bad for the trade. Bad for wine.'

The argument was not going away. 'Listen, get real. People know Parker is as objective as you can be, and they trust him with their money,' confided Eric. 'If you're going to pay thirty or forty dollars a bottle, then you want somebody telling you it's money well spent. Points do that.'

I revealed that was just the price bracket we aimed for with our wine. 'Then you need points. You need Parker.'

What I needed was a drink. Ahead of us stood one of the world's finest vineyards, Indeed, if Mr Parker was right, it was the second-best Malbec vineyard on the planet: the Adrianna vineyard, so high up in the Andes the air felt thin. The wine from here received 93 points.

Time to get down and dirty. The vineyard owner had laid on a class in pruning for this élite group of American businessmen who lived at the sharp end of his business, where sales signalled make or break. We were given sharp secateurs and instructions on how to cut back a vine, make sure to keep the best buds, and the v-shape, in what is known as the 'double Guyot' system that encourages the best grape come spring and summer, named after the nineteenth-century French physician and agronomoist, Dr Jules Guyot, who invented the pruning technique.

We were pruning Malbec, a grape I had never heard of until a few years before, but which now represented the leading lady of my dreams. My fingers were soon sore from cutting, so I hid my slow progress by raising 'What's with Malbec?' with my nearest, far more efficient cutter.

Andy, a youthful seller of fine wines in the Pacific Northwest, was unstoppable on the topic. 'Malbec was just a blending grape when the French had it in Bordeaux. Argentina has taken Malbec and made it a rock-star grape.'

Rock-star grape? How did Americans learn to talk in sound-bites?

'I say rock-star grape 'cause it's just this big, fruity, smooth, drinkable star of a wine.'

Morgan, a fresh-faced wine manager for one of Boston's trendiest brasseries, picked up the theme of French failure, Argentine triumph, Old World decline, New World breakthrough. 'The value factor with Malbec is huge, it can be a gorgeous wine that would cost twice as much were it from France, or California, when I think about it,' she said, all the while struggling to make sure she didn't cut herself rather than the vine. 'People who want a big wine, they love it. People who want a smooth, easy wine, they love it too.'

Greg, a weather-beaten merchant from San Francisco who had his own vineyard in the Russian River valley, looked at the landscape and mused: 'This is unique, the altitude, the soil, the climate. I can see now why Malbec has those thick red skins, that deep rich quality on the first taste. It's all in the land and the soil. Back home, Malbec is the favourite of the sommelier set. And let me tell you, when you have the sommeliers on your side, you're on your way.'

But it was left to Scott, a muscular, tall Virginian who looked as if he bench-pressed his body weight, to make my day. Tearing at the line of plants and branches like a professional, cutting rhythmically at the stem, counting his buds all the while, the fellow went into a rhapsody over the grape on which I had risked a small fortune. 'Malbec is more feminine, not so masculine and intense, there's perfume of flowers and red fruits, and it's always so fresh, it retains the freshness of its fruit, never gets heavy.'

Scott, would you like to meet my bank manager?

'Red flowers, good minerality, smoky character, great with a meat or a sausage, what more do you want? I tell folks back in Virginia that Malbec is one of the world's gems, and get it now.' He paused to cut a vine just above the juncture of stem and sixth bud, his breath visible in bitter cold air. 'Get it now, I tell my customers, before the points for Malbec go through the roof and it costs so much more.'

Ah, there you had it, just when I thought it was about poetry, it was still all about the points.

Scott grinned. 'Have you thought about the kind of wine you want to make?'

Of course I had, but not in terms of points, minerality or market share. One thing to have a dream, quite another to acquire the palate, the nose, the technical know-how that took grape and turned juice into great wine, which people actually wanted to buy. It turned out it was not enough to have the land, even if it was blessed, or plant the vines, even if the grapes were good.

It was not enough to have risked my life savings – and my wife's.

It was not enough.

What I did know, on the basis of that tricky day with my new friends, was that we faced a fork in the road, and soon. Did we make a wine that washed down a good steak with richness, smoothness, balance – a wine for the ages? Or did we chase the dream of a star wine, 90 points plus, our first vintage flying off the shelves – a wine for the age we lived in?

Those were tantalizing choices to make. There were no bad options here, except perhaps bankruptcy. But what began as a dream, an impulse to give it all up, to live by the mountains close to the land, the seasons, the fruits of the earth – well, a day with Eric and his powerful friends had changed all that. They looked at me with a mixture of wry envy and the concerned smile usually reserved for puppies about to be neutered. Nothing personal, just business. So I remembered. You be cool with me, and I'll be cool with you.

# The Study of Virtue

Sonia and I had come to New Orleans on a mission. After three courses in the study of wine, and three exams passed, taking us to London and New York, Bordeaux and Montalcino, Napa and Sonoma, we presented ourselves as candidates at the Court of Master Sommeliers, an organization founded in London in the late 1960s with a thriving branch in the United States, where its diplomas were viewed with serious respect. 'Education was then, and remains the Court's Charter,' they told you in their handsomely produced and rather pompously written literature, 'the premier international examining board.' Education, that is, in the knowledge and service of wine. Examination, we were about to discover, of the ability to recognize a wine, then explain it to a potential drinker and sell it to a happy customer.

Sonia, as ever, had been the driving force when it came to learning. Her view, from the day we purchased Finca Alegría, was that we needed to study the world of wine if we nurtured dreams of making and selling our own. 'You wouldn't dream of opening a restaurant without knowing something about being a chef, would you?' That had been her mantra, along with the tease-line: 'It's turning a vice into a virtue, studying wine.' Truth be told, Sonia had an extraordinary capacity to study, absorb and apply. When a sink was plugged up, she went to the DIY book, grappled with the diagrams and became her own best plumber, invariably celebrating by announcing that she was going out to spend the money saved on a new pair of Prada sunglasses or a set of cookbooks. Her approach to the wine adventure was based on the same principle. Knowledge = independence.

First, we attended the Wine and Spirit Education Trust in the City of London, the grand old lady of wine knowledge, personified by its emblem, the seated figure of a woman evaluating the partly filled glass of wine in her hand. Their Latin motto reflected the culture. *Gustibus mens dat incrementum.* 'Knowledge enhances sensory perception.'

As we plunged into *Behind the Label*, the trust's remarkably dull study-guide for the introductory certificate, I was reminded of learning catechism at the convent, six years old, and struggling to prepare for my first sip of communion wine.

*'I am the Lord your God who brought you out of the Land of Egypt, of the house of slavery.'*

'Wine is product obtained from the total or partial alcoholic fermentation of fresh grapes, whether or not crushed, or of grape must.'

*'Do not have any other gods before me.'*

'France is the most important wine-producing country in the world.'

*'You shall not make for yourself an idol.'*

'Though a large producer, Argentina produces wine of moderate quality.'

As you might have expected, South America merited only passing mention: 'in remaining parts of the world, leading producers are Argentina, Chile, USA and South Africa'. Instead of the forbidden treasures of the New World, we studied the detailed topography, farming styles and wine-making of France, with exhaustive explorations of Bordeaux, and Burgundy, and the Loire, and the Rhône, detouring off briefly to Germany, Italy, Spain, and even Bulgaria and Hungary, before returning to France for a section on champagne, where the attempts of New World countries to make bubbly received the following put-down: 'There are many sparkling wines made by the same method as champagne, and sometimes from the same grape varieties. There is, however, only one true champagne.'

We concluded that the path to success lay in accepting orthodoxy, learning the intricacies of Bordeaux and Burgundy without question, and making as few mistakes as possible in a multiple-choice arena that put a premium on differentiating Pomerol from Pauillac, Cabernet from Carmenère, *qualitätswein* from *tafelwein*. At the second stage, with the advanced certificate on the line, the grape was separated from the stalks. When asked to taste, identify and describe a classic white from Burgundy, a Meursault, I made it sound like a well-balanced, mineral-rich Chardonnay, minus the lashings of butter and creaminess that went with the New World, which was what it tasted like to me, a New Age wine drinker, drenched in California revolution and the global brand of Chardonnay.

Sonia, of course, looked askance at my descriptions and shook her head. She knew what the Francophone judges were looking for: the

Meursault, for her, was no less than 'a French original . . . based on
*terroir*, plus generations of winemaking . . . think of Catherine Deneuve
in a golden evening dress'. *Mais oui*. Why didn't I think of that? She left
the City of London with a gold-star distinction. I came home with a
straight B.

Still, tasting and spitting, smelling and quaffing, decanting and
swirling made me realize what we needed from any education in the
wine adventure. We needed to learn the language of the business. We
had to be able to speak to the players. We needed to understand why
someone could stick his or her nose deep into a goblet, then declare
'barnyard', or 'sweaty leather boots', or 'rotten plum', and actually
consider it a compliment. The bizarre world of wine talk. From flowers
no one had actually ever smelled, violets, acacia, elderflower, to every
fruit under the sun. Lychees, anyone, or gooseberries perhaps? And,
anyway, no matter how hard I tried, sniffing into the goblet, I just never
smelled pungent boots, or farmhouse filth, or musty paper cartons. And
if I did, I refused to drink it, just like any other sane wine drinker.

So I did not lust after the industry's ultimate honour, Master of
Wine, or MW, the most impressive two letters next to every wine writer's
name. Frankly, I knew I would fail. It sounded to me like a decade of
hard labour, with the unbelievable challenge of being expected to blind
taste a glass of wine, anywhere, at any time, and recognize its provenance,
its vintage, its creator. We saw friends through the assault course that
led to the MW, developing the skill to identify instantly a 1995 Château
Latour, or a 1947 Pétrus, or a 2000 Opus One. A life skill, maybe, but
with my DNA, not worth the risk. Long before I got to the magical
MW, I was sure, I would end up in that other two-lettered fraternity of
wine lovers, AA, Alcoholics Anonymous.

So, no MW for me. What I did see was the business imperative. If
you wanted to enter the world of wine, you had to learn the language,
you had to establish some street credibility and, above all, you had to
acquire the confidence to define what kind of wine you liked. What
kind of wine you returned to. What kind of wine you wanted to make.

That is what led us to New Orleans. And the Court of Master
Sommeliers.

Only a city that lived through a hurricane called 'Katrina' could come
up with the idea of a cocktail named 'The Hurricane'.

New Orleans. A city that always had one more for the road. A city that lived for midnight. A city that prided itself on being semi-inebriate. Only the 'Big Easy' would celebrate its catastrophe with a sledgehammer of a drink.

As defined by the city's star chef, Emeril Lagasse, a 'Hurricane' was based on the following mix: two ounces light rum, two ounces dark rum, two ounces grenadine, one ounce orange juice, one ounce sour mix, one teaspoon of sugar, with wedges of orange for garnish.

We winced at the hangover such a cocktail might unleash, but there was a spiritual lament in the parish of New Orleans, dating back to the days of the slave trade and the Underground Railroad that produced more free people of colour than anywhere else in America at the beginning of the Civil War.

> Bury me down in New Orleans
> So I can spend eternity above ground
> You can flood this town
> But you can't shut the party down
> Ain't no drowning the spirit.

I chose New Orleans to take the exam at the Court of Master Sommeliers because it was one of my lucky cities. And I needed every ounce of luck this time to pass this test. Not any test. A test that would make us certified sommeliers.

Gathering in the Sheraton Hotel on Canal Street at the unlikely hour of eight o'clock in the morning to start tasting wine, Sonia and I looked decidedly out of place. Everyone else was a wine steward, a head waiter, a chef, a restaurant owner or a wine buyer. The men in dark jackets and sober ties, the women in tailored suits that emphasized business rather than bodies. Everyone else was handing out business cards with invitations to wine and dine the next time in Beverly Hills, Vancouver, Denver, New York. The twenty-somethings tried to intimidate us with knowledge, research, tasting, how much they preferred this vintage to another. Poor things had not worked out we were not worth intimidating. Two days before, practising for the big day, a bottle of champagne had exploded in my hands and landed all over our dining-room floor. As we mopped it up, we knew we were remedial students when it came to the most important skill being tested. The actual practical business of being a sommelier: opening bottles with expert panache. Plainly, we were not Michelin star material.

But we were experts at hiding our fear, listening to the young men and women who might one day happily be persuaded to buy our Argentine wines.

'I tried an Alban Rhône blend the other evening, it was an exceptional California rendition,' informed Ron, head waiter from Baton Rouge, Louisiana.

'Never had an Alban that wasn't in the 94–98 point range,' countered Tracy from Southern California.

'Much prefer the Southern Rhône Grenache blends,' interrupted Dan, manager of a New Orleans restaurant that catered to presidents holding summits, the famous Commander's Palace. He seemed the most amiable, plus I recognized credibility when I saw it. This man, I felt, was the one to trust.

But next to us was California Tracy's boss, a heavily bejewelled manager of a four-star restaurant in Orange County. 'I'm not worried about the practical, the tasting and presenting,' she said. 'It's the theory that makes me nervous, remembering all those place names and putting the wines together with location.' But she let us know, with her look, that we should have heard of her restaurant if we knew our stuff.

So what was the use of our fancy Oxford and Cambridge degrees if we could not even open a decent bottle of red wine without impersonating John Cleese? We had the theory nailed down. All those dull facts about appellations, soils, pruning methods. But the thought of uncorking a bottle of champagne at shoulder height, keeping the noise down to a quiet *pshhh* rather than a fourth of July firework display, pouring glasses of bubbly almost to the top in one continuous pour, remembering to serve women first, walk clockwise around the table, always show the guest the label, remember to leave the wire basket on the cork with your thumb firmly on it all times, just to make sure you don't blind one of your guests with a propulsively ejecting cork. Oh God. Or the idea of decanting an old French red over candlelight, avoiding any hint of a bubble or a splash, pouring evenly at a forty-five-degree angle into a decanter, then serving the table in correct order without leaving a trace of deep-red claret anywhere. Well, we didn't have a tablecloth without red wine stains in the house. Nor, frankly, the budget to keep practising with decanter-worthy old Bordeaux.

But at least we had tried to learn from the best. Washington DC was home to the venerable Willard Hotel, the original lobby where a century ago presidents were lobbied by those who knew, where presidents once escaped the White House for a drink at the bar, where Abraham Lincoln arrived one morning in 1861, just before his inaugural, declaring: 'I'm Mr Lincoln, and I believe you have a room for me.'

I asked my friend, the manager of the Willard Hotel, to let me practise with his chief sommelier. Luckily, the day before we left for New Orleans, the British Foreign Secretary had held a meeting at the Willard Hotel, discussing the future of Afghanistan and Pakistan. Perfect timing. I could hear his talk, have a brief word, then bid him goodbye and disappear to the hotel dining room to meet my mentor, the delightful Caterina Abbruzetti, who patiently corrected me as I struggled to open a bottle of low-quality champagne and decant a cheap red. She was too kind to say so, but her Italian look was unmistakable. I was, as my Roman friends would say, a real *stronso* at opening bottles. Maybe it was the sad tell-tale drip down the neck of the bottle. Or the loud crack that accompanied the champagne cork flying off. But on my way home, armed with Caterina's tips, I bought a case of the cheapest bubbly, and the cheapest red, known as 'Two Buck Chuck', and we practised for two hours, determined to avoid humiliation. At the end of the night we were still bad, but maybe not *stronso* bad. We were ready for New Orleans.

But still. I needed a dose of my customary good luck in New Orleans, listening to the talk of Spanish *tempranillo*, checking whether Rogue Mountain was in Oregon or Washington State, delving into the maps of Bordeaux and Burgundy for the last time. New Orleans had always been a friend to me.

Soon after I arrived in the United States, just after the end of the first Gulf War with George Bush Senior as President, I had come to the city. I travelled south to oil-rich Louisiana and the Gulf of Mexico off-shore to look at energy policy, America's dependency on the Middle East for oil, and how the superpower required some kind of Middle East peace to keep its economy burning brightly. It had been my first experience of Cajun country, and the fusion of Creole and Anglo that made New Orleans unique.

I snagged an interview at the Governor's mansion outside Baton

Rouge. Governors of Louisiana have been legendary ever since a man called Huey Long took control in the 1930s, made 'Every Man a King' his populist slogan and ran the state like a medieval fiefdom until he was shot inside the State Capitol. His final words, the stuff of a classic American novel and Hollywood movie: 'God, don't let me die, I have so much more to do.'

I met the Governor, a bright-eyed, witty fellow named Buddy Roemer, on the very day he decided to ignore the pleas of a fellow Southerner called Bill Clinton to stay a Democrat. No, Governor Buddy Roemer decided that day to leave the Democratic Party and throw his support to the Republican President George H. W. Bush, with his remarkably high popularity ratings, immediately after that first Gulf War. Governor, we all made our mistakes. Me included. Like so many stories, the idea of looking at America's energy policy in 1991 after one Gulf War seemed sharp. But my timing, terrible. Seventeen years later, it was the story of another election, another President. But being seventeen years early did not a career make, right? The election that followed was not about energy policy, or independence from foreign oil. It was the economy, stupid. In the memorable words of the Ragin' Cajun himself, Jim Carville, a political guru who invented the slogan for that son of the South, Bill Clinton.

# Good Luck

No one likes to admit it, but luck can play an extraordinary role in the making of a career. One principle stalked the media industry. Any journalist was only as good as his or her last story.

World exclusive. The Pope just happened to stop to bless a child in front of the microphone, making the question about his health impossible to avoid. Bless you, Father.

The paratrooper in the early hours on day one of a war just happened to be one fluent English-speaker, worth serious syndication revenue. Thanks, mate.

Boris Yelsin just happened to lose that infamous temper in front of my camera, walking across Red Square one glorious summer afternoon, declaring an end to the Soviet Empire. Cheers, comrade.

Being in the right place at the right time? Maybe. Or maybe just damn good luck. For me, some cities signalled just plain bad luck. Take Berlin. Berlin represented, always, my Marlene Dietrich. Full of promise, but a real bitch.

First, there was the hunt for Miss Germany. She had won the Miss World title in London, then fled back home when her past, specifically some stunning images in the nude, became an issue. Now that was a promising story. Stuck outside her parents' apartment in Berlin, with a TV cameraman hired locally that morning, I did the unthinkable in the fiercely unionized TV world of the 1970s and acted as the sound technician, recording an exclusive interview with her, fully-clothed. She spoke of her previous boyfriends, how they took intimate photos, how her life had turned so quickly from Miss World to disaster. This was tabloid heaven. Then I learned how naïve I was. The British TV unions forbade anyone other than a card-carrying union member from using recording equipment. It was a strike, or reprimanding me for recording the sound. No contest in the 1970s. The union won; the story never aired. *Auf wiedersehen*, Miss Germany.

Then, at the height of the Cold War, on the twentieth anniversary of the building of the Berlin Wall, we left Checkpoint Charlie to cross from West to East, from capitalism to communism, from our world to theirs. So we dashed hither and thither, filming East Germans in their rather bare shops, in their rather sad apartment blocks, and leaving their decidedly drab offices. I convinced myself that we had shaken off the minders of the East German security police, and sent my news network a message via the British military in West Berlin, saying I needed space on the news that night for a rare look at life in the Eastern bloc. The only event we were supposed to film was the afternoon military parade, the centrepiece of that anniversary on the communist side of the wall. I was greeted by a smiling officer of the secret police from the infamous Ministerium fur Staatssicherheit, the Ministry for State Security, other-wise known as STASI. 'Give me that film, or if not you will be spending a night or two with us,' he said with a Germanic grin.

I asked my West German cameraman to hand over the film in the camera, knowing we had another reel safely in his bag. 'OK, now you can film the parade, and then you leave,' said our STASI minder, satisfied. He who laughs last.

Well, not me. When we opened our remaining secret reel of East German life, we discovered it was unusable, a cameo in total darkness on a bright August afternoon. Wrong exposure. Bad luck, or my assignment had been sabotaged from the beginning, with the help of the cameraman. His military-parade pictures were perfectly exposed. I ended my day filing a short, truly miserable news piece, showing the East German army goose-stepping past the Politburo, military might on display, from tank divisions to long-range missile units, the Soviet bloc seemingly united, defiant as ever. Just what the STASI had ordered. Berlin, I concluded, was a bitch to work in.

But if Berlin spelled humiliation, I cherished wartime Beirut as my lucky dateline. From the moment I arrived, as Israel invaded Lebanon in the summer of 1982, Beirut became a part of my heart. Stories to remember, friendships to savour and evenings by the shore that seemed so peaceful, precisely because the day had often been so violent. To the outsider looking in, Beirut appeared to be the crucible of the age, the inferno that claimed lives on all sides, the shorthand for endless conflict. Yet, to me, Beirut was where living so close to death validated my life.

The thrill of being a war correspondent outweighed the danger. We worked as a team, cameraman, soundman and me, smelling for danger on the lonely roads of front lines. I learned to gauge the time between outgoing and incoming shells, and their parabola of death drawn across the sky, as they fell near us, exploding. It helped to have a veteran with us. That old mate Don McCullin, war photographer, perfectionist in the art of survival, student of life and death, often travelled with us, his experience of Cyprus, Vietnam, Cambodia, Biafra, Congo keeping us all alive.

One evening we were trapped on the rooftop of the British Army's headquarters on the outskirts of the city, pinned down by heavy sniper and rocket fire, crawling on all fours, shouting out our fears like frightened children who have just discovered the f-word. Screaming, for any pause in the bombardment. Suddenly we heard the US battleship *New Jersey* out at sea open up with its long-range guns, firing at the very Syrian and Moslem militias who had us in their gunsights. The longest, most harrowing hours, saved by the sound of heavy artillery. The story won me an award from the Royal Television Society in London, but it belonged to a camera team behind whom I cowered, two towering figures named Sebastian Rich and Richard Rose.

There was the morning we broke through to a mental hospital in the Palestinian suburb of Sabra, to discover kids who had not been fed properly in weeks, their screams horrific, their squalor shameful, yet their faces speaking so powerfully of the wish to live, not die, on the very front line of West Beirut. Their images on the news that night syndicated around the world, all the way to Calcutta and Mother Teresa. She begged for a ceasefire so she could come in and rescue those children forty-eight hours later. When, years further on, a Washington friend, Christopher Hitchens, published an indictment of Mother Teresa as a publicity-seeker, I had to acknowledge that the saintly nun had indeed stolen my story. But the memories of her carrying mentally disabled toddlers to safety, in the arc-light glow of world media, left me grateful for the media savvy she exercised with such professional efficiency. No one else, not even the President of the United States, could stop the fighting in West Beirut. Mother Teresa succeeded with the simple tactic of putting herself in the firing line, and defying the combatants to kill her.

And then the memorable afternoon we drove north from Beirut to the port of Tripoli, stopping for a superb seafood lunch and a fine bottle of Ksara red wine along the way, daring to go farther than anyone else in the days before, to the final redoubt of the Palestinian leader Yasser Arafat. Not so much the theatrical father of his people, but rather a cornered animal, his enemies circling around him, waiting for the kill, tightening their blockade by the hour. So much so that he dispensed with any swagger, or sermon, instead cutting our interview short to enable us to escape his camp before nightfall, the last interview before the battle for Tripoli began in October 1983; the look on Arafat's face as he waved goodbye still stamped on my memory because, that evening, the ultimate survivor looked like a man who had given up on the cause that made him Mr Palestine.

Beirut's luck never left me, even when I had to leave for the last time. By 1985 and 1986, many Westerners, especially journalists, had fled the city. Kidnappings added a new level of danger, a danger that was harder to smell. Yet Beirut still called me back and rewarded me as ever. When rivals from the BBC, and the American networks, even the wire services, left after published threats to kidnap foreigners, I stayed on and won praise from major newspapers in London, New York and Paris for continuing to report from Lebanon, not to mention the thanks of ITN's syndication team who sold my reports to others. And just when my naked ambition could have cost me my life, I was rescued by my best friend, a driver named Abed Moughrabi.

Abed, a stocky, impish figure of a man who limped from a bullet-wound inflicted by a Syrian soldier during Lebanon's civil war a decade earlier, a spirit who never moved without caressing his prayer-beads, decided almost everything in the course of a working day. When it was safe to go out. Where we might travel. What supplies we needed, not just for personal consumption, but to bribe whomever we might encounter. His ancient Mercedes acted as our home. Abed himself acted as our guardian. And because Abed was paid handsomely when we were in Beirut, he never wanted us to leave.

Not until the spring of 1986. I had journeyed to Beirut from my base in Jerusalem to put together a story on the Western hostages. The American journalist Terry Anderson, kidnapped a year earlier, was a friend and tennis partner. The British missionary Terry Waite, in town trying to open channels to the kidnappers, had been a valuable contact for years. We had worked together in some unlikely places, Iran, Libya, Uganda. This was my story, and I convinced myself that I alone could get in and out to do it. Such arrogance. Such was the climate of fear that I travelled alone, without a TV crew, checked into the Commodore Hotel in West Beirut quietly, then made my calls as usual, the loyal Abed ferrying me back and forth across the city in his Mercedes.

One morning he greeted me in the lobby, very serious. 'Mr David, please pack your bag and I will drive you to the airport immediately,' he said, with a glare.

Taken aback, I joked whether his beloved wife had stopped talking to him, or whether he had betrayed Islamic law by drinking. He cut me short. 'Mr David, you're a danger to yourself. You no longer see the danger.'

Those words hurt. As the correspondent and team leader in a TV operation, I had always prided myself on not taking unnecessary risks, not putting others in unnecessary danger, thinking not gung-ho but smart. Abed knew that better than anyone, and he knew the pain he was inflicting.

'Mr David, I cannot work with you any more. You are too dangerous for me.'

His words punched me in the gut. I could not work in the city without him. He was telling me to get out, and never come back, even at the risk of losing our friendship. I understood. He knew I was in imminent danger. I told him I had no airline reservation.

'Mr David, make no reservation here at the hotel,' and then his voice dropped to a whisper. 'We drive to the airport. There is a flight to Cyprus at eleven.'

The glance he shot the hotel concierge urged silence. Abed was telling me to leave this place with no evidence of my next move. I settled my bill, saying I wanted a night down by the coast at Byblos, a favourite watering-hole on the other side of the city, and that maybe I would come back tomorrow, requesting my favourite room if available.

Abed drove me to the airport without a word. He shut down on me, forcing me to leave, rather like the lover who knows the only way to end it is without words.

And so my love affair with Beirut ended. The day I left was my luckiest. Just a few days after I boarded that 11 a.m. plane to Cyprus, John McCarthy, a young British journalist who worked for a sister company, staying in the same Beirut hotel, was kidnapped. He spent more than five years as a hostage before being released.

# Let the Good Times Roll

All said, it put my judgement day into perspective, in the ballroom of the Sheraton Hotel in New Orleans, before the Master Court of Sommeliers.

We had acquitted ourselves respectably, we felt, on the wine-tasting. Presented with a glass of white, and a red, we had taken the examination through the professional's roadmap. How pale, or golden, or straw-like did the white wine look against a white napkin? How purple, or violet, or black the red wine? What about the 'legs', the drops of viscosity that might be seen clinging to the side of a glass when you swirled the wine?

And then what about the 'nose', the smell? Lemon, or vanilla, or gooseberry, all strong indicators of a certain grape? Or blackberry, maybe cherry, even spice on the nose of a red wine? How much oak in the flavour and the smell, because oak was such a lead indicator wine style?

According to the study-guide, 'The taste of the wine, which is called the palate, reveals the true nature of the wine.' Thank you, master sommeliers, very helpful.

Our assignment was identifying two wines. What were they? Where from? Which year?

On first taste I was still groping for the answer. Eventually, a process of elimination formed in my head, then my nose, finally in the finish at the back of the throat. Rather like most politicians of my acquaintance, I did not know what I was for, but I did know what I was against. I was not absolutely sure what wines we had been given. But I deduced the white was not a Chardonnay, or a Riesling, or a Sauvignon Blanc, or a Viognier. I plumped for a Chenin Blanc, probably from old-world France because I tasted minerals, not oak. On the red, I finished more convinced, indeed I drank every drop even though it was barely nine o'clock in the morning. A robust Cabernet Sauvignon, blended with smooth Merlot, California-style. To my delight, Sonia concurred as we left the room together. To our enormous relief, most of our classmates backed our judgement. Even if we were all wrong, there was safety in numbers.

Next came the kind of written test that numbed the brain. Where is the Red Mountain wine district? What about Rogue Valley? Is the Clos D'E in Mercurey or Pomerol? What year yielded a better Bordeaux, 1984, or 1995, or 1998? Where is the Appellation Contrôlée with the semi-comic name of Fixin? Is Château Lascombes a second-growth Bordeaux, or a fourth-growth Pauillac? We snorted at the question, 'Which of the following is not a wine region of Chile?' The answer, of course, was our beloved Mendoza.

Remembering useless and useful information was a skill. Fortunately, I spent a lifetime learning by rote. Telephone numbers of old girlfriends? Still locked in the memory. The capacity to recall exactly where I was on a certain day twenty-eight years ago? Also clear. Where did I leave my key twenty-eight minutes ago? Not so clear. But I knew I had passed that tedious part of the exam, probably with a high number.

Two down, one to go. But here was the problem. We knew that to become certified sommeliers we had to pass all three tests, with more than a 60 per cent mark. Blind tasting? Felt OK. Theory exam? No problem. But ahead lay the walking barefoot on broken glass segment. My only experience as a waiter, serving burgers at a motorway cafeteria while a student in Britain, did not cut it in this company.

It was time. We needed to be the king and queen of composure, Sonia said as we marched into the ballroom for the final act. 'Remember who we are, darling.'

'I know who I am, thank you,' I glared at her. 'What I don't know is whether I can open a bloody bottle of wine without my hands shaking.'

All those years of live television in both our cases. Sonia was the serene anchorwoman at moment of crisis. I relished my minor reputation, coined by *The Times*, as the 'gloomiest man on British television'. I frowned relentlessly. I used my hands to punctuate points. If I didn't know the answer, I admitted it. Towards the end of my TV days, I realized the secret lay in being comfortable with yourself, a knack that had eluded me painfully in my early years in the business.

But walking into that ballroom I froze, looking at the four master sommeliers sitting at a round table, ready to see if I would make a worthy certified sommelier. I stammered out answers on cocktails.

'What is Pernod? I'd like a Sidecar, do you know how to make one? What is a Negroni?'

'A Negroni is gin, sweet vermouth, and Italy's finest Campari,' I said, with a flourish, as I imagined a fancy sommelier, trying to impress, would speak.

'Tell me, what is vermouth?'

Oh shit. What the hell was it? That horrible bitter stuff my uncles drank back in the 1960s. A liqueur? Fortified wine? Brandy?

I was busted. The examiner's eyes told me he had seen I was not certified material.

We ventured into dessert wines. Name a botrytized sweet white? Name a *vin doux naturel,* a natural sweet wine? Oh, and by the way, we're eating herb-crusted *lamb au jus,* what would you recommend to accompany it? Much better, we were back in wine territory, not horrible cocktails. So I was on track again. I knew it. A Syrah from the Northern Rhône, I recommended, and the response was a knowing nod. All I had to do now was the practical. It all hinged on serving a bottle of champagne decently.

But he was not going to make it easy. He outlined the scenario. 'I am here with my wife and a couple of friends,' he play-acted. 'I also have four friends about to join us. We would all love to have a glass of this champagne. And don't bother to offer me a tasting. It's a '66 Krug. I know it's good.'

Eight glasses? From one bottle? That was pushing it. First, I set to work, fiddling with the foil. For God's sake, get a grip, stop shaking. I did manage to cut the capsule that seals the cork with a sense of purpose. Twisting the bottle back and forth, not the cork, I even succeeded in popping the champagne with a soft thud, not a gunshot. So far, so good. But wait a minute. Disaster. I had been showing the judge my behind the whole time. Mooning the judge was not good strategy. Then I remembered that I was supposed to present the bottle to the host first, confirm the name of the champagne, with the year, before opening it. Disaster two.

Trying to make up for my *faux pas,* I took the open bottle out of the bucket, made sure the label was out front, then presented it to the examiner. He looked away, quietly appalled. The thought flashed across my mind. The last thing you do is open the damn bottle, then ask the host to confirm it was his order. It's too late. OK, make that Disaster Three. I felt so foolish, trying to be a waiter. Who am I? And why am I here? Worse, why am I actually paying to be here?

All that remained was to pour eight glasses of champagne for an imaginary table of four men and four women, cradling the bottle from the bottom, holding it steady, never allowing the neck of bottle to touch rim of glass, then delivering three-quarters full flutes in one continuous pour, free of bubbles rising and falling. Just for a few moments, I entered a peaceful zone, my flutes a picture of professionalism. Halfway though glass six, however, I realized I was running low on champagne. The order was for eight glasses. My eighth looked like a sorry dribble, an afterthought at best, maybe one third full.

'I imagine you would like to taste, sir,' I said, offering the final glass to the examiner.

'I told you the order was for eight guests, so eight full glasses,' he replied pointedly. 'No taste necessary, as I told you at the beginning.'

I gave up. 'I'm not a professional waiter, sir,' I admitted.

His disgusted look said it all. And you never will be if I have anything to do with it.

It was over. There was nothing left to do but wait. I had nothing left to lose, not even my pride.

# Katrina Bottles

So often in my journalism years I was struck by the way we media road-rats lived such schizophrenic lives. By day we might have witnessed death, and destruction, and the suffering of many around us. By nightfall we invariably found a path to a decent meal, and a drink or two or more, often enjoying comforts unimaginable to those we had seen in the hours before. That stark juxtaposition, the sense of living in two worlds, side by side yet so brutally apart, came back to me in New Orleans.

Still, this being New Orleans, *laissez les bons temps rouler*, let the good times roll. We had made new friends among the survivors of the Court of Master Sommeliers. That night Sonia and I joined them for a memorable meal at Restaurant Nola, oozing the sophistication and raw excess of the city. A salad starter, with rare yellowfin tuna served on a bed of spinach laced with coconut-curry vinaigrette, a perfect fit with a classic Chablis from Burgundy. Then scallops to die for, in a San Marzano sauce with basil. My mother in London could have murdered the main course, a shepherd's pie with lamb loin corn, smoked mushrooms, stout gravy, covered in dill-cheddar mashed potatoes. A magnificent Syrah from the Northern Rhône. Dessert . . . all caramel, chocolate, cream and magnificent indulgence.

As for the conversation, it unearthed a rare, untold story from Katrina, one tale that affirmed the good life. And what was New Orleans, if not a city of survival and *joie de vivre*?

All around New Orleans sat the open wounds of Hurricane Katrina. Neighbourhoods such as Lakeview, where the levee of the 17th Street canal broke, letting Lake Ponchartrain fill the city with water like a bowl, were being rebuilt, but on almost each street stood an empty house with the tell-tale sign 'No Trespassing', or the painted notes on the wall left by rescuers in the aftermath, denoting whether they had found bodies, or no sign of life at all, or – something so poignantly in between – a dog barking. People had left, for ever, and some sections of the city would never recover. When I asked a taxi-driver to take me to the Lower Ninth ward, the poorest in the city and the zone worst affected, he laughed and told me that not even the police ventured there, years after Katrina.

Above all, American leadership lay buried in the wreckage of New Orleans. At time of crisis, the United States always looked to its Head of State, its President, with a respect and sense of unity that few other societies managed in my experience. Rallying round the flag and their leader was never an issue for Americans. But not after Katrina. Whatever the historians concluded about the presidency of George W. Bush, whatever impact they attributed to 9/11, or the wars in Iraq and Afghanistan, or the economic meltdown that accompanied his final days in office, one defining moment for that presidency stood out, derived from the tragedy of New Orleans.

George W. Bush buried himself, and his presidency, in New Orleans. In a matter of days he lost the confidence of his people. The turning-point for the presidency of Bush Junior lay not in New York, or Baghdad, or Kabul, or on Wall Street, but sitting by the window on Air Force One flying over the flooded city of New Orleans. It was the President, divorced from the agony of the people below, watching his countrymen and women beg for their lives from rooftops. It was a 'decisive moment', as classic as any image taken by the legendary French photographer Henri Cartier-Bresson.

I had witnessed personally how detached President Bush was during the worst, first days after Katrina. I arranged for my boss, Kofi Annan, to speak to the President. Annan wanted to offer the help of the United Nations to the people of America. 'The UN stands ready to help the people of the United States, Mr President,' was his message. 'Just as America has always been so generous to the world, so the world wishes to help your country.' And the UN offered practical aid, from blankets to food packs, to schools in a box, as well as instant tent cities, plus the expertise to set up such relief centres and handle traumatized communities. Whether it was earthquakes or tsunamis or war refugees, the UN had such experience of how to get practical help quickly to displaced people. The message back from the President? Thanks, but no thanks.

After the waters receded, New Orleans recognized how the physical wreckage mirrored the body blow to its sense of self, once a proud emblem of the country's fusion of African, French, Cajun, Creole, Latino, Anglo. Yet the disaster divided the city along racial lines. The

African-American community in many cases fled the Gulf Coast never to return, just as previous generations had migrated to escape slavery. Those who came back brought with them despair and determination in equal measure.

Given the tragedy that had engulfed New Orleans, I looked round the table that night of the sommelier exam for a sign that the spirit of New Orleans had survived. It was provided by our classmates, the sommeliers of some of the city's best restaurants. Yes, they had memories of frantic last-minute efforts to secure homes and businesses, evacuating with the sure knowledge that they were going to lose so much. Yes, they recalled returning to New Orleans to discover so much more damage, to their neighbourhoods, their homes, their restaurants, than even their worst fears had imagined. And yes, nothing prepared them to lose what every sommelier considered semi-sacred: the wine list. The schizophrenic notes of the jounalism years echoed throughout the conversation that followed.

'You just couldn't imagine, returning to a cellar that had been baking in eighty to a hundred degree heat for two-three weeks, ever since the power cut off in the first hours after Katrina hit,' recalled Greg, then the sommelier at Stella, a French Quarter restaurant renowned for its expensive top-drawer wine list. 'You couldn't believe it, but you had to believe it. Your wine list had gone, and insurance only picked up so much of the tab. I was looking at 61 Bordeaux, one of those remarkable years, everything from Château Pétrus, to Château Lafite, to Château d'Yquem.' He didn't say it, because he was listing wines in a tone of such reverence, but I was thinking: those wines were close to stewed fruit after weeks of no temperature control.

Dan, the open-hearted fellow who had emerged from the day's test full of such insights about what lay in store for us from the examiners, remembered returning to the cellar at Commander's Palace, where on an average night he could sell a bottle worth more than a thousand dollars, on a good night he'd move a bottle in the five figures. 'At first you tried to act as if this was a routine clean-up, cleaning out the courtyard, sweeping away the debris, then the closer you got to the wine, the more your stomach just tightened up at the thought of what had been probably lost,' he chuckled grimly, a wince creasing his face. 'I broke the lock on Mr Dick's cabinet, as it was called, and there lay two cases of one of those wines that represented the very best in the world:

1945 Clos de Vougeot from Musigny. A red burgundy to die for, old vine, Grand Cru, absolutely priceless. And you knew in an instant that you could never sell it because of the temperature.'

Russ, then sommelier at Delmonico's, the star restaurant of superstar chef Emeril Lagasse, the irrepressible spirit who invented the Katrina cocktail, chipped in. 'At first we didn't drink the wonders of the world that lay around us. But then the insurance companies paid up on the policies we had, valuing vintages at what they had been bought for, not what they were worth. And, heck, one day we concluded we could drink it, we had to. We couldn't sell it, and we certainly couldn't throw them into the Mississippi. So we drank, and drank some of the finest cellars in the world. We tasted wines you would never dream of trying. In our restaurant that meant about 6,000 bottles.'

'We called it a Katrina bottle,' added Greg, a puckish look on his face. 'And each bottle had a certain something. A 61 Pétrus tasted like it should, but with a roasted character, slightly bitter-sweet, splendid and sad in the same moment. Feeling liberated about drinking 61 Bordeaux was something. We had to drink, because collections were dying in front of our eyes.'

New Orleans, the city that lived for midnight. The city that woke up and smelled the vino. The city that staged its own, unique wake for what was lost in countless cellars during Hurricane Katrina. And, once again, New Orleans had brought me luck. I had something to celebrate. Didn't need to be smart. Just lucky. I was a certified sommelier. And Sonia too, with a gold star in her certificate.

*

Dan, restaurant manager, New Orleans:

My view of all of us taking the sommelier exam that day was quite simple. I wanted all of us to pass. I despised folks who felt better if others failed at something, that somehow they were enhanced by succeeding where others fell down, and clearly we had some of those that day in New Orleans. I just believed that, if we all succeeded, we all won. Think about it. New Orleans, the city where I lived and worked in the restaurant world, could have been boasting more master sommeliers than any other city in the world.

That would have been good for the city, good for the restaurant business, good for me.

I wasn't shy about saying it. And I didn't hold back when I came out of the room, having uncorked that champagne. I had nailed the test, probably the best they had seen all day.

Just as well. Because I had underperformed on the theory. In fact I concluded I failed that part. But on the practical I felt untouchable. The minute I saw they had given us cheap bubbly, with plastic corks, I knew this was all about striking up a rapport with the examiners, those questions about Negronis, and Sidecars, and vermouth were designed just to trip you up from the fluency of serving a respectable glass of lousy champagne.

So the first thing I see when I come out of my master sommelier test is this couple sitting by the window. She never picked her nose out of her book, studying some wine bible, but listening intently at the same time to everything going on around her. He was working the crowd, cleverly encouraging people to reveal what they had been asked without seeming to question. You could detect the combination. This Englishman, saying, 'Tell me more,' while making notes in his head, and his bride sitting there, taking it all in while appearing to be buried in making notes from her book. I must have been their idea of perfect witness, because I just spewed out everything that had happened in the test. All the questions, all the answers I gave, then suggestions about what wines to recommend. If they asked about a suggestion for lamb chops, and everyone had the same question, then give them a Syrah from the Southern Rhône. I even remember trying to show them how best to open a cheap champagne with a plastic cork. And again, he was all encouraging smiles and tacit thank yous. She was all spectacles, and book, and big ears.

I concluded that this couple represented a force to be reckoned with. The Englishman was focused on the experience. His bride was hell bent on getting a result. He was passionate about every-thing he did, you could tell. She had notes written on her eyelids, she was so studious and restrained. For a moment I thought this was an odd match-up. He was so obviously a performer, loving the sound of his own voice, delighting in the chase. She seemed so enigmatic, restrained, demure, comfortable in her silence, beautiful yet so enigmatic. But then I thought of serving some famous couple in restaurants down the years. And I thought of Bill and Hillary Clinton. The dreamer and the doer. The odd match-up suddenly didn't seem so odd. He gave the impression of being across it all, of understanding the detail, but that's all it was. An impression. She was the determined one. The partner who did the serious work once he had opened the door. The one who converted dreams into reality.

Then the Englishman told me he worked for the United Nations, and that fascinated me.

Ever since adolescence, and a Model UN conference where I played the role of the US Ambassador to New York, saying no with bullish stubbornness to some objectionable Security Resolution, I had loved the idea of the United Nations. The place where the world came together to discuss peace, and avoid war. The organization that tended the sick, fed the starving. The force for good that can save us all. It saddened me that the UN had sunk in the eyes of many people, and that America's view of the institution had become so negative.

I always had one image in my mind when I thought of the UN: a soldier standing in some god-forsaken corner of the world with a blue helmet on his head. There were so many people for whom the only taste of freedom, and safety, and human rights, came in the shape of the blue helmet.

So watching this Englishman from the UN, dressed like some high-end *maître d'*, but fretting about the sommelier exam, biting his nails and mopping his brow on a muggy New Orleans afternoon as he listened so intently for all the help he could get, proved something of a shock. But I could see how that passion for everything might produce an advocate for the UN, especially in a city as staid as Washington DC. He gave away very little about what he actually did, seemed to be acting as a liaison with the Congress, and the White House, and so on.

And the two of them downplayed their vineyard. Sitting with them that night at dinner, I had the impression that they grew grape to sell to some winery down there. So I was seeing a small farm with no greater ambition than a seat on the porch and a beautiful view of the mountains. But then I caught up with them in Washington DC, and they brought their first vintage to dinner.

Their wine was extremely well balanced. It did not drink like a young, tight wine, suggesting to me that it would age well. It had an incredibly long finish, soft tannins, the alcohol not too high. I kept having this strange thought: it was not French, but it was French. It drank like a fine claret, with wonderful complexity and the potential to age.

I tried to tell David to think about the business plan. But it was hard to know if he was listening. My message was – establish this wine as your award-winner, your heart and soul, your premium label. Then come in behind it with something down-market, something far cheaper and exploit the line 'from the makers of SonVida', etc.

As I said, the dreamer and the doer. He's the dreamer. She's the doer. I had faith that she was listening

\*

# Next Year in Jerusalem

A cocktail party at the White House had nothing on this.

Sonia and I stood at the door of the world's largest wine show, VinExpo, where the romance of wine met the hustle of commerce. Every other year, the magnificent city of Bordeaux hosted wine producers wishing to show off their wares, the price for a small stand measuring in thousands of Euros. We came from 135 countries: 46,621 producers, distributors, importers, marketers and, of course, the professional schmoozers and boozers. The world's wine, tasted for free under one exhibition-hall roof. Two hours later, we had walked from one side of the convention centre to the other, threading past rows of lavishly produced stands, set up as glamorous pop-up wine bars, with bottles piled high and glasses filled at the merest hint of a potential distributor. But not a drop for us.

Sonia and I held hands, feeling insignificant. Of course no one served us. They knew better. But just in case they proved useful one day, we harvested visiting cards. Would we ever grow big enough to make a stand in VinExpo worth it? We had not even thought to print up business cards with the name of our company, Casa Altamira. Our 46,619 new friends at VinExpo looked at our name-tags, puzzled. 'Why are you here?'

Wine as big business. The business of wine knew why it was there, looking for deals, hunting for sales and new markets. I heard buyers talking nervously about prices on a bottle. I heard of the surge in wine sales in the millennium, now a memory drowned by wines lakes and fears of bankruptcy. Too much good wine chasing too few buyers.

Finally, one of those good wines was within my reach. 'The wines are better than ever,' confirmed Claude Boudamani, winemaker and sales director for the global powerhouse Lurton, pouring me a delicious new red blend from Portugal. 'But the market is down; the crisis is real. Just look at the Americans. They're still drinking, but not at the same price.' He took a sip of that Portuguese red, savouring its long, surprisingly elegant finish, astonishing me by revealing that ten different grape varietals came together in one glass. 'And what am I supposed to with a product line like this, aimed at the twenty-five- to thirty-dollar market?' he asked.

'I share your pain, *monsieur*,' I confessed. His price target, twenty-five to thirty dollars, was precisely the market we planned for our first wine.

The next stop, far from the France stands, almost at the end of the hall, displayed a winery in the Bekaa valley of eastern Lebanon. Château Kefraya, at the foot of Mount Barouk, had a story all of its own, beyond the vineyard and the castle that housed the winery. I visited once, at the end of a day I could never forget. A day when the skies over Lebanon shrieked with battle. The Israeli Air Force, commanding American-made F-16 fighter planes and F-4 Phantoms, seeking out Russian-made Migs belonging to the Syrians. That day, back in 1982, the world went on high alert. American jets in dogfights with Russian Migs. It was exactly the kind of clash between surrogates that Cold War historians had always feared, potentially the trigger for a wider war between the superpowers. Ronald Reagan in Washington DC chose to be pragmatic, not dogmatic. The ailing Soviet leader, Leonid Brezhnev, had his own internal issues to worry about in Moscow. As the jets streaked across the skies of Lebanon, the superpowers warned their respective allies in Jerusalem and Damascus to back off, for the moment, when it came to fighting each other. For the real war was between Israel and the Palestinians who had occupied Lebanon for decades, paving the way for the conflict between the Israelis and Hezbollah, the militia that became such a mainstream political force in the early years of the twenty-first century.

But on that day in 1982 it helped that American hardware had triumphed in the Bekka valley. Eighty-six, yes eighty-six, Syrian Migs shot down with just one crash on the Israeli side. A staggering defeat, and a vivid exposé of the Soviet Union's technological backwardness. Years later, I heard how the Soviet Politburo, the young Mikhail Gorbachev among them, took the news. Gorbachev told me: 'The disaster in the Bekaa opened the door to a much broader conversation about the state of our Empire. That news, that day, meant denial was no longer an option. Like a canary in the coal mine, that day warned us of the crisis coming down the tunnel. If we lost so many planes in the Bekaa, what else might we lose?' For Gorbachev that was the moment to seize the initiative on reform.

'And fortunately for us, the fighting between the Israelis and the Palestinians stopped just a few days before our normal harvest time, in late August,' recalled Émile Majdalani, Château Kefraya's commercial director. 'Still, we made our 1982 wine with Israeli soldiers outside the winery, and with the fuselage of an Israeli plane on the edge of the vineyard after it crashed. The soldiers imposed a night curfew, so we worked a night shift that year, from seven at night till five in the morning.'

He offered me a glass of the château's signature red, a wine that had won plaudits in the wider world.

'The funny thing is that we all think the 1982 war vintage was our best ever,' concluded Majdalani. 'And the Israelis came back in 2006. That time they were going after Hezbollah. Of course, we didn't have Hezbollah fighters in the vineyard, or in the winery, or in our company for that matter. But try telling that to an Israeli commando. Thank goodness, in 2006 they stopped fighting just three days before the harvest.'

# Harvest of Tears

By the time I was sent to Lebanon as a correspondent in 1982, witnessing death was no longer such a shock. By then I had reported on unimaginable suffering and pain, often on a scale that defied belief, from the likes of Uganda, Ethiopia, Afghanistan and Pakistan. As for the wish to kill, I had seen bloodlust at work in the terrorism that haunted old Europe, in the military dictatorships that dominated Latin America, certainly in the tribal conflicts of Africa.

But nothing prepared me for Lebanon.

Lebanon represented such a crucible, such a tragedy, such perversion of humanity. *Pity the Nation* was the title of a devastating book written by my long-time Beirut confrère Robert Fisk, a book that I reviewed out of loyalty for a London magazine. But, in my heart, I struggled with his view of Lebanon, so desperate, so bleak, so bereft of hope.

Pity the nation that dispatched fighters from one village to the next, intent on slaughtering those who had been neighbours, co-workers, friends in some cases, destroying everyone and everything in their path.

Pity the nation that had Christians, yes Christians, murder whole communities of Palestinians, men, women and children. No mercy shown, as we discovered when we found piles of bodies rotting out on the streets days afterwards.

Pity the nation that suffered foreign invasion, and foreign occupier; the Syrians coming from the east with their insidious use of fear, torture, kneecapping and murder; the Israelis from the south with their carefully calibrated blend of overwhelming force and psychological operations: psy/ops that put an entire population on edge, in real fear of a thousand-pound bomb, or a tank round, or a phosphorous shell that could sear an arm or a cheek down to the bone.

A quarter-century later, those memories, and the nightmares they fed, led me to join the UN Secretary-General's Crisis Group with a plea for instant action, never an easy task at the UN, when during the summer of 2006 the Iranian-backed Hezbollah movement launched attacks on northern Israel from their bases in southern Lebanon, and the Israelis replied with aerial bombardment that reminded us all of 1982. I argued that, this time, the world at large had to move, put a buffer force between the two opponents, not allow the three-month carnage I had seen all those years before. The UN had a small, peace-keeping operation still in the south, the legacy of wars past. Surely we could reinforce those units quickly and effectively? UN Secretary-General Kofi Annan led the charge, his deputy Mark Malloch Brown worked the phones, and in just four weeks the Europeans produced some 14,000 boots on the ground, led by French Legionnaires and Italian Bersaglieri, regiments with long memories of Lebanon.

And my nightmares? They spoke to blind fear laced with panic, not the kind of emotions the war correspondent normally admitted to, but then I never bought into the particular brand of bullshit that went with the war-correspondent ethos. A few correspondents were heroes. Some took unbelievable risks for the story. But most of us focused on doing simply the best we could, one day to the next, consumed by survival. And, if we were honest, dominated by fear.

That fear was in my DNA, in my family's folklore certainly, but it didn't help me when I tasted the raw, overwhelming violence of war for the first time, first-hand, up close and personal, in Lebanon.

In 1942 my mother moved as a bride to the North London house I grew up in, to work as a conscript in a nearby munitions factory. Tales of the blitz peppered my young years; indeed, the house and almost all others on our street carried signs of bomb damage for ever. Comi-tragic as it later seemed, she was trained at the factory, along with other women, to use a shovel as a weapon in the event of a land invasion and a German 'knocking at the front door', as she so quaintly put it. The hook behind the front door stayed for years as a memento of the shovel. Part of mother's milk was hearing about the Luftwaffe bombing, usually when she went to start the morning shift and the night workers left, the human target so much bigger at that hour. I learned how she recognized, and distinguished, the enemy above. I learned how the bombers sounded as they droned heavily overhead, how the fighter-planes screeched as they turned in pursuit of a kill, how the dreaded 'doodlebugs', the pilotless predators of 1944, first-generation drones, cut their engines. In an instant. In a click. In a second that must have been oh so cold, and pregnant with terror. And I learned how my mother, clearly, then waited in silence below to see if our house took the hit, her life measured in seconds.

My mother taught me about the fear I experienced in Beirut. But nothing prepared me for that. Lebanon, as ever, took me to the crucible. One day above all.

I remembered the date, 12 August 1982, known as the Glorious Twelfth on the grouse moors of Scotland because the shooting season started on that date. Nothing glorious for those of us who happened to be in Beirut that day. The Israeli army had crossed into Lebanon more than two months before and, on 6 June, surrounded the Palestinians in Beirut. What historic irony. June the sixth, the anniversary of the Six-Day War of 1967 that made Israel master not just of modern-day Israel, but also of the West Bank and Gaza Strip, those Occupied Territories that so consumed politicians, generals, diplomats and human-rights campaigners for decades afterwards. Now, on 12 August 1982, the final act loomed in what was the supposedly do-or-die conflict with the Palestinians.

I had to hand it to the Israelis. They knew how to get our attention. At 5 a.m. – and to the minute – the bombardment began. I jumped out of bed in West Beirut, defying a hangover, to crouch under the window-sill, peering over the edge to identify the orange-red flares, heralds, trumpeters almost, to the exploding shells that rattled the window so violently. I grabbed my crotch instinctively and prayed, the catechism of my Catholic upbringing my first, and maybe last, resort.

I retreated to the bathroom, away from the window, looking for anywhere that might protect me. If my mother knew about doodlebugs, then I knew about F-16s and French Mirages and Daggers. To avoid anti-aircraft fire from the hand-held, hand-cranked guns used by the Palestinians, they flew high, so high, so smartly, so elegantly if you watched them on the end of a TV camera lens. As they circled above, they dropped flares to distract any shoulder-fired, heat-seeking missiles, then they swooped and plunged like sharks in sudden and lethal dives. It was like watching a young heavyweight take on a much lighter, and much older, prize fighter. No contest.

The F-16s honed in on their targets close to my hotel, followed by the bombers and the deafening weight of naval gunfire. The explosions, the shaking were too near. I was not a hero. I crouched, intoning a curious combination of prayer, absolution, farewell to loved ones, imagining a first child, due later that year. When I opened my eyes, I screamed deletive expletives, staring at myself reflected on three walls of mirror encasing the bathroom. If a shell hit, I was to be scythed apart by shattering glass.

I had to get out of there. Get to ground level. If a shell hit, it would hit above. There was better chance of escape on the ground. I ran down four flights of stairs to the lobby of the Commodore Hotel. With no thought of how I looked, or whether I had shaved, ready for face-time on a TV camera, I descended two steps at a time, stopping only to bang on the door of the cameraman and plead for him to get in gear. Downstairs, we found ageless photographer Don McCullin, a son also of North London and the blitz, Finsbury Park in his case, one hard-nosed, battle-tested veteran, survivor of Khe Sanh, Hué, Saigon, the red-letter days of the Vietnam war, and a man who saved my life with sage advice on more than one occasion. That morning he hovered at the door of the Commodore alongside Catherine Leroy, the petite blonde, highly strung and furiously driven French photographer who was my neighbour on the fourth floor. (Indeed, I looked after her cat whenever she was away.) If McCullin and Leroy held back, then the rest of us stayed, the pecking-order in courage and savvy well established.

McCullin, maestro of the brutal calculus of war and journalism, took me aside for a chat, sounding like the coach to a young, inexperienced player in the changing room before the game. What he gave me was a master class in survival. 'It's all down to the few minutes as the bombing ends, a few decisive moments,' he insisted, pinning me up against a hotel wall because he thought I was turning a deaf ear. Decisive moments. 'It's in those few moments that you make your mark,' said my mate Don, and with him in my face I remembered his iconic images, the shell-shocked American grunt in Vietnam, the US Marine athletically throwing a grenade at the Vietcong, the Palestinian family evacuating Beirut with a cart carrying everything, the cityscape behind them an inferno. Decisive moments. 'And remember, you're no good to ITN dead.' Don was a survivor, the war correspondent who lived to tell the tale. He grinned, touching me on the shoulder almost playfully, and the man was rarely playful. 'Not much use to ITN alive either, in your present rather pathetic state.' Clearly, my fear was writ large, let alone the hangover.

What followed amounted to the longest twelve hours of my life. I ran back and forth between the lobby and my room, using the bathroom more times than I cared to remember, quite petrified and quite cowed in the face of an aerial bombardment that, in my mind, dwarfed anything the Germans, or the Allies, conducted in the Second World War.

That night I called my mother in London. The telephone lines still worked. But I did not tell her what I had seen. I confined myself to reporting merely that I was safe. I did add that, for the first time, I understood what life must have been like during her younger years, as a bride on the street where I was born and raised.

I did not tell her of stumbling out, as the bombing ended at precisely 5 p.m., into the dappled sunlight of a glorious summer afternoon, along rue Souraty, a small shopping street parallel to Hamra, the main artery of West Beirut.

*Decisive moment 1.* I did not tell her of the middle-aged man lying in a pool of his own blood, cut to pieces by the blow-out, specifically the glass, from a building hit by a massive bomb.

*Decisive moment 2.* I did not mention what we found on rue Assi, an apartment block reduced in seconds to rubble, most likely by a thousand-pound bomb, with dozens of people manhandling lumps of shattered concrete, using their bare hands, only to find bodies but no recognizable features.

*Decisive moment 3.* I left out the mother and child, struck by shrapnel down on the Corniche, the mother too traumatized to speak, her silence magnified by the wailing of her son, his face and torso pitted with metal.

I did tell my mother that I had learned, from the American Ambassador, that President Reagan had watched breakfast news in Washington DC, then called the Israeli Prime Minister, one Menachem Begin, shortly before 8 a.m. Eastern time that day and told him: 'For God's sake, Menachem, stop it! It's upsetting me and Nancy, and all of us here!' But I did not share my outrage about being informed that ITN had cut my script to delete the words 'indiscriminate bombing'. On the worst days that summer in Beirut, weak-kneed foreign editors back in London censored coverage, fearing that the Israelis, and Britain's Jewish community, via that most powerful of lobbies, would launch formal complaints. The twelve hours of bombing had shaken me badly, and

ITN's behaviour triggered true anger, indeed a furious row with a colleague at headquarters that left neither of us with a way back to future conversation. Never. Ever.

ITN's picture agency had a local cameraman, a young Palestinian with a keen eye for the close-up, stationed outside the American University Hospital off Hamra on that Thursday in August, and I wished that my editors in London had watched his raw videotape as I did the same night. The litany of video tragedies, decisive moments in my judgement, spoke much more powerfully than my anger down the phone line to London. There was a young woman, clearly heavily pregnant, who had lost a leg, the blood gushing like a water fountain, no other way to describe it, as they cradled her out of the ambulance to instant amputation. There was a child whose eyes, quite simply, suggested imminent death, his arm still smoking as they took off bandages to reveal a limb burned back to the bone, the result of a phosphorus bomb. And there was an elderly man, his face somehow frozen in time by the cameraman's close-up, one cheek, one eye, one ear so charred by an incendiary blast that he looked more like a portrait in a still-life picture than a spirit still fighting for life, if you listened to his cries on the tape.

But they didn't hear the cries back in London, or New York, certainly not in Tel Aviv. And anyway, somebody would have argued that a Palestinian took the pictures.

Nor did they go to sleep that night, as some of us did at the Commodore Hotel after a few bottles of strong red Ksara wine from the Bekaa valley, washed down by Arak, Lebanon's powerful, aniseed liqueur, knowing only the dead had smiled that day in Beirut.

# The Cedar Revolution

I survived Lebanon. More than that, I came to admire the country, its people, their capacity to make the most of the hand they were dealt. But nothing prepared me to find a Lebanese brother by the Andes in our small village of Mendoza.

Sonia met Karim Mussi first, at a gathering of local winemakers in La Consulta, the pueblo closest to our vineyard. By tradition they assembled once or twice a year at the town's Italian restaurant, Los Tilos. First, to taste each other's wines with a plate of pasta or a simple steak, or *bife*. Then to exchange ideas. And finally, to discuss objectives that united rather than divided. Argentines did not do this naturally. Rivalry sat embedded in the culture, often resulting in bitter competition. Our new friends and rivals found common cause because they recognized that together we stood a better chance of moving our wine industry forward in our rather remote stretch of the Uco valley.

Sonia gave a talk to that effect as she presented our first, newly bottled wine, too young to drink with anyone other than friends. 'Success for one of us represents success for all of us around this table,' she told them. 'So let us celebrate whenever one of us gets an award, or a high rating, or points.'

The first to congratulate her was a young winemaker by the name of Karim Mussi, who owned an old, fairly small winery close to our land. 'You spoke to my head and my heart,' he told her.

A few weeks later, Karim Mussi stunned himself and the many in the Argentine wine industry by winning a place in the world's top 100, as selected by the industry's bible, *Wine Spectator*. At number 66 in the list, his Altocedro Malbec Reserve 2006 placed second in the six Argentine wines that made it into the world rankings. 'This Argentine red is rich and pure, with nice drive to the beam of raspberry, plum sauce and macerated blackcurrant fruit,' the magazine's lead writer noted. 'Mussi's Altocedro, which is sourced from a single 2.47-acre plot of 100-year-old Malbec vines, is one of the most exciting wines I tasted this past year.'

My e-mail message to Karim was immediate: 'Wow. Today all of us in the Uco valley celebrate with you. We are so proud of what you have achieved. Enjoy the moment. You deserve it. *Mabrook, habibi.*' (My Arabic didn't extend beyond *mabrook*, the word for 'congratulations'.)

Mussi messaged me back, almost instantly, clearly touched. 'I have received a lot of calls, but none quite like yours. It's as if we know each other for a long time already. *Soukran.* Thank you, my friend.'

AltoCedro. Not by chance did this breakthrough winemaker name his brand Tall Cedar, the national tree of Lebanon, the symbol indeed of the democratic revolution that swept the country at the beginning of the twenty-first century. Because our neighbour Karim was the great-grandson of Lebanese immigrants on his father's side, Catholic Maronites from the Matn district just east of Beirut, near Mount Lebanon. And his mother's family came from Bethlehem on the West Bank, Christian Palestinians who left Palestine in the time of the British Mandate between the two world wars.

Almost whenever I looked at Karim, I saw a broad smile that seemed to stretch from one ear to the other. When I watched him run his hands through jet-black hair, or stroke the semi-permanent growth on his chin, fretting but somehow at the same time enjoying the worry beads of life, I recognized him from another place, another time. I knew I knew the face, and instinctively the personality too, even perhaps the philosophy behind the man. I had met him before, in another guise, along Hamra in Beirut, and in Balbeck in the Bekaa valley, along Radio Street in Ramallah on the West Bank, or beside the Church of the Nativity in old Bethlehem.

To listen to Karim, better still to amble with him through his vineyard on a late summer's afternoon, was to walk through history. He represented, indelibly, the fourth generation of Arabs, who arrived in Argentina almost a century before, speaking not a word of Spanish. Hence they carried a slip of paper with the name 'Mendoza' written on it in Arabic and Spanish, their ticket to a train that from Buenos Aires transported them 1,000 kilometres west to the Andes and a small community of Lebanese and Palestinians merchants based in Mendoza. He voiced the philosophy of those first immigrants, derived from an Arabic adage derived from the nomads of deserts past. 'Wherever you find the sky that warms you, and the sky that enables you to work, that is your country.'

Karim explained lovingly how he bet everything on an old-style family winery on the outskirts of La Consulta, when others constructed state-of-the-art factories with gleaming stainless-steel tanks, the latest crushers from Europe, the newest laboratories from the United States. How he did persist in using the hundred-year-old basket press he inherited, not a museum piece but a fine instrument, in his judgement, designed to extract the juice from fresh grape without destroying the skins and valuable colour. How he worked to preserve the huge concrete vats, built a century before, to ferment grape, turning sugar into alcohol slowly, retaining the aromas of the grape, preserving more polyphenols from the juice, just as they did back then, the 'almost natural' process he called it.

And then he turned to the vines he used. He credited a tiny piece of land, one hectare, a little less than two and half acres, owned by an elderly gentleman named Manuel Villafane, as the key to that wine which made him a star in the global 100. The Malbec vines boasted more than a hundred years on the odometer of viticulture. In Karim's world view, those century-old vines had so much to offer. He talked of the vines as human beings. As centenarians they had knowledge, patience, wisdom, experience. They produced tight clusters of grape with small round berries, not too many seeds, for concentrated flavour; strong fruit, full-bodied grape. For him the old vines carried the secret. The magic lay in marrying their grape with good oak, French and American barrels, down below in his medieval and decidedly cold cellars. Humbly, because this man oozed modesty, he concluded that his forebears a century before could have made wine as good as his, given the exceptional quality of the grape they produced. All they lacked was a market asking for the product.

I had my own view of Karim, and every evening I sat with him, tasting one of his magnificent Malbecs, or *tempranillos*, or his iconic brand, called Desnudos and featuring an artist's impression of a naked lady, one year a Greek goddess, the next a chubby middle-aged house-wife. I watched him work with history. His most prized possession on this land – and never underestimate a Lebanese Palestinian's bond with the land – stood towering at the entrance to the vineyard. Tall cedars, certainly a century old, maybe more. 'The people who live here in La Consulta often use the cedars as reference point,' he explained. 'They say, "Turn left at the cedars," or, "When you reach the cedars, look for the building on the right."' Karim sighed. 'You know, the cedars have been the witnesses to so much history, that's what makes them the most valuable element of the whole property.'

I saw Karim as a throwback. Certainly to his great-grandparents a century before, making their way against all odds from Lebanon and Palestine. But I detected another chain in this man's quest.

All the way back to the Phoenicians, 6,000 years ago in the land of Canaan, the coastal stretch of territory that became the republic of Lebanon in the modern age, they made wine. The Phoenicians left an extraordinary legacy: the origins of the modern alphabet; the earliest of dyes, purple from the port of Tyre; the concept of trade, having as expert seafarers introduced import-export in the East. And, many archaeologists believed, the Phoenicians gave us *vino*, mainly from the city of Byblos on the Lebanese seaboard to the Old Kingdom of Egypt and throughout the Eastern Mediterranean, particularly Greece. Ship-wrecks dated at around 750 BC revealed perfectly preserved cargo bays, and cases of ancient wine.

Karim identified, and articulated, a process that so many had accomplished for so long. The humble vine was brilliantly malleable, adroit, wise in adapting to terrain or climate. The process of refining a drinkable fermented beverage from the grape had always been fairly rudimentary and required only so much effort. Trade flowed from wine. So too interaction between cultures. Then there was wine's role as the centrepiece of religious rite for thousands of years. No wonder the smart money said it all began in the Eastern Mediterranean, its spiritual birthplace either Lebanon or Palestine.

My Lebanese-Palestinian friend (or was he Argentine?) laughed when I told him what I thought of his place in the eternal quest. 'Listen, David, history helps,' he told me, and that winning smile creased his face. 'But you know what you really need in the wine business? You need luck, and an understanding bank, and above all, you need big balls.' At that moment I knew the man was an Argentine.

# Give Peace a Chance

Whenever I gave a talk about the Middle East, certainly in the United States, often in Europe too, I heard the same refrain, born out of frustration laced with ennui: 'Peace can never happen.'

My response sometimes surprised people. 'You know, so much has happened in the years since I lived in the Middle East, so much that I never, ever believed possible in my lifetime, that I have to believe peace can happen.' Occasionally, certainly with a pro-Israeli crowd in America, and certainly after 9/11, I found a way to add: 'And you know what else? Peace had better happen, because the consequences of unending conflict for all of us are simply too dire to contemplate.'

Three decades after I first went to the Middle East, I believed passionately that peace was not just possible but achievable if only we looked hard enough. And yes, that was another of my dreams. But yes, at the same time I saw substantial pieces of the socio-political jigsaw coming together, as I watched and worked on the Israeli-Palestinian conflict from another place, in another age.

My starting-point was the Middle East I left in the late 1980s, having written a book that focused on the lives of Israelis and Palestinians living side by side, yet apart, in the land of Israel and Palestine. *Prisoners of God*, I called it, because I saw the two peoples locked in such small confine, both citing God in their claims for territory. Looking back, I had a rare window during the period I lived in the Middle East, first in Lebanon, then Israel. Just as I experienced Lebanon in the age before the kidnapping of Westerners froze access, so in Israel I enjoyed perhaps the last period when it was safe, indeed routine, to get in your car, drive down to Gaza for the day, even the weekend if the weather was good, or venture down to Hebron, Nablus, Jenin on the West Bank, taking in everything, from the refugee camp to the mosque, to the bazaar, to the Jewish settlement, the kibbutz, talking to people on both sides, the political prisoner in Gaza, the Israeli colonel in charge of him, breaking bread over a meal on either side, even on occasions bringing Israeli and Palestinian together for a rare insight into how both sides interacted.

I knew I had sensed something powerful at work in those years as a scribe shuttling back and forth between Jerusalem and Gaza, Tel Aviv and the West Bank. Privileged to listen, I heard both sides saying the arranged marriage was made to work, this enforced relationship between Palestinian and Israeli, as long as it was business, nothing personal. And what intrigued me, as I devoted years of my life to working in Israel and the Occupied Territories, was the 'state of No War, No Peace'. How people on both sides worked around the no man's land symbolized by those words.

Hundreds of thousands of Palestinians, for example, woke up every morning in Gaza and the West Bank, then went to work for the Israelis. Indeed, many crossed over into Israel to do so, often for minimum wages, often as cleaners, waiters, farm hands. The 5 a.m. call in those days was not to the mosque but to the labour market in Palestine Square, at the bus station that straddled Omar-al-Muktar Street in the heart of Gaza City. Hundreds, then thousands, gathered in a matter of minutes. Street sellers offered thick coffee and the refreshing *sahlab*, a wonderfully aromatic blend of crushed almonds, milk and mastic, while the *ra'isin*, the labour contractors (back then they were often Israelis), negotiated a deal for a day's work through the windows of their trucks, a whistle from a lead worker signalling for his gang to climb aboard and head north to Ashkelon, or Ashdod, or Tel Aviv.

The Palestinians had nothing left to lose except their misery. No matter, it seemed at the time, the humiliation, or the degradation, or the subjugation of national pride. Palestinians worked via the Israeli machine. They survived that way. Brutal maybe, enforced marriage certainly, but it was co-existence of a sort.

And on the other side, it intrigued me how thousands of Israelis, some newly arrived from the global diaspora, took the plunge to go and live in the heart of Palestinian land on the West Bank, some even on the edge of the Gaza Strip, a few of them zealots yes, but most in my experience attracted by the prospect of a four-bedroom house with all mod cons just a short drive from Jerusalem, even Tel Aviv, at a stunningly low price. Zionist pioneers with microwave ovens they called themselves.

I could drive forty minutes from Tel Aviv in those days, and watch a new city being built. They called it Ariel, Hebrew for 'Lion of God'. But

God had little to do with the mission. The settlement's founder, a former aircraft engineer called Ron Nachman, told me back then how he had identified a broad swathe of the Jewish community in and outside Israel, not persuaded by the Bible or the coming of the Lord, as he put it, but by naked self-interest and a brazen quality of life. He built shopping centres, two industrial zones, a country club as a result. He hired virtually all his building workers, deliberately, from the nearby Palestinian village of Salfit as a strategy. And his settlers at Ariel made a point of going into Salfit on a Saturday and shopping at the village market to make a point.

Exploitation certainly. But also co-existence of a kind. Forced? Certainly. Limited co-existence? Undoubtedly. Based on terms defined by the occupier? Of course. Apartheid? Having lived and worked in white-ruled South Africa, the answer had to be yes; even Israeli colleagues called it apartheid.

Yet the abiding lesson I took from that period was that two states, living side by side, doing business with one another, acknowledging each other's domain, was not just feasible in political terms, but entirely plausible, a consequence of the passage of so many years locked in one small piece of land together. Peace was achievable, precisely because two peoples, Palestinian and Israeli, had come to know each other during the decades of occupation. If only. If only the Israelis grew to respect the people who lived alongside them. When I heard Palestinians make that demand, I also heard Aretha Franklin singing. R–E–S–P–E–C–T.

Did the settlers in Ariel and the villagers of Salfit like each other? NO. And it was spelled in capital letters. Did they co-exist? Yes. Lower case, but still yes.

Did the Palestinian men of Gaza riding the Israeli pick-up truck to the building site in Tel Aviv care for the boss? You must be kidding. Did they work together? Yes. Almost every day back then.

Did the political prisoner in Gaza accept the rule of the state of Israel? Most certainly NOT. Did he recognize the state of Israel? Yes. Of course.

Peace was achievable because these two peoples had come to know each other, warts and all. No illusions on either side.

In the years that followed, the 'Realist School', as it came to be known in Washington DC and the capitals of Europe, had us believe that the time came and went for the working co-existence I saw on the ground in the 1980s. That the time had passed for moderates who preached two peoples living side by side, two states recognizing inter-dependency, two economies that had to do business with each other. That the men of violence, on both sides, had scuppered the pursuit of peace. And that the next generation of Israeli and Palestinian had seen too much blood to settle for some form of co-existence. Especially when forces beyond the arena of the Palestinian-Israeli conflict – think Osama Bin Laden and al-Qaeda, think Iran and Hezbollah, think the Taliban and the Moslem Brotherhood – joined the battle. The arguments in their arsenal hit home like the rat-tat-tat of gunfire.

They cited the failure of the peace process signed on the White House lawn in 1993. The assassination of Israel's peace premier Yitzhak Rabin in 1995. The Palestinians' use of the suicide bomber as a weapon of choice, and indiscriminate destruction in Tel Aviv, Jerusalem, Ashdod, Haifa. The building of a monster wall between Israel and the West Bank. The expansion of Jewish settlements on the West Bank. The corruption of government under Palestinian self-rule. The abuse of power and resources by one Palestinian leader after another. The election of the Islamic fundamentalist movement Hamas in Gaza. The sub-sequent election of a right-wing, hawkish government in Israel. And, finally, the desperate plight of the inhabitants of Gaza, the most densely populated place on earth, a million and half people suffering 70 per cent unemployment, with UN rations meeting just 60 per cent of what man, woman and child needed, with 60 million cubic litres of untreated sewage being poured into the Mediterranean every day because all infra-structure had collapsed.

The Realists, so-called, had all those facts on the ground to make their case. And as a UN officer working on the Israeli-Palestinian issue all too frequently, I heard the argument time and again from pro-tagonists on both sides, even my own UN colleagues: 'Peace can never happen.'

But I disagreed. Peace, not war, was inevitable.

First of all, it was high time to look at recent history through the prism of the glass half-full, not half-empty; and high time to ask why the most visceral enemies on the planet, keepers of the flame of biblical conflict, had come as far as they had. I never dreamed when I lived in the Middle East that I would see in my lifetime what followed quite quickly. I never imagined that I would see the Palestinians awake, as they did in the late 1980s, and issue the *cri de coeur* for freedom that accompanied the intifadas, those uprisings that so stunned the world at large.

I never thought, even for a moment, that my old sparring-partner Yasser Arafat – how many times had I seen him dance in the eye of a needle in speaking to my TV camera? – would ever come out and sign an agreement with an Israeli government that recognized Israel, and so convert him from arch-terrorist to partner for peace, nay recipient of the Nobel Peace Prize along with one of my heroes, Yitzhak Rabin. Just a few years before, I would have dismissed out of hand the idea of Rabin and Arafat shaking hands on a deal in Washington DC. Rabin, an erstwhile tennis partner and never slow to voice his true thoughts over a post-game drink, spoke to me once in guttural terms about his loathing of Arafat. And Arafat, such a vacillator, such a procrastinator, forever addicted to the short-term compromise in pursuit of survival, was such an unlikely partner in peace, yet he took a decision for the ages and signed an agreement that gave him, at best, half a loaf. Dream on, David. You were wrong about those two.

I went back to Gaza for Arafat's return home in 1994, and the emotion lingered for ever: was I dreaming, or was I reporting, in semi-disbelief, the most remarkable and implausible act of compromise and conciliation? Co-existence? Arafat and his PLO and Israel? Trust me, it was like taking a hallucinatory drug that day, watching the Old Man ride into Gaza City, Mr Palestine or Godfather of Terrorism depending on your viewpoint, home at last, free at last to see the land of his birth, in the eyes of his people, every inch the equal of Mandela, or Khomeini, or Gandhi, and fêted by the Israeli body politic as a man to do business with. Arafat, a man to do business with? Dream on, David. You were wrong about Israel never ever accepting the man and his movement.

But it didn't end there. I never dreamed that I would see the old warhorse on the other side, Ariel Sharon, Prime Minister of Israel, make the very long march that led him to the bully-pulpit of the organization I represented and he despised, the United Nations, to declare with absolute clarity that the only way forward lay in a Palestinian state, two states, two old enemies, living side by side. As Sharon made that historic concession before the UN's General Assembly, I looked anxiously for my boss, Kofi Annan, to remind him of the significance of an arch-warrior saying those words. My boss, of course, needed no such reminding, but he was too gracious to tell me to quiet down. 'You should hear Sharon on the phone to me sometimes,' remarked Annan. 'It's an amazing moment.' The only time I ever heard Kofi Annan use the word 'amazing'.

So what brought the Palestinians and the Israelis, the arch-enemies Arafat and Sharon, to that juncture? Well, for all his many failings, one George W. Bush did utter three simple words which, by common consent, even among peace sceptics, changed the Middle East for ever: 'a Palestinian state'. Once again, it happened at the United Nations. And it broke with history once and for all. We had waited half a century to hear an American President say those words and so enshrine Palestinian statehood in superpower strategy. In my view, there could be no turning-back once an American President espoused a two-state solution. Again, I never dreamed that might happen in my lifetime.

And then there was the clincher for me, based not on my dreams. Rather it stemmed from the clear, cold intelligence via my UN role of what transpired in the negotiations for peace in the years after George Bush's breakthrough statement, and Ariel Sharon's Damascene conversion, and Yasser Arafat's remarkable make-over.

The broad parameters of a deal between Israelis and Palestinians lay out there, clear for all to see. Both sides knew, almost to the last inch, what the other side needed to make a deal. And both sides were astonishingly close on giving each other the bottom line in terms of land. Evidence lay in a document I saw at one point, in late 2008, at the crux of negotiations between the Israeli government and Arafat's successors, revealing that the Palestinians stood to receive 94 per cent of the West Bank, plus land swaps of territory to make up the difference, plus a safe-passage motorway to link the Gaza Strip to the West Bank. Respect lay in such numbers.

The same intelligence showed that both sides appreciated *realpolitik*.

They had to make Jerusalem international. And at that moment they concurred in principle. The Holy Basin, as they chose to call it. The Western, Wailing Wall, sacred to the Jews. The al-Aqsa Mosque, otherwise known as the Dome of the Rock, so revered by the Moslem world. The clear implication, as I read documents acknowledged by both sides, was that they understood the need to share Jerusalem as a capital. Mutual respect lay in that compromise.

And, finally, I learned with astonishment that the Palestinians swallowed the most bitter pill of all. The right to return of Palestinian refugees, a sacred pillar of Palestinian thinking, had now been sobered by the reality of negotiations. A symbolic number of the elderly, no more, would return to Nazareth, or Tiberias, or Jaffa, not the hundreds of thousands who waited in the refugee camps of the Middle East. That was so painful for the Palestinians to accept. Yet so imperative for an Israeli government that could not sign off on a deal that might return vast numbers of Palestinians to Israel proper, and in time make Jews a minority in the Jewish state. Respect shown by one side for the other's existential fear.

I stopped dreaming when I saw those documents. And when negotiators leaked them to *The Economist* magazine, triggering a cover story, I started to believe. 'The contours of a peace deal are clear,' the magazine's lead editorial concluded. 'But who has the courage to draw them?'

How far the Israelis and the Palestinians had come. That was the untold story from where I sat. How close they could be to peace, yes peace, in my lifetime. Dream on, David.

And then it happened. One afternoon, in the aftermath of yet another bloody chapter of fighting over Gaza, this time the Israelis and the Palestinians both accused of war crimes, I accompanied the UN official in charge of the millions of Palestinian refugees across the Middle East to a series of meetings with the US Congress on Capitol Hill. Gary Ackerman, a caustic, wry Jewish Congressman from New York, an avowed Zionist, listened out of duty rather than concern for the plight of the Palestinians, expressing the age-old doubt that they would ever see the light and negotiate seriously. As we were leaving, I asked him what advice he gave to the latest Israeli government, the leaders who inherited the peace proposals we both had seen.

'I tell the Israeli Prime Minister, and I told him this the other day,' Congressman Ackerman said. 'It's time to show the Palestinians respect.'

I gave the Congressman a high-five. Poor fellow. He had no idea why.

# The Crash

All politics is local, so they said, all economics personal. I had to confess to a decidedly local, personal interest in the crash of 2008.

We had been so patient. We had stayed with our grape every step of the way, from harvest, to being crushed as raw fruit, to fermentation in steel tank, to French oak barrel over a twelve-month period, then back to tank for blending. We had tasted, as it evolved, first just grape juice, followed by subtle growth through fermentation, next an explosion of fruit, a young wine, then a vintage maturing rapidly in the barrel, teasing us with its aromas, its deep colour, its notes of one fruit, then another, and its zest for life. We had harvested in the autumn of one year. We had waited till the second spring, eighteen months, to see what kind of wine we had. The best brains in the industry told us to wait some more, to let our vintage sit in the bottle before we released it. Nothing had prepared us, disciplined in instant deadlines, to the endless wait of the winemaker.

How many times did we ask ourselves if there were better ways to spend our time? And certainly much better ways to lose our money.

We had been so diligent, employing specialists to design a label that reflected our dream, refine the words that appeared on the back, choose a bottle shape, make sure of the alcohol level, agree on the terms that defined a wine from our corner of the world. We had paid lawyers, in the United States, Argentina and Europe, to protect our name, make sure our brand did not conflict with others, create a trademark that would survive us. We had sweated when the Americans said they needed the wine presented in traditional cases of twelve and the Europeans sought the product in wooden gift boxes of six. We had done the final blind tasting to set price, taking our wine, placing it alongside others of similar quality, inviting retailers to tell us the bald truth about how much our wine should fetch. Without knowing what was what, they all savoured six glasses of red wine, one of which was ours. Both of us prayed quietly. Please let our wine win, and if not, please, dear God, please, let it not come last. Everyone wrote down their order of preference, first to last. Our wine, SonVida, we found out, did us proud. It came first for three tasters, and was placed second by two other professionals: obviously those with less discriminating palates, we thought privately and protectively.

We were ready to deliver our dream to friends, associates and the market, with folks in Washington, New York and London eager to sell it. We stood ready to push the button, and put our first vintage on the boat. And then the gods decided not to smile and started pelting our lives with sub-prime derivatives, bank bailouts and the Troubled Assets Relief Programme.

The question for the gods was, would there be any buyers left after the crash of 2008? The questions for us were harder still. Could we launch a wine in the worst economic crisis in living memory? Would we take on the market when everyone knew it was time to stop spending? Should we risk everything on our wine when our own safety net had been shredded so dramatically by the fall on Wall Street?

We agonized. If we did not dare, would we end up living with 'coulda-shoulda-woulda', the regretful phrase that taunts life's losers. No guts, no glory. Nothing ventured, nothing gained. Self-belief had always sustained Sonia's journey, from Argentina, under military dictatorship, to Cambridge, at a time of war between her country and mine, then on to global television as one of the world's most recognizable faces. Neither of us had ever shied away from a challenge.

We held our breath as we watched every bank we used in America, Britain and Europe go into freefall, overnight, saved by government bailout. We held hands, night after night, as strong investments crumbled first in Europe, then the United States, finally Latin America. We argued, no pain, no gain. But what if we just ended up with no gain at all? Just pain. Sometimes it was best to be brave. Sometimes it was best to take cover. The challenge was the wisdom to recognize the difference, knowing when bravery was just another word for stupid.

We were not brave enough to risk any more. As we took out another bottle every week to taste how it was doing, our lovely wine only improved. With every passing week. As it aged, it opened, revealing our land and our dream. Just as the best palates in the industry had told us it would. Except no one would ever know. SonVida Malbec 2007. The best wine you never tasted.

To my mind, I was not, nor had I even been, a gambler, a risk-taker, a betting man. As a child, I once lost an old British shilling on a horse named Rings of Clyde, price 33/1, that finished last in a race called the Stewards' Cup at Goodwood in Sussex. I watched the race with my grandparents, from intense hope of riches to intense pain, as my chosen stallion laboured past the finishing-post last, my dream of having thirty-three shillings shattered. For a few days at Oxford, I worked in a betting shop, marking up the prices of horses on a chalk board, and even then watching the occasional big winner celebrate by giving me a pound, even a fiver. But Rings of Clyde made sure I never felt the slightest temptation. Later in life, on my better days, my sons and friends could persuade me to put a dollar or a pound on a hole at golf. But I was no Michael Jordan, known for the hundred-thousand-dollar wager on a hole. A drink in the clubhouse was my betting limit, but not out of self-righteousness. It was fear of my DNA.

The little I knew of my father told me he had lost almost everything to his gambling habit, as my family put it politely. Certainly he squandered the benefits of a well-paid job, of many opportunities to earn money on the side. At a few moments in my journalism career, I had bumped into old-timers in the print world of newspapers who had known my father from his days as a trade-union shop steward at the *Daily Mirror*. Naturally I was curious. I had so few memories. I learned he held a position of influence and some privilege. As the union man, he was the one who hired staff, sometimes for a fee, or offered freelance printers the occasional night-shift, invariably in return for a back-of-the-hand bribe, cash only accepted. Some printers, quite patently, did not want to talk about him. But I insisted. I needed to know who my father was. The picture they painted suggested a spirit living semi-permanently on the edge, borrowing from one to pay another, constantly promising colleagues and drinking partners discharge of debts come pay day. In his final months they said he lived in fear of a visit from the loan sharks. What did he gamble on? The horses, I was told. How often? Every day that they raced.

So gambling, risk-taking, betting on the future, I left that to others, I told myself. But at least we can drown our sorrows, Sonia sighed, as she opened another retirement account statement. If our investments were all in the red, she mused, then being able to drink the ones in red wine was so much better than feeding them to the paper shredder.

# Riding the Tiger

For us the crisis was personal. For the leaders of the G20 (actually 22, the Spanish and the Dutch gate-crashed at the last minute) it was a crisis of credit, currencies, commodities. Banks were collapsing, stock markets plunging, jobs disappearing, and everywhere all hope was turning to governments and public lenders, crying get us out of this mess. The G20. Specifically, the twenty men and women who ruled the twenty most powerful nations on earth. The Group of Twenty was meeting in late 2008 in the cavernous Grand Hall of the Building Museum of Washington DC. Their job was to decide how to handle the Great Crash of 2008. I was there with the UN Secretary-General, whose message was simple. Don't forget the bottom billion, the poorest who will be hurt the most, as they always are, in hard times.

In the world of diplomacy, everyone had an agenda. My professional agenda, for all presidents and prime ministers gathered, was to make sure the UN put that point across. My personal agenda was to say hello to all the people who I had known before they become important and started running countries.

I saw my favourite gentleman in the room. Lula, President of Brazil, the only leader present who knew what poverty meant. He always had my vote.

This fellow, with a salt-and-pepper beard and a warm smile that endeared him even to his enemies, knew how far we had all come, and what a journey lay ahead. He was the only man in the room, I suspected, apart from my own boss, who knew what it was to be hungry and not have shoes. The seventh of eight children, his father had left his mother two weeks after he was born. By the time he was seven, his mother finally said enough. She piled the children into the cargo hold of a truck for a thirteen-day journey to the big city, to move into the same house as his father's second family. This fellow did not read until he was ten. He started work at twelve as a shoeshine boy. At fourteen came his first factory job. At nineteen he lost a finger on the assembly line, and ran from one hospital to another to another before receiving treatment. No wonder he joined a trade union. No wonder he led demonstrations. No wonder he ended up in prison.

I had met him at the height of a campaign that said so much about how far Latin America had come in his lifetime. It was the early 1990s. The first democratically elected President of Brazil in a generation had been accused, by his own brother, of taking kickbacks from those awarded government contracts. For the first time, the people marched, protesting, in a way that would have been unthinkable earlier, in the long years of military dictatorship. The revolt of the *caras pintadas*, it was called, the 'painted faces', because the demonstrators painted their cheeks and foreheads in the colours of the national flag, then etched them in black.

I went to a TV assembly factory on the outskirts of the country's industrial hub. At three in the afternoon the workers blew the whistle and marched out on strike, joining hundreds of thousands of others for a huge rally that went on long into the night. Having lived in Moscow in a period when Russians had learned how to demonstrate freely for the first time since the 1917 October Revolution, I recognized the same unbridled joy, bordering on obsession, in these people. Given freedom, they marched. Given a voice, they formed an overwhelming chorus. Given a choice, they voted with their feet and their pay packets. In my experience there was no stopping a worker who had exchanged time and money for the right to express their view.

That evening, as the city rocked to the sound of an all-night demonstration, I went looking for the voices of political leadership in this country. I tracked down two figures who sat either side of the age-old divide in Latin America. One, a sociologist-turned-Senator, the aristocratic scion of a military family, sometime professor at the universities of Paris, Cambridge, California, a man steeped in the ways of the ruling class, an intellectual comfortable in several languages, an academic who could float from economic theory to anthropological speculation, a man born to rule, a man destined to be President himself.

And then there was the other fellow, the shop-floor operator who still wore overalls, the trade unionist who had become leader of the Workers' Party, the man born and raised to challenge the *status quo*. Amazingly, side by side, displaying such a contrast in style and substance, they agreed. The President of the day was finished, they concluded jointly, merely a matter of time before he resigned, whatever the consequences for the country and its young democracy. If I was categoric about the outcome in my report back to my TV network, it was because I'd witnessed something so rare in Latin America: the street and the ruling class agreeing on what came next. And so it was. The President fell. The sociologist joined the interim government. The workers' leader went back to the street.

Two years later, I paid another visit. It was election time, and those two men were fighting each other for the presidency of their country. The sociologist had become the standard-bearer for an economic policy that promised to stop inflation, and return stability. The worker trumpeted a social compact between unions and government as the key to future prosperity for all. For a while the workers' champion had the lead, but inevitably it slipped away.

I spent an extraordinary day with Lula and his wife in their strong-hold, the kind of grimy, industrial city that belonged to the age before the debates over climate change and global warming and sustainable development. They made, in that city, cars named quite inappropriately after a saint, San Bernardo. For decades, the multinationals of Europe and the United States had turned the place into a semi-squalid smoke-stack, churning out cars for the emerging market of Latin America with scant regard for the environment or for the living conditions of those who worked on the shop floor. We walked the streets, we toured the factory where he had worked on the line, we ate at one his favourite steakhouses, we sat with him over coffee as he conducted an impromptu politician's surgery with his constituents, hearing very simple pleas for jobs, schools, clinics. In one case, a mother of ten asked passionately for free contraception. It embarrassed his handlers, mindful of our TV camera, but not the man himself.

The man who would be President. Later that evening he talked to a crowd, up on stage. His well-worn shirt and baggy pants did little for his full figure, but he danced in syncopation with a huge crowd that had been carousing for hours, waiting for him. He led them through a rhythmic speech, more body language than policy. A close-up, mopping the sweat of his brow and beard. Here was the man of the people, for the people, by the people. But could he ever win?

In fact, he knew. Before we left, he came to shake my hand. 'Thank you for coming to see me here, in this place that is so special to me,' he said. 'Please come back and see me another year, another election, when I will win.'

One of the privileges of working in the media, especially broadcasting, was such access. The invitation to ride in the campaign bus. The seat on board the President's plane. But all that paled in comparison with the opportunity to climb on-stage with a politician, and see for yourself the adulation, the adoration, the intoxicating combination of theatre and pulling power that drove leaders to seek high office, and in some cases cling on to it well past their due date. I always sensed a much clearer understanding of a politician, and what made them tick, once I had joined them on that stage.

Luis Inácio da Silva, known simply as Lula, the worker who surprised so many, not just by winning the presidency of Brazil, but by putting on an immaculate suit, making friends on Wall Street, walking the fine line between pleasing his supporters at home and the moneymen abroad, transforming his country into a global leader on everything from debt reduction to biofuels. Shaking his hand in the Great Hall of the National Building Museum, I reminded him of that day in San Bernardo, and he, quite clearly, could not remember the moment, or me for that matter. When I told him that no other politician had ever forewarned me he would lose, he smiled, 'But I told you to come back when I won, didn't I?' He paused. 'Maybe it was a good thing I lost one, two, three elections,' he said, holding up his fingers one by one, 'because when the time came I was ready to ride the tiger.'

In the circumstances, it was patently indulgent to tell President Lula how I felt like I was riding the tiger with our wine adventure in Argentina, the country that was his neighbour, my wife's home, in my dreams the piece of land for generations that would follow me. But I could not resist mentioning our project briefly, extending an invitation for him to visit one day.

'Ah, but then, this is not about wine,' Lula replied, with a knowing look in his eye, clasping my hand with both of his, and in doing so reminding me of the worker who lost a finger to a factory lathe. 'It is about love. It is about the universal hunger to express love. To leave love behind you.'

# The Spin Machine Works

Every summit had its class photo. Madame President of Argentina, immaculately dressed, chose precisely the wrong moment to coif herself. Unfortunately, she missed the obligatory group photograph of world leaders. When she returned, the oversight was noticed. So all other twenty-one men and women, arguably the most powerful in the world, were obliged to return to the rungs, pose again, with the Prime Minister of Australia clearly showing his impatience that she had made them endure a second photo call, surely the dullest part of their day.

'So who the hell are you?' Prime Minister Kevin Dunn shook my hand. I had never visited Australia. I had no knowledge, beyond the truly embarrassing small talk about cricket, or criminals, or Chardonnay. So I opted for flattery, remembering that this fellow had been the first to acknowledge how badly Australia treated its indigenous people, the Aborigines. 'You know, if I never do anything else, that's OK,' he told me. 'The day we signed the Bill recognizing our debt to the Aborigines, there wasn't a dry eye in Australia. Thank you for reminding me of that, mate.'

I looked around to see who else I could greet at the risk of another who-the-hell-are-you. I could see the dynamic President of France, Nicolas Sarkozy, earnestly conversing with the ageing Prime Minister of Italy, Silvio Berlusconi, immaculate in his dark suit and trademark pale-blue tie. Always a Cheshire-cat grin, and wisps of hair covering a pate that had been bald until recently. Now there was a man whom I had known in his less august days, as he was building his media empire with an Italian cable channel, Canale 5.

Back in the 1970s, I had been stuck in the northern Italian city of Turin, covering the trial of the leaders of the Red Brigades, the urban guerrilla group that shot, maimed, kidnapped, bombed and murdered its way to a stranglehold on Italian life.

One evening, when I could not face another heavy Lombardy meal with my Italian colleagues, I channel-surfed in my hotel room. On Canale 5, a young, buxom housewife was taking off her clothes, one item at a time, every time a male caller answered an anchorman's question correctly, accompanied by hooting and whistling from the audience; then putting an item back on to the dismay of the largely male crowd when a caller gave a wrong answer. And yes, she did get down to her underwear by the time the programme ended.

The following day, back in the courtroom, I asked everyone I could find whether they had seen the show. My Italian friends responded with disbelief, bordering on ennui, at how behind I was. 'You didn't know that this has been a big hit for months already on Canale 5?' I was told. 'Watch on Fridays, it goes very late and not one tiny bit of clothes is left.' Their eyes said it all.

At the end of that week, I filed an eight-paragraph story for the Reuters world wire:

Turin, Italy, Reuters – Every time Giuseppe the plumber answers a question correctly, Angelina the housewife takes off a piece of clothing to the roar of the crowd.

Some nights she gets down to her underwear, on Fridays it can go all the way.

And it's all live on TV. Welcome to the decidedly new world, the bread and circus, of Italian cable . . .

Not all my stories on the Red Brigades, my access to the *capo de tutti capi* of the movement behind the iron bars of his cage in the courtroom, generated that many headlines and that many hits for Reuters.

My account of the TV show *Housewives Strip* appeared in hundreds of newspapers across the world, from the almighty *New York Times* to the then venerable London *Times*, from the *South China Morning Post* to the *Melbourne Age*, becoming one of the most widely used stories of that year.

I should have asked Silvio Berlusconi, the man behind the show, behind Canale 5 and the cable revolution in Europe, for a fee, I joked down the years. But Silvio Berlusconi did more than build an empire on striptease TV. He went on to make billions, own one of the greatest football teams in the world, AC Milan, and in between got himself elected Prime Minister of his country a few times as well as avoid more than one corruption charge. Somehow he also found the time for a multitude of younger girlfriends. Somehow, standing in the Great Hall of the National Building Museum, I did not think that was the moment to remind Signor Berlusconi of his beginnings, especially as he was still with the President of France. Far better to share my story with his rather ravishing interpreter, Italian of course, all style and stand-out looks, and make her laugh with my tale of channel-surfing in Turin. She pursed her lips, winked, and assured me that Signor Berlusconi did have a sense of humour, and that she would find a way to tell him my tale. 'He is a vain man, so it will appeal to him, your story,' she said. 'To be the centre of attention, it's such a drug for people, *si*? Especially my Prime Minister.' *Ciao, bella.*

What was the story from this first summit grappling with this global financial meltdown? I had read the communiqué long before its release. I had agreed with the Secretary-General the statement he would make, taking it to him for final approval, just as they served dessert and bumping into the British Prime Minister along the way. 'How's the UN treating you? he asked. 'Quite a change from journalism days, I imagine,' he added. Gordon Brown was being gracious, acknowledging that his brother Andrew, a respected journalist, had been a colleague.

I knew the talking-points as I spoke to the media outside. The world had been changed by this very meeting. No longer did just the big industrialized nations meet to decide how to handle the future. In this crisis, the call had gone out to many others, India, China, Saudi Arabia, Brazil. And the new order had spoken with one voice about concerted action.

Back inside, in a hall studded with world leaders, I wondered how the world would receive the final communiqué, with its talk of coordinated action, planetary stimulus and early-warning systems. I imagined the headlines, stressing joint moves, stimulus for all, the new players at this table, the Chinese, the Saudis, the Indians promising to play constructive roles, namely bankrolling America's massive debt. And, of course, the Secretary-General reminding that the world's poorest not be left even farther behind as the world hurtled deeper into recession.

# Head Held High

As the official summit wrapped up, it was time for the real business to begin. The journalist would die – sorry, maybe kill is a better word – for such an opportunity. Precisely because it was the kind of moment a journalist never saw, away from the cameras, and the formal communiqué, and the pre-scripted sound bites. Private conversations, a whisper here, a nudge there, a handshake that lingered, 'We need to talk.' The rare, almost invisible process of politicians doing business.

And so what to say to the departing American President? He had finished with the Secretary-General, now he was winding up an exchange with the President of Mexico. 'I've told my successor to be very careful when it comes to Mexico,' he said. 'Treat Mexico with dignity, understand Mexico's pride, respect Mexico. *Viva Mexico!*' He punched the air.

It was my turn. Everything that came to mind seemed disingenuous. The usual phrases. It's been a pleasure working with you. Thanks for the time you've given us. I do appreciate . . . 'I hope, Mr President, that you'll enjoy the next chapter of life.'

At least I was honest.

George W. Bush, 43rd President of the United States, slapped me on the back with his trademark, good-old-boy bonhomie. 'Thank you, David,' he said, looking down at my summit credential, checking my name. 'I'm going home to Texas with my head held high. Yes, sir, my head held high.'

# Irish for O'bama

It was the biggest crowd, and the most memorable party, of my life.

I had never been a part of a sea of humanity like it. I had seen many crowds, but none like the one that greeted President Barack Obama. All colours, all races, and all bedecked in Obama paraphernalia, buttons, hats, scarves, flags, as well as all layers of clothing needed to stand all morning in subzero temperatures, waiting, looking out at the brilliant dome of the Capitol for one man to raise his right arm.

Large crowds have their own dynamic. Impossible to forget the million-strong audience that waited patiently to hear Generalissimo Francisco Franco give his final speech in the Plaza de España in Madrid. This was not the 1930s, but as late as the 1970s. Yet here was the last contemporary of Hitler and Mussolini, offering the fascist Nazi salute. *'Arriba España!'* he shouted in that high-pitched, whiny voice of his that always seemed out of keeping with the image of a ruthless dictator.

Or the joyous crowd welcoming Yasser Arafat back to ancient Jericho on the West Bank. All ages gathered, carrying pictures of the man, many flashing Churchill's V-for-Victory salute. And Arafat, so ambivalent a figure when speaking English, such an orator in Arabic, gave the speech of his life. Barely a dry eye in that crowd that day.

A very different all-singing, all-dancing throng greeted the Soviet Jewish dissident Anatoly Sharansky when he reached the Wailing Wall in Jerusalem. He was there, after years in the labour camps of the Soviet Gulag, where he had lived off rodents and insects, so emaciated, he later told me, that he spent the evening constantly pulling up his new trousers, to stop them falling down.

But of all the crowds I had witnessed, none compared to the one that gathered for Barack Hussein Obama on the freezing January morning that accompanied his inauguration as the 44th President of the United States. Just by raising his hand and taking the oath of office, Barack Obama made history.

They came from every corner of the United States. They came from Africa; the family next to us in the security line was from Ethiopia. They came from Europe. I lost count of the British, French, Scandinavian voices as we marched in orderly file on to the Washington Mall. They came from Latin America. Among the thousands waving the stars and stripes I could see flags from Argentina, Brazil, Peru, Bolivia. They wept. They danced. They sang. They kissed. And they shared.

Nearly two million people came and went that morning on the Washington Mall. This was a crowd battered by stress elsewhere in their lives, deeply pessimistic about the future of their country, fighting two wars abroad at dreadful cost, and, worried for themselves, fighting to pay for the cost of living.

Two million people fell silent – and the new President spoke.

'Our nation is at war . . . our economy is badly weakened . . . homes have been lost, jobs shed, businesses shuttered . . . no less profound is a sapping of confidence across our land, a nagging fear that America's decline is inevitable.' Few rhetorical hurrahs that day, rather sombre thought for a sombre moment. 'We remain a young nation, but in the words of scripture, the time has come to set aside childish things . . . what is required of us now is a new era of responsibility.'

An elderly white male, bespectacled, apple-cheeked, proudly wearing the hat of a military veteran, turned to a young African-American next to him, 'Welcome to the new America.' They hugged, even cried.

'We did it . . . we really did it . . . it's here.'

The last time I had attended an inaugural, eight years earlier, the crowd had been measured in the low thousands, and the atmosphere could hardly have been more different. While a cold wet Saturday in January 2001 had much to do with the turn-out for George W. Bush, the nature of his election made America a house divided. I spent the morning in the Press Section at the Capitol Rotunda, watching Mr Bush assume office, saying: 'Sometimes in life we are called to do great things.' Dubya did not do Cicero.

A month before, the US Supreme Court had stopped the counting of votes, and in effect declared Mr Bush the winner over Vice-President Al Gore. I regretted not calling it as I saw it, as if this was happening anywhere other than America. I had written the script in my head so many times: 'If I were reporting to you from Zagreb, Croatia or Buenos Aires, Argentina, I would be telling you of a right-wing, constitutional *coup* . . . yes, here in the United States, a hundred million people voted in the election, and yet one vote decided it, five to four in the Supreme Court . . . and the casting vote belonged to a Justice who had actually told us before the vote that she wanted a certain candidate to win . . . This being America, of course, few will dare to report matters this way. But just look at the facts, and let that idea of a right-wing constitutional *coup* sink in . . . '

I had only myself to blame for not reporting the Supreme Court decision as a *coup*. Facts are stubborn things, said America's second President John Adams. I should have stayed with the stubborn facts. The nine Justices of the Supreme Court did determine the outcome in the year 2000. They did stop the counting of votes when the other candidate might have won. And the vote did come down to one person out of 100 million: Sandra Day O'Connor, the daughter of a rancher out in the American West, a brilliant jurist and livewire thinker, a conservative appointed by a Republican President. And yes, amazingly, she had told a reporter about a month before the election that she wanted Mr Bush to win. Her reason, beyond politics? Her husband had warning signs of Alzheimer's disease, and she wished to retire from the bench, go home to Arizona and take care of him. Her freedom to do so required a Republican President to appoint her successor.

A few years later I saw Justice O'Connor with her husband at a rather glittering party in the home of Ben Bradlee, the *Washington Post* editor, whose pursuit of the Watergate story brought down Richard Nixon. Justice O'Connor did not evade my whispered question: 'Ever look back at that decision, and wonder whether it was right?' Her answer lay in a clear shake of the head. 'The country needed a resolution of the election,' she answered emphatically, and searched for her husband's hand.

How would Al Gore have handled 9/11? How would he have dealt with Osama Bin Laden? There might have been no war in Iraq. The economy might not have crashed. The planet might have bought time to save itself from environmental meltdown. Thinking of Gore as President, I did not necessarily see some happy ending. Al Gore was a man of ideas rather than the executor of policy. After decades in Washington, he was still an enigma to those who spent time with him. I wanted to believe in him, as many did, but somehow he never closed the deal. Yet, given his zeal for climate change and the Nobel Peace Prize that came with it, losing the election was the making of him.

# Shame on Us

I had met Senator Obama on a few occasions, dealing with UN matters, specifically the crisis over Darfur and the war in Afghanistan. First impressions endured.

In my UN role, I learned much about a politician from the way he or she conducted a meeting. Bearing in mind that many meetings last less than thirty minutes, and that they often held eight to ten such sessions in a day, I grew to appreciate how the disciplined politician had little time for small chit-chat at the beginning, beyond normal courtesies, then made time at the end to seal the conversation with a personal exchange which went beyond business, often seeking off-the-record insights and depositing off-the-record thoughts. Equally, the smart politician did not make speeches, revisiting well-worn arguments, but rather asked questions, sought clear responses, then delivered personal position while displaying that he or she had listened to what was said to them. The priceless variable lay in the politician's ability to leave you, not just with a clear idea of what he or she thought, but with an addendum that maybe you might think anew about the way a certain issue was being handled.

For all of the above, read Barack Obama in the early days, well before he ran for President. In his first few weeks in the Senate, in early 2005, I bumped into him on a day when the issue of Sudan, and the allegations of genocide in Darfur, had resurfaced. Six months earlier, in September 2004, George W. Bush's first Secretary of State, the very likeable Colin Powell, had gone to the Senate and used the word 'genocide'. One of Powell's advisers had forewarned me, and I made a point of attending in person that day, so as to be able to send Kofi Annan an e-mail: 'General Powell has just called Darfur genocide, now we may get some real support.' At the UN we had for months been negotiating quietly for the US to provide logistical support, such as transport planes, helicopters, engineers, to get men and *matériel* into Darfur, which lay 1,500 miles from the sea and had no roads. So many meetings at the White House, and the Pentagon, and the State Department ended with our interlocutors offering the thought: 'The President feels so strongly about this crisis, he wants action, and soon that will be clear to all.' We concluded that, if the President's men used the G-word, action would surely follow.

How wrong we were. The months passed, General Powell had stepped down, and I was being told that the United States had little or no capacity for operations outside Iraq and Afghanistan. Equally, I was routinely treated to speeches in meetings with members of Congress who blamed the UN for failing to act, who denounced the UN as complicit in mass murder, mass rape, mass starvation in Darfur. Rock bottom arrived the day that I rushed to Capitol Hill, minutes before a press conference, to talk a Republican Congressman out of calling for Kofi Annan's resignation on that issue.

'Congressman, you can hardly make my boss a scapegoat when it is your government that cries genocide, then declares time out on taking concrete action to prevent it,' I argued.

Shortly after that damage limitation, in the other house of the US Congress, I bumped into the newly arrived Senator Obama. He invited me to walk with him back to his Senate office, firing away immediately on the humanitarian crisis in Darfur. 'How many people have we got now in those refugee camps? How many times do we have to say genocide before the world does something about it?'

I replied that the world waited for America's lead. After all it was America which recognized it as a genocide.

'OK, point taken, shame on all of us,' he said.

We walked downstairs, to ride on the underground train that linked one building to another in the belly of the US Capitol, and he sought straight-up answers on some decidedly delicate matters: what the United Nations knew about mass murder, when the UN knew, what action the UN had taken in response, what kind of messages we sent to the government in Khartoum. I answered some, but fell back on my broadcast days to say I did not know the answers to all, that I would get back to him as soon as possible.

'I appreciate that, I appreciate your honesty, never speak of that which you don't know, something politicians ought to heed,' he said with one of those trademark, wide-as-a-mile smiles that stretched from ear to ear and won you over in an instant. Then came the Obama line, and I remember how he paused. 'It's not enough to cry genocide, there's a historic responsibility that goes with the word, and the responsibility lies with all of us in the international community. We need leadership, and concerted action here.'

We disembarked from the train, and he extended his hand, making clear that our meeting was over. But not before he sought more insights. 'Where are the Europeans on this?'

I answered that the Europeans had registered the crisis much more vividly than the United States, explained how my old TV network, among many others, had been hammering home images of ethnic cleansing, rape, starvation and death, adding: 'But the Europeans wait for you guys to lead.'

He looked away in faint disgust. 'Where's the Secretary-General on this? He has to get to Darfur and stand with those people.'

I assured him that Secretary-General Annan made calls every day, seeking support for a UN operation that could avert even greater tragedy.

In my position, you rarely asked to speak to the Secretary-General of the United Nations unless warranted. My boss walked around with a long list of calls to return all day, every day. That night I phoned Kofi Annan direct at his residence in New York: 'Saw Senator Obama today, we discussed Darfur . . . He urged you to go there yourself and make a stand . . . In his words, sir, you have to get to Darfur and stand with those people . . . Clearly a force to be reckoned with, and a force for good from our perspective.'

# Game-changer

As we left the inauguration of President Barack Obama on the Washington Mall, I held the hands of my youngest children firmly. Two million people, walking at glacial speed, past the porta-potty lines, to get back to the main streets, the metro, and above all a warm house. We walked with a couple from Atlanta, a city I knew well. I had courted Sonia there, while she presented the news for CNN. Atlanta stood out for me, a city as segregated as any I had ever lived in, and they included Johannesburg and Jerusalem. One side of Atlanta celebrated the city's history as the final bastion of the Confederacy and slavery. The other celebrated Martin Luther King Junior, and believed not much had changed, despite the proclamation of the New South.

'Atlanta is changing, trust me,' said the white gentleman at my side.

'Forget Atlanta, America is changing, right now,' added his African-American wife. 'Obama is a real game-changer.'

He needed to be. He had his work cut out for him.

If there was one thing the Americans were supposed to know how to do better than anyone else, it was surely capitalism. Unfettered, unbridled, unrestrained capitalism. Since the Reagan revolution in the 1980s, when first I lived there as a visiting professor at the University of Michigan, the United States had prided itself on being free of government intervention. Free markets relied on the 'hidden hand' of the market to get things done efficiently, to self-correct, to step back from the brink, to regulate itself. Now it turned out the hidden hand had been dealing with financial crack cocaine.

To save the system from collapse, the government had bet the farm, putting as much money as it could, lending banks tens of billions of dollars to get the lending bloodlines of the economy pumping again. But still credit did not move. Instead, many banks used the money to buy up rivals. Others paid themselves grotesque bonuses. Whatever emerged, it was time for a game-changer in how Wall Street did business.

And beyond capitalism, where did America the superpower stand?

The United States, from its earliest days, saw itself as an example to the world, of freedom, of individual rights, of good.

Yet, to the world, it was an example of the rhetoric not matching reality.

America talked about free markets, but the world saw a Wall Street collapse that took markets and economies across the world down with it.

America talked about democracy, but the world remembered hanging chads on ballot cards, indicating votes not registered by the punch machines, and an election decided by the Supreme Court.

America talked about human rights, but the world recalled Abu Ghraib, or Guantanamo Bay, or torture defined as 'enhanced interrogation techniques'.

America talked about peace, but there were wars in Iraq and Afghanistan.

The question had to be: could the United States continue to preach its way as the best way? And if it did, would it be believed? To take the theme one step further: was it time to reconsider whether the United States could shape the world in its own image?

For generations, certainly since its emergence as a major power in the early years of the twentieth century, the United States had run its international affairs assuming that it must encourage others to become more like itself. As economies, as nation states, even as societies. But for President Barack Obama, the challenge was to be the first American president who could *not* take for granted the power of the American ideal.

# Life, Liberty and Vino

The man who penned those American ideals, 'Life, liberty and the pursuit of happiness', was the extraordinary Thomas Jefferson, author of the Declaration of Independence, third President of the United States, proud Virginian and lover of fine French wine.

'We are doing what Thomas Jefferson couldn't do – and that's make wine in Virginia,' said Jason Tesauro as he poured me a glass of his aromatic yet surprisingly earthy Viognier wine.

But surely, I queried, Thomas Jefferson was America's first winemaker. Didn't he plant vines at his fabled Monticello mansion in south-western Virginia? Didn't America's third President bring France to the Americas in everything he did, whether it was a secret mistress, a fine claret or the custom of eating tomatoes? Wasn't that how historians explained his lifelong affair with an African-American slave, Sally Hemmings? I wondered whether the sales patter wasn't a shade economic with the truth.

'Listen, my friend.' Jason was riled. 'Jefferson planted French vines, vinifera, in Virginia, but he didn't know how to prevent phylloxera, the louse that ate the vineyards of the world until we Americans came up with the idea of grafting vinifera on to American rootstock resistant to the pest, that lousy louse.'

He paused for effect. That 'lousy louse' had surely been rehearsed time and again by Jason, a young son of the South, proud of the Old Commonwealth of Virginia, raising his glass and scrutinizing it with keen eye. 'So yes, we are doing what Jefferson couldn't, and we're making some damn fine wine in the process.'

Good luck, my friend. Sonia and I might not be brave enough to try to sell our wine, but Jason was, and so were plenty of folks around him. What did they know that we didn't?

I realized that if there was hope to be found, it was by learning from those who worked the marketplace. So, on a bleak Sunday afternoon, I was at the Washington International Food and Wine Festival, in the Ronald Reagan Building, just off Pennsylvania Avenue, close to the

White House, barely a few weeks after the Obama family moved in.

The Ronald Reagan Building was no architectural masterpiece. High on glass, low on style, an atrium framed by corridors and corners, offices and meeting rooms. But vast enough for an introduction to the zoology of wine: thousands willing to pay for a ticket to enter the Washington International Food and Wine Festival. With a ticket came an empty wine glass, and the chance to get as much wine poured as any bladder and liver could handle. A test of fortitude, and sobriety. Dozens of stands offered a taste of Italy, or Spain, or Chile, or South Africa, or Argentina, or Virginia, or even suburban Washington DC vines.

With a vineyard less than an hour from the Reagan Building, close to the suburban turnpike and the strip malls that surrounded the city, Margie Russell, all twinkling blue eyes and warm smiles, offered me a glass of her signature blend, named 'Long-bomb'. The winery's founder, a man called Whitie, had been a star quarterback on an American football team. His wine label celebrated the long pass, the long bomb, or the 'Hail Mary' as it was sometimes called, a desperate but thrilling throw, the last-chance saloon in that sport.

'How robust is that?' she asked, as I sipped a red wine that smelled (how to put it diplomatically?) like fumes. I felt it strip the enamel off my teeth. 'The Long-bomb sure packs a long finish,' she added. 'We have a Canadian winemaker who understands cold-winter growing.' Only a cold-hearted spirit could have failed to admire their courage and daring.

Then came the man from La Mancha, the flat, baked plains of old Castille in Spain. 'We are the land of Don Quixote, with all the history of Toledo and Goya, and now we have winemakers from France, from Australia, even from Britain,' said Juan Carlos Ramírez, an immaculately dressed new-age Spaniard, looking decidedly out of place in suit, tie and cufflinks, producing a lively red, strong on first taste, less smooth when the raw finish reached the back of the throat. Not sure that the British winemakers sounded so appealing.

'We are so dry, and so hot, with temperatures well over a hundred degrees in summer, so little rain,' he added, as if that explained all. I knew La Mancha was famous for the EuroLand wine lake, subsidized by the paymasters of Brussels, generating volumes of the undrinkable, only fit to be distilled into cheap alcohol.

The quality improved when I reached the Italian stand, where the exhibit spoke to the broad church of Italian wines, tripping off the tongue, classic Barolo, Chianti, Nebbiolo, Barbera, Dolcetto, Prosecco, Pinot Grigio. 'My wines come from vineyards, where families touch their vines, smell their earth and work their land every day,' said the boss, a striking middle-aged brunette named Bridget Thibodeau, who had created an import business specializing in Italian wine. 'The people I work with in Italy don't sit in their offices and wait for some "flying doctor" consultant or enologist to come and tell them how to make wine. They live in their vineyards every day of their lives, just as their grandfathers did.'

Finally, the stand where we belonged. Argentina. As ever, my adopted country paraded dazzling women out front. By late afternoon, dozens of young men seemed to have settled in, as if at a bar, drinking copious amounts of Malbec and Torrontés, Argentina's distinctive floral white wine, barely bothering to listen to the presentations of Víctor, from Mendoza, or Inés, from Buenos Aires, or Roberto, from Patagonia. 'Malbec, from old France, from the region of Cahors is the grape that has found its true home in Argentina . . . Argentina has it all, the *terroir*, the families, the history, the skill and the style . . . Mendoza is the new capital of the New World when it comes to wine.' The words flowed, but the wine flowed better for this Sunday-afternoon crowd of young professionals, on a rare day off from Congress, or the law firm, or the lobbying shop.

'What I like about Malbec is its plum qualities, soft, luscious, plummy,' said Mike, who mixed a government day-job with being a *sous chef* several nights a week.

'Malbec is a favourite of mine,' added Anji, a tall thin-faced woman who worked at the Obama White House as a secretary. 'And it's always great value, whether I'm drinking high-end wine or something down the price scale, for everyday drinking. I'm never disappointed in Malbec.'

Maybe our Malbec did stand a chance, if we could bring it into the United States.

On my way out I stopped again at the Old Virginia stand, where Jason was still working his crowd, by now semi-inebriate, nodding to his warm, commanding voice. I had to give it to Jason. He could sell.

'Five thousands years before Christ, they made wine. And they drank it, just like us, with family, and friends, when they married, when they celebrated . . . damn good wine.'

Once again, Jason's fine salesmanship triggered questions in my head. Hadn't archaeologists concluded that maybe, even before the Phoenicians and the Holy Land, the prehistoric communities of Georgia in the Caucasus had embarked on the wine adventure first? Hadn't they found giant urns, dating back to 10,000 BC, in what became the Georgian capital of Tbilisi?

I wanted to tell him about a wonderful evening in Tbilisi, the night Georgia declared independence from the Soviet Union, drinking their Tamada, a big, rough red made from a grape called Separavi, and a more subtle white called Mtsvane, floral and chunky. Georgians knew how to celebrate their freedom, and the end of Moscow's diktat. They drank from dusk to dawn that night they took their leave of the Soviet Empire.

But Jason was in full flow. 'So drinking our Viognier or our Cabernet Franc, it's all part of the chain that goes back thousands of years, to the Middle East, to the valleys of Lebanon, to the sea of Galilee . . . My family, from Palermo, Sicily, spent centuries making wine . . . and now we are in Virginia, bringing the Old World to the New, putting our ear to the ground, listening to our land and asking ourselves what will grow well there . . . We are part of that long chain of people and history.'

What a sales pitch. If you've got it, flaunt it.

And if you haven't, don't let anyone know.

# Bon Courage

Maybe Sonia and I were too cautious. After all, we had the vineyard, the house and the wine. We had fallen short on courage.

Why not just bring it into the country ourselves? After all, we had made a few hundred cases. How hard could that be?

Wine, as if we might not have noticed, was an alcoholic substance. It was not as simple as shipping an extra large piece of luggage on the plane.

Once upon a time we would have had to face the Bureau of Alcohol, Tobacco and Firearms of the United States. Pleasant company: wine, a cigar and a gun. But Firearms had been moved away to another regulator. Goodbye guns, hello . . . taxes? The new regulators were TTB, the Alcohol, Tobacco, Tax and Trade Bureau. A glass of wine, a cigar and all the 'sin taxes' the government meant to collect from the enjoyment of both. Firearms were so much more romantic.

TTB was the regulator. No one could import wine into any state of the United States without an import licence. The importer sold it on to a distributor, maybe a different one for every state. The distributor then sold it on to the retailer. These three levels were known as the three-tiered system, a hangover from Prohibition reform, trying to prevent monopolies.

From my point of view, the three-tiered system was an expensive toll system, where I paid three times, three margins, to get my wine on a shelf.

Now, all politics is local, and so is all retail. I turned for help to my local wine store, and my favourite salesman, a Cuban called Pepe Almodóvar. Ever since we married, and bought a house just off Washington's new Embassy Row in Northwest DC, Pepe had guided our evening wine choices. A diminutive, wisecracking Cuban, Pepe worked the large wine store round the corner, and down the years had introduced us to his favourites, picking up a bottle of red Burgundy, or a white Alsace, or a Sauvignon Blanc from New Zealand, placing it in our hand as if it belonged there, with a knowing wink, a cheeky smile and the advice: 'You'll like this, trust me.' Pepe picked more winners than losers in our view. He educated us to understand Old World versus New, France versus California, Spain versus Chile, Italy versus Argentina with a passion that defied a grey day, a bout of the flu or a stressful week at work.

When we showed pictures of the land to Pepe, he exulted: 'Beautiful place, so grow some grape on it.' When we planted vine, he insisted: 'Let the grape mature a little, not too long.' When we sold our first harvests of grapes to a leading local company, he challenged us: 'Make a wine, a quality wine, and I tell you I will sell it, all of it.' Through the ups and downs of the adventure, Pepe had been a constant compass, reminding us of the ultimate goal.

But there was one subject that I knew divided us. Fidel Castro. I had worked in Cuba during the 1990s, reporting on the crisis that Castro's revolution faced after the collapse of the Soviet Union, Cuba's long-time patron and financier. Cutting sugar cane by hand, taking oxen and plough back to the fields, living without electricity, the country had returned to a semi-medieval state, Fidel's will imposed via Communist party cadres, militant youth leagues and a secret police that imprisoned dissidents without trial. Yet by the standards of Latin America, Cubans still enjoyed health, education and welfare. Simply put, Cuba stood poor, but refreshingly free of the shantytowns, squalor, starvation and suffering that I saw in other parts of Latin America.

'That's bullshit,' declared Pepe, himself a supporter of Fidel in the late 1950s before he defected on his father's boat across the Florida Keys in 1961. 'Fidel has been the worst face of communism, celebrating the misery and ruin of the country.'

Still, my Cuban friend represented our best hope of bringing our wine to market, and he had hand-picked the importer, the figure who sat at the crossroads of our wine dream. Without the importer, we could not move our bottles from Argentina to the United States. Without the importer, we had no access to the next link in the chain, the distributor, who moved bottle from warehouse to the shop shelf. Of course, these folks did not work for free. There was a price to pay for shipping cases of SonVida from Buenos Aires to Norfolk, Virginia. There was a cost to moving bottle from warehouse to wine store. Without Pepe, such an engine-room driver, encouraging us forward and promising to support us on arrival, I would not have found the courage to revive the dream of a wine.

Luckily Pepe's choice of an importer was not far out of Washington, past Arlington Cemetery and the Pentagon, heading west on Route 66 to the town of Manassas. On the face of it, a fairly typical suburban community, dotted with town-home developments, strip malls and industrial parks. But it was also the site of the first battle of the American Civil War, a reminder of how close the old South came to seizing power in Washington.

I drove out on a breezy four-lane highway. One sweltering afternoon in the summer of 1861, Congressmen and their wives had ridden out in their carriages, picnic baskets and parasols to hand, children dressed in their best outfits, to watch the battle of Bull Run, in Manassas. They had expected easy victory over the supposedly ragtag army of the South. President Abraham Lincoln had dismissed the concerns of his generals, that most in the Union army had never seen action before. 'You are green, it is true, but they are green also,' Lincoln told them. 'So you are all green alike.' The battle proved a disaster for Lincoln and the Union, their vastly superior forces routed by the Confederates, including one Stonewall Jackson, a man who achieved immortality in the South that day at Manassas.

There were two versions of history of how Colonel Thomas Jackson, of the Virginia Brigade, earned the name Stonewall. One had his commanding general pointing out the colonel as fighting an exemplary rearguard action: 'There is Jackson standing there like a stone wall.' According to this version, the general told his men they could count on Stonewall Jackson's rearguard. 'Let us determine to die here, and we will conquer.' The other, less flattering version of history, had the same general, who did indeed die that day, furious that Jackson had not reinforced him, pointing across the fields at the colonel, shouting: 'Look at Jackson, standing there like a stone wall!'

I headed to the outskirts of town, just off the main highway, where Union soldiers ran from the battlefield, leaving their weapons, artillery and ammunition behind them, mingling with the horses and carriages of politicians who thought war was a spectator sport, all of them fleeing in blind panic on the road back to the capital.

My own battle would be won by charm, or I would end up fleeing in blind panic. I learned just how dramatic was the gap between our financial expectation and reality.

Harrison Jones, dapper, witty, incisive, one-time law student turned man of wine ('There has to be more to life than the law') acted as my guide. The meeting began with me opening a bottle of SonVida, and it surely helped that he loved his first taste. 'It's very pretty,' he declared, with a refined Southern accent which reminded me that his native Tennessee had always sat on the line between North and South. Indeed, during the Civil War it was literally torn between the two, its landmarks of Chattanooga, and Memphis, and Shiloh the scenes of terrible battles. 'Yes, sir, your wine is pretty. Enough fruit to make my mouth water, and enough of a finish to make me want another glass. It makes me miss Argentina, just sitting here and tasting it.'

As the afternoon wore on, I learned Harrison could be less than complimentary about others and that soft Southern accent could be a weapon of some precision. Speaking of a South African red he had recently tasted, he judged 'that was like licking a sweaty horse's back'. Then there was a Bordeaux blend that had sat too long in a warm cellar, which 'smelled and tasted like a musty, saddle blanket'. Finally, an Italian classic disappointed with it strong tannins, 'enough to knock your teeth out'. In the circumstances, I was happy to settle for 'pretty'.

Nothing personal, just business, he added, as he took me through the numbers, stressing that he tried to break it gently to me. 'There's a small cake, and the best way to handle it is to think of it being split in three,' he said, straightening up at his desk and taking a quick sip of SonVida. 'One third for the importer, one for the distributor and one for you.'

I sipped. This meant we made just a few dollars per bottle. Our distributor had a truck and salesmen, our retailer had a store and sales-men, and the fine Tennessee gentleman tasting my wine also had sales-men and a warehouse, and needed to get the wine in a container on a ship. But still. None of them had our costs of production, in the vineyard, in workers, and in the winery. I needed a calculator to be sure, but I believed I had just heard we might not break even on this venture.

Harrison consoled me by selecting one of his favourite Argentine reds for me to take home. 'You need to be brave to make wine,' he waved me off, 'but it's worth it. You have a pretty wine.'

# Bon Courage

*

Pepe, wine salesman, Washington DC:

You know, I've been selling wine for almost fifty years, but I'd never come across a couple like these two. I've watched them from the very beginning. They showed me pictures of their land, and I thought immediately to myself: we have to get them to make a wine, because it's such a beautiful place and such a beautiful story. But there the romance ends, because this is a hard business, and it's changed so much over the years.

Back in the 1960s, people didn't come into a liquor store looking for wine. They came in for a case of vodka, or bourbon, or bottles of gin. In those days, people bought a bottle of wine for cooking, and I was happy to sell a bottle or two of fine wine a day. Can you believe that? Today, I can move cases and cases of wine in a few hours. Back then I was so happy if I sold six bottles in a day. I sold Château Pétrus for eight dollars, Margaux for four, fine burgundy red for less than that. I used to move a Spanish Rioja, and a fairly decent one, for 59 cents a bottle back then. In the late 1960s France made a move, people started to recognize French quality, they liked the élitism that went with good French wine. Then California entered the market, and that's when wine took off in the United States, and I suppose the world. There was a shift, quite dramatic, customers no longer asking for a case of vodka, maybe a case of wine instead. Chardonnay was a game-changer, with Chardonnay the market moved from spirits to wine. People didn't want to drink gin and tonic any more, or even Martinis, and they didn't want to be seen drinking that. They wanted elegant, smooth, fine wine.

We didn't see wine from Argentina until the late 1980s. And frankly most of it was poor. I had the impression they kept the best wine for themselves at home. We had an Argentine Ambassador, here in Washington, and he had a winery, a large operation, and he started bringing it into the American market, mainly Cabernet Sauvignon, Chardonnay, Sauvignon Blanc. But the quality was still ordinary. Then in the 1990s I saw the change. The quality improved, also the marketing. For a few years now Argentina has been the coming country. I have always said the same thing about Argentina: great quality at a fraction of the price. The new kid on the block with a great story to tell and a great product to sell.

For David and Sonia, the key has to be quality. I have been tasting their wine for some time, as they have experimented, and I think they have a winner. But they must not sacrifice quality for quantity, thinking they are going to make money fast that way. They must not bastardize their wine and start chasing volume. I've seen it happen with others, and the minute it does, producers lose their pants, or their shirts, or whatever Englishmen say.

As for Cuba, well, the Englishman doesn't understand what I see. Like so many Europeans, he sees Cuba, and Fidel, and *communismo* as a revolution that takes care of the masses. That's garbage. I left Cuba in 1961, on board my father's boat with twenty-one others, because I saw that Fidel was a gangster with a fake law degree. I thought I would be back within six months. Now I don't want to go back, because I don't want to see my people living in misery and hunger.

So David and I have to keep the conversation about wine. Because Cuba is a dangerous topic. If we talk about wine, it's a wonderful dialogue. If we mention Cuba, it's as toxic as a cheap Italian Chianti that is oxidized and rotten. And that's me being kind to Fidel Castro.

\*

# Out of Africa

Only those who had lived in Washington DC for decades, or those born there, didn't notice the dog days of August. The city built on a swamp, mainly by African-American slaves, usually endured a few weeks of almost unbearable humidity, and mosquitoes to boot, stifling, tiring days that had you thinking of the Great Lakes of East and Central Africa.

So when the good news came, one sweltering afternoon, as I attempted to stay awake in a meeting inside the US Senate, Afghanistan's future the topic, well, it was most welcome, as they said in the Middle East. The *Gallia*, a Panamanian-registered cargo ship that had left Buenos Aires in July, had docked in Norfolk, Virginia, with 250 cases of SonVida aboard, 3,000 bottles of our dream. Ten years, four months after we first saw an onion and tomato field nestling in the foothills of the Andes. Two years, three months to the day after we harvested in the rain. A year and two months since we first bottled. Nine months after we abandoned the original launch date in the face of the global economic meltdown. SonVida, that first vintage, our first wine, had landed. It was my brother's birthday, 5 August.

I stopped on my way home to see Pepe at our local winestore, hoping against hope that the recession, combined with a deserted Washington DC, had not dulled his appetite to take the lion's share of the first SonVida.

'What are you talking about, you crazy Englishman?' my Cuban friend replied with a trademark, puckish grin. 'This isn't Fidel Castro's Cuba, you know. Here we know a thing or two about free markets.' He paused to hug our daughter Alegría, giving her a gentle squeeze while he teased me. 'Just get me the wine as soon as you can. Then I will sell it faster than you can dream of.'

Clearly the look on my face suggested scepticism because Pepe went into overdrive, as if I needed convincing. 'Listen, Englishman, if a madman from Argentina, by the name of Che Guevara, could launch a revolution in Cuba, then I can sell your SonVida.'

That night, as Sonia and I celebrated the long-awaited arrival by dipping into the small reserve of our wine we had brought back with us in previous months, another call came. The UN wanted me to go to Congo on a mission. I checked the weather map. The cool season in Kinshasa.

# 'They walk on Gold. They live on Misery'

Somehow that thought, first given to me by a United Nations trouble-shooter decades before, remained indelibly etched on my mind whenever I thought of a country as terrifying as it could be magical, a country that inspired almost as much as it horrified, a country called Congo. Years later I was the troubleshooter dispatched to cast a fresh pair of eyes on the biggest, most expensive operation the UN had ever conducted. My mission? To ask the questions on the minds of those who paid a large slice of the bill, namely the Americans. To investigate allegations of corruption and abuse within UN units. To witness first hand the reality of peacekeeping in a country where there seemed to be no peace to keep. Above all, to see for myself a measure of the suffering endured by millions.

Congo, the land immortalized by Joseph Conrad in *Heart of Darkness*, a novella I read and thoroughly disliked at Oxford, diagnosing that it represented one of those works students said they appreciated when in reality they struggled with the material, the style and the white man's patently shallow expiation of guilt. 'The horror! the horror!' intoned the lead character, Kurtz, on his deathbed. Exactly. A book not to be celebrated as a masterpiece, in my view, bereft as it is of definition of the African beyond a grunt here, or a chant there, or a wild incantation.

And then came Che Guevara, baptized Ernesto. Leaving aside the revolutionary legend, Che was a trained doctor from Córdoba, Argentina, who adopted Cuba as the country of his heart and Congo as the theatre most likely to replicate the revolution he had led alongside Fidel Castro. Che Guevara's *The African Dream: The Diaries of the Revolutionary War in the Congo*, published more than three decades after his death in 1967, stood out as a truly rare example of truth-telling among communism's élite. 'We can't liberate by ourselves a country that does not want to fight,' Che wrote to Fidel from the hills of Eastern Congo. 'You've got to create a fighting spirit and look for soldiers with the spirit of Diogenes and the patience of Job – a task that becomes more difficult, the more shits there are doing things along the way.'

To visit Eastern Congo was to step into a land of fairy-tale beauty. You could take in its mountains, its lakes, its volcanoes, its rich farmland, and you recognized immediately one of the most magical places on earth. From the air, in an ageing Russian helicopter that had you white-knuckled with fear but also breathless with anticipation, you surveyed lush forests that served as potential lung for the planet, interspersed with gold mines that might make a nation fabulously wealthy. Crossing Lake Kivu, in a hydrofoil that skimmed water so sublimely blue that you imagined some digital Photoshop trickery at work, you glimpsed a riviera that once was the summer playground of the Belgians, magnificent villas boasting swimming pools, tennis courts, even ballrooms. Visiting the remarkable Viruga Park, courtesy of some of the most dedicated park rangers in the world, you spied up close some of the last mountain gorillas on earth. Sad to report, the plight of the gorillas grabbed the world's attention while the world so often averted its eyes from the human suffering writ large in the magical Kivus.

All around you was the vast, natural, untapped potential of this land. Congo had it all. Copper, gold, zinc. Cassiterite, tin to you and me. Wolframite, the basis for tungsten. Cobalt, and cobalt with a purity ten times higher than almost anywhere else in Africa, they said. You knew instantly why King Leopold of the Belgians had lusted after Congo so in the final years of the nineteenth century, seeking what he succinctly and shamelessly termed 'a slice of the African cake'. You knew why he had financed the ruthless mercenary Henry Stanley after Stanley shot his way to discover Dr Livingstone down the Congo river, the waterway that a century later still boasted one sixth of the world's hydroelectric potential. And you knew how mercilessly the King had imposed his will, sending white men in the guise of missionaries, and doctors, and teachers to enslave the people of the so-called Congo Free State through the use of the whip and the gun. Conservative estimates put the number of dead during the Belgian period at ten million.

The modern era had not spared Congo, or the Congolese. One-time friends and neighbours became hungry predators as the country collapsed under the madcap leadership of Mobutu Sese Seko, the pocket tyrant fêted by Presidents from Richard Nixon to George Bush Senior, and a despot treated kindly by the media after he staged the 'Rumble in the Jungle' fight between Muhammad Ali and George Foreman in 1974.

Gold, diamonds, copper, tin. Then there was coltan, the mineral that acted as an essential component of every mobile phone. When, in the late 1980s, Mobutu became the first African head of state to see President Bush the First, the phone industry was clamouring for access to Congo, or Zaire as it was then called, and the richest deposit on the planet of coltan, almost two thirds of the global reserve. By the time I visited Congo twenty years later, at the end of Bush the Second and at the dawn of the age of Obama, a quarter of humanity, almost two billion of us, had cells or mobiles. And five million Congolese had died.

As a UN representative, you hesitated before producing statistics like that to make your case. The people in power, especially my main client base in Washington DC, at the US Congress or inside the administration, invariably concluded that the United Nations had a statistic for everything. But when it came to the Democratic Republic of the Congo, and when the job at hand was to convince the American body politic to stump up the money for UN operations there, I went to the mattresses, and those numbers, time and again.

More than five million dead. Seven million displaced. Almost two million confirmed with HIV/Aids. If those statistics didn't focus the attention of those who held the purse strings, then I would repeat them, adding refrains, hoping to punch home the point. Five million dead, a number not seen in conflict since the Second World War. Two million HIV positive, three times the entire population of Washington DC, the city with the highest incidence of HIV in the United States. Seven million displaced. Imagine all the good people of Iowa, or Arizona, or Connecticut on the move.

And then came the last chilling, numbing, horrifying fact. No statistics this time. Because no one knew how many women had been raped, or how many times, or by how many men.

Except, that is, to put the number of rape victims in millions.

Africa's 'World War', they called it. The 'Silent Holocaust'. Genocide by predators. And nothing prepared you for the faces that lay behind those statistics.

Sifa, a ten-year-old girl with a child's eyes and a wonderful, innocent smile, gang-raped by seven armed men in her home town of Shabunda in Eastern Congo, playfully asking the doctor who accompanied me on a visit to the rape victims' hospital in Bukavu when she might return home. 'One day, my child,' the doctor said as he stroked a cherubic face so far removed from the evil inflicted on her. Then he led me away to explain that he had operated on Sifa three times. 'She will never go home, and she will never bear children,' he concluded.

Rosalie, a seventy-six-year-old grandmother from the town of Mwenga, once a strong-willed and broad-shouldered matriarch capable of carrying a full load of firewood at the end of the working day, reduced to a ghostly, hollow-eyed spirit after being raped repeatedly in the fields where she had lived all her life, and in the presence of her son-in-law, shattering one of the special relationships in Congolese family culture. 'Why did you save me?' she asked after a second round of surgery failed and her husband refused to have anything more to do with her. 'Why?'

Fesa, a bright-eyed twenty-six-year-old, mother of two children from the town of Nyanzale, raped three times by three different armed rebels in front of her husband and children, then abducted by the same group and taken off into the forest hinterland of North Kivu to be their sex slave, cook and porter when they marched to the next battle zone. 'After three months, I only guess how long, because I lost all sense of time, I got away when they went to look for food, and left me alone,' she told us at the clinic in Goma that dealt with hundreds of such cases every month. 'When I returned to my village, it was to discover that my husband had been shot, along with my children.'

I wanted to look away, but spirits such as these held you in rapt attention, the terror of their memory bank denying any such attempt to avert your gaze or cover your ears. 'This is not about sexual desire. Seven men don't line up to rape a seventy-six-year-old woman or a ten-year-old child out of sexual lust,' the doctor explained. 'This is rape as a weapon of mass destruction. Rape as terrorism. Rape as a strategy, designed to destroy the identity of a tribe, or a community, or a region. When you destroy the women, you take away the future, because they will not give birth to a next generation.'

My heart and my head, still spinning with the image of that ten-year-old victim smiling so innocently, raced back to a diary kept by a Belgian army officer in the 1890s who clearly had a conscience. He described a fellow officer who kept a harem of local women. One local beauty refused to share his bed. He had her lashed fifty times, to the point of death, then he gave her to one of his soldiers for the night.

'You felt like a ghost, not of the past, but of the future,' concluded Salim, the hero of V. S. Naipaul's *A Bend in the River*, a 1989 novel set in Mobutu's Congo. 'You felt you were in a place whose future has come and gone.' Naipaul spoke to me in a way Conrad never had.

The largest country in sub-Saharan Africa, its territory twice the size of Western Europe, but Congo did not have a national airline. Waiting for a flight to Kinshasa at the UN airstrip outside the war-ravaged town of Goma, fresh from those hospital visits, a message from Sonia in Washington came through. 'Great news! SonVida has arrived, and Pepe thinks it's so rich he's upped the price and given us a big display. The kids and I just spent an hour watching in wonder, and people were buying our wine!'

For so many reasons at that airport terminal that day in Africa, the dream of tomorrow which lay behind our wine paled in comparison with the memories of the afternoon.

# Independence Cha-Cha-Cha

Kinshasa represented an assault on the senses. Its prime location on the Congo river yielded magnificent sunsets, great barbecue on a sandbank, and arguably the best freshwater prawns in the world, *cossa-cossa* they called them, served with a rare garlic and chili sauce. In the throbbing commune of Matonge, just off the boulevard Kasu-vabu, its nightclubs still hummed to the sounds which the Congo exported to the world in the early years of independence, rock-rumba, and soukous, and African jazz, pioneered by the bandleader Joseph Kabasele, author of a favourite African anthem of mine, 'Independence Cha-Cha-Cha'. In the cool season, you drove the Champs-Élysées of that city, the boulevard de 30 Juin, with its wide lanes, department stores and commercial landmarks, and you imagined how Congo saw itself at independence on 30 June 1960. Even five decades on, *les Kinois,* as the people of Kinshasa were known, expressed undeniable pride that their city was destined one day to surpass Paris as the largest Francophone metropolis on earth.

But the city, which uniquely shared a great river with the capital of a neighbouring country, Congo-Brazzaville, offered so much evidence of decline and decay. Five decades after independence, boulevard Lumumba, the road in from the airport named after the country's first elected leader, communist Patrice Lumumba, was swallowed by darkness come dusk, teeming masses appearing at the side of the road the minute your headlights veered left or right, searching for the next giant pothole. Grafted on to the quarters of the original city, with those grand avenues, vast shantytowns of shacks were thrown together in total chaos, ramshackle huts of cardboard and packing boxes that the poor rented out to those even poorer. Forget electricity. No running water, no sewers, no transport and no garbage collection, which meant huge piles of trash on almost every street corner. Kinshasa had the earliest documented case of HIV/Aids, and the virus was rampant in the slums.

Kinshasa was officially nicknamed 'Kin La Belle' ('Kinshasha the Beautiful'). The Kinois who drove me patiently from one meeting to another, stressing that the supreme objective was to avoid those potholes and hence preserve valuable tyres, explained a change. 'We call it Kin La Poubelle.' ('Kinshasa the garbage-dump'.)

And there perhaps lay the greatest resource Congo boasted, beyond those diamonds or all that copper, even that reserve of coltan. Its people, irrepressible, indomitable, indefatigable. And their unquenchable sense of humour. 'Better late than dead on arrival,' deadpanned the Kinois, Eric the driver, as we took eternity to reach the residence of the American Ambassador one afternoon, and I fretted about being late for an important meeting designed to solidify American support for the UN mission. 'Never forget – a bad day in the bush is better than a good day in the office,' he added.

One particular line of Congolese jokes that year tickled me.

'What did they use in Zimbabwe before candles?' (*Pause.*) 'Electricity.'

'How come they don't know the results three weeks after the elections in Zimbabwe?' (*Pause.*) 'Here in Congo we know the result three weeks before the election.'

And then the clincher:

'So what did Robert Mugabe say when they asked him how he planned to say goodbye to his people in Zimbabwe?' (*Pause.*) 'Why, where are my people going?'

Robert Mugabe. What mixed emotions that name, and that figure, lit inside me, some fuse, some explosive combination of memory, excitement, regret, dismay, overlaid with more than a tinge of guilt. Quite simple. Robert Mugabe launched my career as a broadcaster. He gave me one exclusive after another as white-ruled Rhodesia transformed itself into Zimbabwe governed by his black majority, so sealing the sunset of the British Empire in Africa.

He took me into his confidence at critical moments of the negotiating process that transformed him from Marxist-Leninist guerrilla chief to democratically elected leader of his country. He asked me to travel with him when he visited comrades-in-arms in Ethiopia, Tanzania and Mozambique, ushering me into meetings as if I belonged to his delegation. I joined him as he performed his 5 a.m. ritual of calisthenics and meditation, a legacy of his prison years. I introduced him to the white Rhodesian general who had fought him for years, the beginning of a relationship that was to turn bitter enemies into necessary allies in the first years after independence. In the days before he returned home from exile, I sat with him for hours as he brainstormed about what he would do with his country once he won power. We broke bread together in London, Maputo and Harare, most memorably on the night he was elected leader of the free Zimbabwe. His first wife Sally always welcomed me with a hug. She said I brought Robert good luck. I always thought of it the other way round. Robert Mugabe brought me a serious measure of professional success, an inside track to the man of the moment *circa* 1980. Indeed, my first book was the first biography of Africa's hottest new leader: 'an in-depth profile of the man who is the most influential and articulate of Africa's statesmen', according to the jacket notes of *Mugabe: The Man behind the Myth*, published in London in 1981. Astonishing when I looked back, but he called me David and I thought of him in those days as Robert.

I still did, years later, when I found myself at the US Marine Training Base at Quantico, Virginia, giving a talk about United Nations peace-keeping operations to a group of Marine colonels. The second question from the floor spoke for itself.

'Your book about that madman Mugabe is on the internet for thirty bucks,' shouted a chiselled, crewcut colonel from the back of the auditorium. 'Is it worth that, is it worth reading?'

My friends knew me as a spirit usually with too much to say, but that day at Quantico I stumbled and fumbled, lost for words. What to say about the book that encapsulated a golden year spent with the politician who helped make my career in premier-league journalism? How to answer the question of whether my thirty-year-old version of events stood the test of time? And how to respond to the chilling truth that accompanied Mugabe's life? As Archbishop Desmond Tutu once remarked to me, in that crystal-clear, xylophone cadence of his: 'Robert was the darling of the world, so dear to all of us, then he became a monster.'

Responding to the Marine colonel, I observed, briefly, that I was not sure *Mugabe*, the first biography, was worth thirty dollars when the early paperback edition had gone on sale at one pound, fifty pence. Credibility was barely preserved, but at least it was done with a chuckle. You could not chuckle about the bigger picture.

# My Friend the Tyrant

Robert Mugabe the Statesman, *circa* 1980. Robert Mugabe the Monster, decades later. Robert Mugabe, my one-time gateway to success.

How could you have been so wrong? How could you have so misjudged a character? How could you have missed the megalomaniac, who signed off on a democratic future for his country, then spent the next thirty years making it a brutal one-party dictatorship where people starved to death and life expectancy lowered to the medieval norm of thirty-five? How could you not have diagnosed the mass murderer, who called in the Fifth Brigade of North Koreans, of all armies, to destroy the Ndebele tribe that voiced opposition, and their leader, Mugabe's coalition partner at the Lancaster House peace talks, Joshua Nkomo? How could you have been so blind to the cruel despot who sent thugs with such *noms de guerre* as Stalin Mao Mao to organize mass rapes in opposition villages, teenagers gang-raped in front of parents who were forced to chant, 'Long live Mugabe . . . Long live Fidel Castro . . . Down with Tony Blair and George Bush.' Did you never detect the tyrant, capable of bulldozing the shantytown slums where the poorest of the poor took refuge in the face of an economic crisis that had inflation demanding trillions, yes trillions, of his ravaged currency to buy a loaf of bread? And what about the homophobe who crucified politically one of the state's founding fathers, indeed its first President post-Independence, simply because he was homosexual?

I made the classic journalistic argument to myself. I wasn't the only one, after all, who got it wrong. Those way above my pay-grade, those with real power, those who could have ejected Mugabe from the country's future, made the same mistake. I recalled the late Peter Carrington, aka Lord Carrington, British Foreign Secretary, introducing me to Robert Mugabe in the basement of Lancaster House, the splendid site for peace talks in London's St James's that once had Queen Victoria aghast at its beauty, with the words: 'Meet the man who holds the key to the future of his country. And just remember, he's too smart to be led down the garden path by *News at Ten*.' I went back to a long, slightly tipsy evening with the one man who did hold the key to war or peace in Southern Africa in those last weeks of the 1970s. General Peter Walls commanded the Rhodesian Army, and my days and nights with the Rhodesian Army outside Umtali on the border with Mozambique taught me they were natural-born killers, capable of slitting a throat or lining up a firing squad with impunity. Walls could have ordered his men to enforce a peace deal or hijack it. 'Mugabe is a winner, because he has his thugs in place, and because people like you ignore that, preferring to deposit in Mugabe your naïve hopes for Africa,' Walls told me over dinner as peace talks reached make-or-break moment in November 1979. 'You want Africa, by the Africans, for the Africans, all right, and Mugabe tells you what you want to hear.'

A few days later, because I was interviewing one after the other, I introduced my friend Peter the General to my friend Robert the Marxist. 'General Walls, I presume,' said Mugabe, with the trademark, somewhat artificial grin that usually belied nervousness. Walls, never a man to back away from a challenge, replied somewhat hesitatingly: 'I'm sure we will meet again.' Mugabe stayed in the moment, his stare sure, his handshake lasting; the general blinked. Somehow I knew that the white general knew he had met his match in the African revolutionary. One of the last white demi-Gods in Africa faced his nemesis, knowing the odds were stacked against him, that Mugabe held the cards which mattered, namely the political cadres and battle-hardened thugs in the bush to guarantee him the votes come election day.

That long-playing record of my memory bank was rich, and the image of bringing yesterday's general together with tomorrow's leader was special, but it provided no excuse. However much I told myself that the world at large bought into Mugabe, the Marxist they could work with, I saw the tell-tale signs of his tyranny. I knew of the innate arrogance, to begin with. I sat with him one afternoon at his London apartment in Bayswater, across the road from Hyde Park, in the eye of the storm of peace-making in 1979, Sally in the kitchen preparing yet another meal for his entourage and me. And I sensed instinctively the fix was in, days before a peace agreement was signed, months before an election was scheduled. So much so I was reminded of talking to the mafia in Sicily or Calabria in my Italian days. 'Who can win if not us? Who can possibly match our military comrades?' he asked me, as he detailed how any vote would go in Fort Victoria, or Plumtree, or Gwelo, always referring to the strength of his military in the same breath as his electoral prospects. 'I believe we have done the most mobilization of our masses during the years of our struggle. Our object in the war was always to create the base for power. We will not be wanting. We have taken care of ourselves.' The man boasted supreme conviction, based partly on his theology but more on his facts on the ground. Mugabe was trained by the Jesuits. So was I. The sign language was unmistakable. God was with Robert in Robert's view. But, just in case, he had the deck loaded, courtesy of the men with guns, courtesy of a command structure that meant they followed orders, courtesy of his willingness to intimidate, torture, rape and murder. That separated us.

Robert did kill, and I knew that too. He had talked to me, at his house of exile in Maputo, of the agonizing decisions to execute those who defied discipline, as he put it. Such a euphemism covered so much. 'I hate those decisions,' he told me. 'I remember my days in prison, and I recall how men were sent to death, not for a reason but for a mistake.' When I asked him how many men under his command had been condemned to death, he looked away, crossed his hands as if in prayer; that unnatural half-smile again, accompanied by a nervous shuffle of the shoulders. I knew then that Mugabe lived in a world apart, a world of impunity, and our conversation had reached a fork in the road.

When he flew home to Zimbabwe, on Sunday, 27 January 1980, and I found myself in the cockpit of his odyssey, riding aboard a 727 of the Mozambican state carrier *Deta* with him and Sally, the strategy spoke volumes. Despite genuine provocation by the white immigration officers who greeted them – I never forgot the sight of a white terminal worker swearing audibly at Sally, then spitting at her feet – Mugabe presented a face to the world straight out of the modern spin doctor's playbook.

A week before, back in Maputo, sitting in his living room, I had seen a draft of his first address to the people of Rhodesia, to be delivered via a press conference at Salisbury airport that Sunday morning. Asked for my thoughts, I tried to limit myself to telling him that few Rhodesians had ever seen him before, courtesy of censorship. Therefore the tone he adopted was critical. He had to speak to the butcher, the baker, the farmer. The Whites.

I recounted an extraordinary meeting I had with a farmers' leader named Denis Norman. Denis, a Brit in everything he did and said, especially as his burr came straight from the Oxfordshire of my student days, had invited me to his large but workaday farm at Norton, about an hour from Salisbury, and treated me to a wonderful Sunday lunch, his beautiful blonde, blue-eyed daughters with us, so much so that the ITN cameraman, a loveable lad named Peter Wilkinson (later to be Queen Elizabeth's videographer), and I were besotted. Denis gave me a lesson that day in understanding. He explained how the future lay not just with Mugabe and Nkomo, but with whites like himself. 'We can run, as so many others have in Africa in recent years, lose everything we have worked for.' The sigh that followed hung in the air. 'Or we can bet it all on this fellow Mugabe,' he exhaled. 'I'm betting Mugabe needs us as much we need him.'

My mini-speech about such white folks back in his country triggered an hour of vintage Mugabe. Here, in cameo, spoke the leader who convinced Lord Carrington, and Margaret Thatcher, and Ronald Reagan, and Desmond Tutu, and Nelson Mandela, lest we forget, to place their faith in him. Mugabe in such mode was unstoppable as the loquacious hands, the manic eyes, the nervous smiles, the awkward shuffles, the croaky, high-pitched voice all fused in rare syncopation as Robert led you down the garden path of Zimbabwe's future.

'We fought the war to win the peace,' he began. And then he showed you how he was reading himself in to be leader of his country. Industry preoccupied him. He didn't know Denis the farmer, but he had studied him. (In fact he later recruited Denis Norman to be his first Agriculture Minister, alongside a Scotsman named David Smith, no relation, as his first Finance Minister.) This, after all, was a political prisoner who studied for graduate degrees from his prison cell in the 1960s, in between sessions of torture, solitary confinement and personal humiliation. He had learned from the ultimate mentor, the freedom fighter named Samora Machel, who led Mozambique to independence from the Portuguese with Robert as his eager pupil.

'Samora has taught me, time and again, never to repeat the mistake of history. Almost a quarter of a million Portuguese fled when Samora came to power here,' he explained. 'And Machel has always cited one lesson. The whites didn't just leave Mozambique, Samora said, they burned the combine harvesters, and they burned the manuals with which we might have fixed the damn combine harvesters.' It was rare to hear Mugabe use a curse word, even one as mild as that, his mother's catechism speaking to the boy and the man all his life. So, no, he didn't want to nationalize the mining industry (that day he was obsessed by Zimbabwe's mines), or the bakeries, or the farms. 'Tell your farmer friend Denis Norman that,' he added.

He reeled off the frightening statistics that faced him as the new leader of the infant Zimbabwe. I can still hear him in full cry, his voice incandescent with anger about the failure of others, yet also thrilling to the challenge ahead. A million people uprooted from their homes by war; too late for them to go back and sow crops to feed themselves, maybe for years. Nearly half a million children without schools; again a consequence of the war. Just a handful of doctors still working in the rural areas, serving millions of his people. Mugabe saw the tragedy. He voiced the need. Above all, he smelled the opportunity. If ever a man was reading himself into being Prime Minister, this was the one. And this was the intellect, the spirit, the life-force that persuaded so many in power to get behind the Mugabe bandwagon. 'We fought the war to win the peace.'

Robert never, in my experience, knowingly undersold himself, never, ever. There was always a hint of the Anglo-Saxon Lord in his demeanour, his quiet arrogance and his fastidious dress. On occasions I even thought of him as a Scottish laird, so secure in the fiefdom of his superior attire, intellect and political machine. And when he turned that day to the speech he would deliver on his return home, his vanity was breathtaking. 'This first speech has to find a touch of Kennedy, and Lincoln even, grand vision tempered by humility, reconciliation and hope. I must look my country squarely but compassionately in the eye, make them understand why I am with them, not against some of them.' Never knowingly undersold indeed.

All who knew him had their theories, a way to rationalize the sense of dismay, despair and depression that accompanied the daily news diet that so haunted the decades which followed, the drumbeat of death, suffering and oppression from Zimbabwe. Some concluded that Mugabe had handed over power to his henchmen, notorious thugs in many cases, to stay in power. Mugabe had always hated the whites, according to others, a legacy of the prison torture that so scarred the man, and had delivered payback via the lawless land grabs which delivered hundreds of white-owned farms to his militia. Or there was the school that thought Mugabe believed the ultimate threat to Africa's future lay in endless tribal warfare. Hence his genocidal treatment of the rival Ndebele represented political philosophy, a solution once and for all. And then came the 'realists', who deduced that Mugabe had no place to run to, or hide, especially after the collapse of the Soviet Union. 'Not much of a choice – Cuba or North Korea,' to quote one UN colleague who sought my advice as intermediaries tried to persuade Mugabe to take a face-saving trip to exile after the bitterly disputed elections of 2008. In truth, Mugabe was offered an attractive exit – to South Africa. In reality he chose not take it.

No theories from me, because long experience with the man had taught me that the complexities of Mugabe's character, background and temperament made a mockery of such 'one size fits all' explanations. Rather some hard-nosed observations that formed as I attempted to answer those nagging questions. How did we so misread the man? And what did his legacy represent?

With hindsight, from the moment Mugabe signed the Lancaster House peace agreement just before Christmas 1979, he was gifted a sense of impunity by an international community, specifically the British, that turned a blind eye to his evident excesses. So as I joined the Royal Marines in the bush over New Year 1979-80 (alongside the BBC's John Humphrys, my sleeping companion) to wait for Mugabe's guerrillas to turn themselves in, hand over their weapons and be demobilized, Mugabe's commanders told a sizeable chunk of their army to stay out, defy the agreement and deliver the vote for their leader. Deliver they did. All along the border with Mozambique, from Centenary in the north to Chiredzi in the south, more than 2,000 of his fighters ran a campaign of brutal intimidation. They tortured. They maimed and crippled if need be. One favourite tactic was to pour burning coals down the throats of opposition candidates. And back at Government House in Salisbury, the capital, the people who held the reins of power in those last days of Empire knew this as well as anyone. About 300 of Mugabe's men had been captured, and they gave away the plot.

Britain's last Governor in Africa, Lord Nicholas Soames, Winston

Churchill's son-in-law, gambled on the power of persuasion. The portly, rather verbose Soames, and his wise wife Mary, Churchill's most devoted daughter, conducted soirées aplenty in those final days of Britannia, and the gin most certainly flowed in a room that occasionally boasted the young, rather giggly Camilla Parker-Bowles, there with her then husband Andrew, a military aide to the Governor. The Parker-Bowles, whose marriage two decades later moved the epicentre of the British royal family's future as Camilla divorced Andrew, then married Prince Charles, seemed to fit perfectly into a drawing room that looked a world apart from what was happening outside in the country, the emphasis on a stiff cocktail or two and canapés rather than Mugabe's machinations. Delightful company, even if conversation was often limited to tennis, horseback riding and the heat of a Rhodesian summer.

Lord Soames sought advice, and he received an earful from some. His military commander, John Acland, knew all along that Mugabe had betrayed the peace agreement. His election commissioner, John Boynton, diagnosed intimidation and coercion on a massive scale, making a farce of any claim to a free and fair election. And then came the increasingly tragic figure of Joshua Nkomo, the man who signed the peace alongside Mugabe.

One afternoon, Nkomo in person (and the vastly overweight Nkomo was not a figure you could ignore) reported his candidates and campaign workers abducted, savagely beaten in front of hundreds of villagers in the Chibi tribal trust land near Fort Victoria. Mugabe's gunmen told the crowd they had equipment that detected how people voted. 'Anyone who votes for this man,' they said, pointing to Nkomo's candidate, Francis Makombe, 'will have his head cut off.' The candidate was last seen choking with burning coals. That night Lord Soames told us that he needed to sleep on the next move. The following day he adopted a manner that spoke loudly of the dilemma, if not of an answer, as he declared: 'In this particular race, all the horses are going to get to the starting-line come what may. We may have to pull a jockey or two, or even hold an inquiry. But they are all going to start.'

Mugabe read the tea leaves better than most at the Governor's mansion. He understood that the mother of all Empires was not going to ride off into the sunset having outlawed the man most likely to succeed. Therein lay the dawn of absolute impunity. One fact stayed with me. Robert, in one conversation after another that year, told me that he would win fifty-six seats in the new Parliament. In the end, he won fifty-seven. Those comrades-in-arms did indeed deliver.

Then there was Sally. Like so many who knew him in that period, I sensed immediately that Sally's death in 1992, from kidney failure, signalled the end of Mugabe's 24/7 access to wise advice. No matter that the man had a mistress by then, a secretary in the presidency named Grace, who already had two children by him, the woman later installed as first lady after the 'Wedding of the Century', as it was dubbed in Harare. Sally had represented Mugabe's rock, his *alter ego* and his smartest adviser, the man's woman for all seasons. With her deep, ever-optimistic eyes, her wonderful smile and a voice that blended beauty with baritone, Sally knew how, when and where to lighten the man's mood, to tell him to chill; or sometimes she diagnosed the need to push Mugabe's buttons. She had his ear from the moment she took him under the wing of her family when he was a visiting schoolteacher in her native Ghana in the early 1960s. She had held his devotion since she stayed loyal to him and the cause during the long prison years, losing their only child to cerebral malaria, burying him alone because Ian Smith's government refused all pleas for compassionate leave for Robert Mugabe, political prisoner.

Others he might intimidate, or browbeat, or vilify, but never Sally. I lost count of the times I heard her tell him to think again, revisit first impulses, hit the pause switch on his quick temper and consider options. 'Engage brain before you open mouth, Robert,' she told him one afternoon in the Bayswater apartment when he tore into Margaret Thatcher for her leadership of the peace talks. 'Without Thatcher, and this process, our revolution goes back fifty years.' Or the day in Maputo, when he overplayed his hand badly in an interview with me, lashing out at Lord Soames for not letting him stage all the rallies he wanted. 'Robert, assume good in people on the other side for once, just for once please!' she cried. 'Lord Soames seems to want to give us a chance to win this election.' On the morning after election victory, as she hung out the washing on the line at 27 Quorn Avenue, the house the Mugabes rented on their return home, Sally alone articulated the challenge ahead. 'Forget about how many seats we won. It's all about how many hearts and minds we keep in the years ahead.' She stood alone, I so often felt when

I watched them together, in being able to provide checks and balances to his sense of impunity. With her passing, the man did indeed become a tyrant, an all-bestriding colossus in his own mind, and a cruel despot to his people.

The last time I saw Robert Mugabe, it was at the General Assembly of the United Nations after Sally's death. At a reception for African leaders, I waited in line for the chance to exchange a few words, specifically to remember Sally and convey condolences. His long-time henchman, Edison Zvobgo, later to be a critic of Mugabe's, gave me an embarrassing bear-hug, clapped me repeatedly on the back and reminded me of a fairly inebriate evening during the Lancaster House talks years before. From Mugabe, thank goodness, no such recognition or welcome. He shook my hand perfunctorily. I looked into those cold, cold eyes, searching for some emotion, but found none. I filled the silence by extending my condolences. Mugabe said: 'Sally always said you brought me luck. But I think we make our own luck, don't we?' He looked at the floor, then the ceiling, clearly considering our meeting over. But now I wondered whether I might be allowed to revisit Zimbabwe. (Years before, Mugabe's Information Minister had banned me from the country after the publication of the biography, calling me 'a capitalist lackey who just wants to make money out of Comrade Mugabe's life-story'.) Comrade Mugabe, dressed immaculately as ever, suit tailored to perfection in Jermyn Street, or Fifth Avenue, or maybe Milan, tie and handkerchief of red silk, Comrade Mugabe sighed, looked at the ceiling as if appealing for patience from on high, then wagged his right index finger as if to scold me: 'Actions have consequences, my friend. That's what the Jesuits taught us, didn't they?' I took that as a no. I felt undeniable relief. I was still *persona non grata* in Robert Mugabe's Zimbabwe.

# Never Again

When you went on a mission to a country like Congo, and you worked for the United Nations, you inevitably left with fear gnawing at your heart, spirit and brain. Fear that the country's civil war would once again erupt into the kind of widespread bloodletting that had already claimed so many lives. Fear that Congo's many militias would persist in unspeakable acts of sexual violence, destroying countless lives that had still to be lived. Fear that my organization, the UN, would end up being blamed by all, supported by few, the whipping-boy of history. A legendary UN Secretary-General, the Swede Dag Hammarskjöld, once remarked: 'The UN was not invented to take the world to heaven, but to stop it going to hell.' Flying out of Kinshasa on a crisp, cloudy morning, having asked some tough questions of my UN colleagues, I knew what he meant.

My final stop was Nairobi, my home for a while three decades earlier, and always in my experience a safe haven from the ills that afflicted so much of the African continent. The aircraft had just reached the gate at Jomo Kenyatta Airport when my BlackBerry fired into life again with a bulletin from the UN's World Food Programme. On this day of all days, my first time back in Kenya in years, the UN issued an emergency appeal. 'Red lights are flashing across the country,' said a statement issued by Kenya's lead food expert. 'People are going hungry, malnutrition is preying on more and more young children, cattle are dying. We face a huge challenge in Kenya.' By the time I had reached immigration control, and moved quickly through the diplomatic channel, another message appeared. 'The current food security remains highly precarious,' declared the UN's Famine Early Warning System Network, an institution to which I felt a special attachment. My reports from Uganda and Ethiopia in the early 1980s, along with those of countless others, had prompted the UN to build the network, on the basis of never again. Never again the Karamoja in 1980. Never again Ethiopia 1983-4. 'This is Kenya's worst drought in years, food production has dropped dramatically, and this represents an emergency.'

Ethiopia. Somalia. Sudan. Niger, certainly Chad. Those countries had long lived with the wicked cycle of drought and hunger, turning to famine. But Kenya? The country that had been developed more than any other, and as you reached Nairobi you looked at the office blocks, and the business parks, and the skyscrapers. Then you thought of the scores of UN offices in the country, the thousands of aid workers who lived there. But Kenya?

Fortunately, I was staying with an old friend who knew more about Africa than anyone I had ever met, a man trained in the art of survival whatever the challenge. Sir Mohinder Dhillon, Kenya's leading film-maker, once official photographer to Emperor Haile Selassie and thirty years before the ITN cameraman in East Africa, hence my companion in the Karamoja, and Ethiopia, and Kenya. 'Don't worry, my dear David, we have water, and I have my own generator,' said Mo as he gave me the warmest of hugs. 'I'm just so angry about the politicians who deliver starvation and suffering to their people.'

How much had changed. How little had changed. That night we wondered aloud together, over a long, healthy Indian meal, washed down by cold African beer, about the hunger that still stalked Africa. Hadn't we worked to change that, with those chilling tragic stories of starvation and famine from Uganda, Somalia, Ethiopia and Eritrea a generation before? Hadn't we said back then that this could not be allowed to happen again? Hadn't the world, through the UN, put early-warning systems in place to ensure never again? Didn't we once bury a child that died in front of us, at the side of the road in the Karamoja, and leave her shallow grave believing not just that we had done the right thing, but that we would make her death a clarion call for action?

Mohinder, more than anyone else I ever worked with, showed how to give life to those who were dying. He educated me in the art of taking his images, married to my words, and making the tragedy of death one day the catalyst for change the next. He made me look into the eyes of a child and recognize an infant too weak to cry, or swat away the flies, or even blink. He stayed with the dying right till the end, his compassionate eye always at work, knowing that his work gave them dignity, even hope. Never did he turn his gaze away, cover his eyes. Mohinder taught me never, ever to turn away from the most desperate soul on earth. He taught me to try to confront the worst of humanity with the best of humanity.

So how to confront the tragedy of Africa thirty years on? How did you deal with the child starving that day in Kenya? How did you face the annihilation of a society such as Congo? What did you say to the doctor dealing with ten rape victims a day, let alone the ten-year-old girl whose future had been destroyed by a bunch of armed thugs? And what was the answer to a Robert Mugabe?

Flying to Nairobi that day, I was left speechless by an article written by a one-time colleague from the *Financial Times*, among the best and brightest of African commentators, who concluded: 'It is time for Western Governments to admit defeat, swallow their pride, re-engage Zimbabwe, and do business with Robert Mugabe.' Michael Holman, a white Zimbabwean, punctured my conscience with the rat-tat-tat gunfire of thought:

> The first step down this path is to acknowledge an uncomfortable truth. Mugabe has won the battle for Zimbabwe . . . he has presided over a fundamental change to an African economy, his popularity in much of Africa is undeniable, and the landless of Kenya, South Africa and elsewhere look on his work with admiration . . . Never again will a 5,000-strong minority own much of the country's best farmland, and though it has cost Zimbabwe dear, Mugabe has created a lasting legacy, having radically changed the racially distorted land structure he inherited at independence.

Mohinder taught me once again: 'David, you and I believe that Mugabe should be in The Hague as a war criminal. But you and I believed, thirty years ago, that we could prevent another famine. It's not that we were wrong, or that our principles were misguided, or our hearts misled us. It's just that we were a little naïve.'

# The Bull and the Belly Dancer

On a cloudy, grey autumn morning in south-western France, I took the ferry from the citadel town of Blaye, where the Romans planted the first vines and where they still made terrific red wines at a few Euros per bottle, as well as growing award-winning asparagus, the town's other claim to fame. Only the French, bless them, would have awards for asparagus, though I do recall Bill Clinton once telling me, in some detail, how his home state of Arkansas had competitions for water-melons. We crossed the rather muddy Gironde river, the secret to so much of Bordeaux's success, environmentally and commercially, my destination the fabled vineland of Médoc. When I disembarked at Lamarque, to the north in Haut-Médoc, they stacked up ahead of me. One. Two. Three. Three of the oldest, indeed legendary wine communes, boasting some of the best vineyards on the planet.

First St Julien, a village so small I drove through it without knowing I had been there, but a commune that punched way above its size. Almost all of its wines were in the classified growth rankings that meant subtle drinking and high prices, and its wines were well known for their varied aromas, everything from blackcurrant, to cocoa, to cedar box. I do not have a clue how cedar box smells. Still, my wine bible put it succinctly: 'If you were to drink only the wines from this commune for the rest of your life, you could be very happy.'

Then came Pauillac, home to so many of the original stars or First Growths, as they were called back in the mid nineteenth century when Napoleon III demanded that Bordeaux rate its wines from best to worst. *Quel nightmare* that must have been for the château owners. You could hardly imagine the dogfight that would have accompanied that process, neighbours becoming enemies, villages and communes bitter rivals, old grievances settled by the sword of the Emperor's Classification of 1855. The grand names of Pauillac trip off the tongue of any wine student or collector: Château Lafite-Rothschild, Château Mouton Rothschild, Château Latour. All of them the best in the world, if you accepted the French system. From our study days in London,

New York, Washington and New Orleans I had come to love the tale of Baron Philippe de Rothschild. Back in 1855 his family's château was originally classified as Second Growth, second division, a stellar ranking but not top. The twentieth-century heir, Baron Philippe, would simply not accept that. Post Second World War he pursued successive French governments for an upgrade, and finally succeeded in 1973. His is the only château to have changed position since 1855. It was a perennial test question on the Master of Wine Course in London and the exam at Court of Master Sommeliers in the United States. The only time the Classification was ever changed, the only château to move up the rankings. *Quel upgrade.*

Finally, just above Pauillac, came the rather austere-looking commune of St Estèphe, a name that had always teased me with its incredible diversity. As a student on the Sommelier course, I had tasted St Estèphe wines that were sensuous, lush, incredibly ripe and so full of smooth fruit that the word explosion came to mind. Sexy wines indeed. One called Cos d'Estournel stood out. Yet at the same time St Estèphe produced wines as austere as its appearance, rigid Bordeaux blends of Cabernet Sauvignon, the commandant grape in these parts, softened only slightly by supple, warm Merlot. St Estèphe's secret lay in the soil, the French said (but then the French always said that), a little heavier here in the north but still boasting the gravelly edge of the Gironde river, interspersed with clay, the Haut-Médoc *terroir* that emerged from a seventeenth-century revolution when the local nobility brought in Dutch engineers to build canals and so turn marshlands and swamps into riverside gravel banks that spawned the nonpareil of châteaux. Never let it be said that the New World led the wine revolution. The French, as ever masters of marketing and spin, coined the word 'revolution' first. Even in the world of wine.

My destination that autumn morning a grand vineyard, Château Caronne, on the outskirts of the pretty village of St Laurent, just south of St Julien, on a lovely island of vines, but further inland from the Gironde, therefore a little way from the best gravel, and the finest clay, and the top Classification. Some years before, on the advice of my favourite salesman Pepe at my local wine store in Washington, I had bought a case of Château Caronne on the Bordeaux futures market, paid him up front, then waited almost two years to receive it. Indeed, I had to remind him that he owed me a case. By which time it was worth three times what I paid for it, because the reviews had come in favourably. 'Dense, dark, macerated fruits. Rounded, fleshy. Very good structure behind it,' reported one leading judge. 'An underrated vintage. This is very good and needs six to eight years in the cellar.' I didn't wait. Deferred gratification was not a speciality of mine. I opened a bottle immediately with Sonia, and we diagnosed a classic Bordeaux blend, the soft, gentle Merlot wrapping round the strong tannic Cabernet, with blending grapes such as Petite Verdot and Cabernet Franc thrown in to add colour and spice. I could have drunk the whole lot then and there given a week or two. Sonia, ever the disciplined student, insisted we save it and learn from it as it aged.

When I met its maker, a dapper, thoughtful Bordelais named François Nony, selling his wine in Washington DC, he looked quietly appalled when I told him his wine passed my muster test. 'I liked my first glass a lot, and I wanted another,' I said, offering a mischievous grin, English-man to Frenchman. 'In fact I enjoyed the first bottle so much, I wanted a second, but my wife stepped in.' François, who looked faintly out of place in the wine store on a Saturday morning, dressed in Guy Laroche suit and tie, French blue cashmere sweater wrapped over his shoulders, cellphone to ear, took me aside. 'The magic lies in the wait,' he half-whispered, clearly believing the Englishman responded to a quiet word, discreet education. 'Like the best things in life, the ultimate pleasure, the magic, comes not with instant gratification, yes?' The wink told me everything. 'The magic comes when you take time.'

I pushed back, half-heartedly because I liked the man in that instant way of mine, and didn't want to argue. 'OK, but maybe I take the view that I buy today, I drink this evening, and if I like, I will drink tomorrow, simply because I live now,' I replied, laughing at myself.

François paused to put his cellphone away. 'Please take your time, listen to your wife, and drink my wine a bottle a year. Then you will see how good life can be.'

There you had it, the Jerusalem of all arguments in the world of wine, the Final Status issue that stood between the Old World and the New.

To my genuine surprise, as I delved into the world of wine – when I went to the VinExpo in Bordeaux or attended a grand tasting in London – the issue was not Old World versus New World in straight *hombre-a-hombre* terms, namely who produced the better wine. To my genuine amazement, the French accepted how the New World had taken their primordial belief in *terroir* to the laboratory of new-age science and the wine industry to another level. Not a spirit easily astonished, I heard French wine makers from the birthplace of Malbec, the old French domain of Cahors, look to us in Argentina as the trail-blazers for a grape that was never taken seriously in Bordeaux. Over a long lunch in Cahors, when I shared our young wine with local Malbec producers, they preferred it to their own, acknowledging how the grape flourished in the Andes in a way it had never done in France. And my jaw dropped.

No, what I learned was that the Old World drew the battle lines on higher ground. The French, even before the Classification of Napoleon III, had us believe that the defining moment for great wine revolved around the capacity of a wine to age. Hence the unbelievable price, and cachet, attached to a 1947 Cheval Blanc, or Pétrus '82, or Latour '83. The New World prided itself on making great wines for now, today, the moment. But the New World made wines for the ages too. Just ask anyone who ever tasted a Stag's Leap 1976, or a Penfolds Grange 1999, or a Catena Alta 1996. Still, the New World pitched instant gratification. *Carpe diem.* Live for the moment. And the moment was now. Not tomorrow. Not next year. Not next decade. Certainly not next century.

My mentor Nicolás Catena, the pioneer who revolutionized Argentine wine, worried about those who believe in deferred gratification. He knew all too well, from three generations of winemaking in his family and a cellar of their work to match, that our wines from Argentina aged well. Exceptionally well, in some cases. But he feared that Malbec, the star of our stretch of the Southern Hemisphere, did not mature in ways that the Old World chose to appreciate. 'We will be judged by how Malbec grows old, and there can be no guarantees about that, even though our Malbec is the best it can be,' he told me time and again down the years.

I always responded that we had a two-pronged response, a double-whammy of an argument to make, a two-fer, as Americans liked to call it. 'We make great wines for today, for drinking now, but they will age well if you prefer to wait,' I replied. 'Great wines for today, tomorrow, or ten years from now – that should be our philosophy, Nicolás.'

# The Bull and the Belly Dancer

On a crisp autumn morning, walking the vineyard at Château Caronne with its owner François at the height of the harvest in the Northern Hemisphere, I recognized immediately what brought us together. And, as the day wore on, what set us apart.

Harvest time brought so many stresses and strains, wherever you grew grape. A gentlemen in every word and deed, François raised his voice uncharacteristically that morning as I arrived at the winery, the grape coming in by the truckload, the sorting machine humming to the sound of berries bouncing down the line to the crushing machines, the giant cement tanks brimming with Merlot, this year as lush, and as fleshy, and as alcoholic as any they had ever harvested. 'Let's get more workers in here – now !' he shouted at his foreman. 'We need twice as many people to sort the grape by hand,' he ordered. Turning to me, he remarked: 'I have good people, and they care, but every year I have to bring myself as well, for that 30 per cent of extra effort.'

Having lived through my own harvests, I felt his anxiety.

Walking in the vineyard, 110 acres, 430,000 vines yielding 22,000 cases, namely 264,000 bottles of fine Bordeaux claret a year, he reminded me of what came first in our business. The grape, stupid. He fretted about his Cabernet Franc: 'Not as tannic as others, little colour. I don't understand the grape, I just add a little as we have always done.' He stroked his Petite Verdot: 'It brings great colour, and an acidity that I like, it's a little help on the side, a lucky grape for some.' But his Cabernet Sauvignon remained a worry, still on the vine and just a week more of good weather in the forecast.

'My Cabernet Sauvignon is not ready yet, just look,' he explained, stripping away a berry to show a pip still green, then crushing the skin to reveal a juice clearly watery, tasting another berry to diagnose fruit ripening, the tannins too green. 'I will wait as long as I can, and as long as the weather holds,' he said, looking up at a sky brightening by the hour and a sun offering mid-morning warmth after the dawn's chill. 'You see, my Cabernet Sauvignon is my bull. My Merlot is my belly dancer, and this year, she's a voluptuous dancer. So the Cabernet has to be a real bull.' He laughed for the first time since I arrived. 'Every year we make a marriage. And some marriages are made in heaven.'

Over a light lunch at the château, a family home since the eighteenth century, now modernized to meet the needs of family and business, we opened a bottle of our first, young wine from the Andes. Nervously I asked for a decanter to let our wine breathe a little. As ever, I waited anxiously for judgement from a maestro of the Old World.

And always, as the New World waited for the Old World to be expansive, the Frenchman kept the verdict pithy. '*C'est bon*,' said François, sipping our wine, then letting it linger on the tongue before a long, hard swallow. '*C'est bon*.'

I didn't spend all those years asking questions in journalism to leave it there. I pushed, I probed, I chivvied, and the Frenchman held forth.

'I'm surprised,' François declared. 'You were so nervous, almost shy, about us tasting your wine, so much so that I expected less. It's excellent. I could take a little more oak, more barrel-time perhaps, but it's so velvety, and it's well-integrated, a sound balance between fruit and acidity.' He took another sip. 'It has such good acidity that will keep it fresh, but not so much acidity that it kills the fruit at the end of the mouth. The tannins are excellent, and at the end there's this dryness. That's very good, it disappears with oxygenation but it's a dry, smooth finish.' He hesitated, but my face said more, please, more. 'I would put your wine up there with what we do here in Bordeaux, because it's balanced, it's integrated, it's a well-rounded wine not like others from your New World – you know what I mean, those fruit bombs, some call them *café au lait* wines. I call them punch-in-the-stomach wines.'

His winemaker George thought the wine would age well. 'Put fifty cases in your cellar, if you have them, and leave them there for as long as you can,' he advised. 'One day the wine will be worth more than you ever dreamed of.'

I challenged this Old World orthodoxy. 'Years ago I wrote a book, and I'm delighted people read it back then, in the moment, and not years later,' I recalled, mentioning that the book was the first biography of Robert Mugabe, written in the days when Mugabe enjoyed almost worldwide approval, not the ire of a world that deemed him a murderous despot. 'What's so different about wine? Why does wine have to be drunk decades later? Our wine is made for today, tomorrow or whenever you choose, but I want people to enjoy our dream now, not defer the pleasure.'

I hesitated to add that, if I had bought into the philosophy of deferred gratification equating to magic, we would never have pursued that dream of ours in the Andes – and I would never have come to this table as a fully paid-up and indebted member of the wine fraternity.

François took charge of the conversation with a broad smile chiselling his handsome features. 'Don't be so serious, my friend,' he counselled. 'We all know deferred gratification is a dangerous game.' He stopped to remind his foreman that the afternoon harvest had to start on time in a matter of minutes. 'Listen, you want to know the secret of the French, and the Old World, and the magic of old wine?' He took a last sip of my wine. 'You people in the New World, you hold a tasting and you serve the old wines first, then your big fruit bombs from today, and youth wins out, you think, but there's never the magic.' He looked around the table, with a knowing eye on his team. 'When you have a grand tasting in France, you start with the young vintages, then you go to the old wines. By the time you reach that Latour from the '60s, or that Pétrus from the '80s, or better still that Cheval Blanc from the '40s, you're half-drunk. You're ready for the magic. It's all in the Bible. The marriage feast at Canaa.'

*

François, vineyard owner, Bordeaux:

If I had to do it all again and I could start out from scratch, I would do it in the New World. First, as a winemaker, it's a question of microclimate. Having enough strong sunshine, as David has in the Andes, balanced by the cool of the mountains, that's brilliant. You never get everything right, but that's one important start.

And then it's a question of economics. I have a mogul friend in California, he wanted to buy vineyard here in France, money no object. So I looked for him. It was a shock to me, and I live here, I grew up here in Medoc. A hectare of good vineyard costs millions, and I'm talking Euros. I told my friend, bluntly: 'You will never see your money back in thirty years, you will be paying for ever for something that has not yet been achieved. So forget it.'

If I have a worry for David, it's that he seems much too humble about his wine. He needs to bring his ego to the table, and I'm sure he has that ego from those days in journalism. You don't work in places like Lebanon, and Congo, and China without it. And he needs to fake it, if necessary. He needs to say: 'This wine is brilliant, it's well worth fifty, or sixty, or seventy dollars.' He's going to spend so much time selling a small amount of wine at a lower price, when he might just as well devote that time to a higher price bracket. We're not here, as winemakers, to re-educate people. We're here to deliver what they think they want, and what they expect. His wine is much better than his sell. It's as if he is shy of making the sell, or delivering the pitch.

What I do see is that he understands the danger. And the danger is in going too quickly for ratings. For points. You live by the gun, you die by the gun. My view is that you have to build up quality, produce three to four vintages of quality, with a distribution system to match. Then you might go for ratings. Too many newcomers, like David, go for points, get them, then they have no way to follow up. And the people who give points, well, let's just say they have no loyalty.

He's gone for a balanced, integrated wine, not a points-scorer, a wine for the ages in my view. That's wise. But the challenge is to stick with that strategy. Trust me. I know about that, I know how big the challenge is. You reach that point when you know your wine, when you taste how it should be with every vintage, and you master that one year after another. Yet you don't necessarily receive instant market recognition, it takes years. Then the challenge is big, and the mistake made by many is that you lose confidence, you can't keep your nerve, and you start listening to people who say do this or that with your wine. You have to decide what your wine is, and how it is, and how it will be year after year.

You see, instant gratification is impossible in this business. Lots of people think otherwise. And the cemeteries are full of them. So too the bankruptcy courts.

I have told David to pursue his dream, because his children and grandchildren will talk about his life, and his vision, and argue over his decision-making for decades to come. I do the same over what my grandfather and my uncle did with this land of ours. My forebears made so many decisions on this land that affect my life today, decisions that will shape the lives of my own children. They planted our wonderful belly dancer, Merlot, on the high ground, when it would have done much better further down the island of vines. They wanted quantity, so they planted dense vineyard. Today we crave quality, less is more. They made judgement calls about rootstock, soil, canopy, and it's taken me years to put things right.

And then, despite all the effort, and the labour, and the rebuilding, you have no way of knowing whether the next generation will take on the adventure as you did. My children might want to be doctors, or lawyers, or accountants. What I leave them will be a place, a piece of land, a lifestyle. I know they will love the place, because it is in their blood. I have no way of knowing they will put their shoulder to the wheel of the business that goes with it.

It's a game for the ages, the wine business. Not for today, or tomorrow. I hope David learns that.

*

# At a Price

So how long does the average wine buyer take to decide on the purchase of this bottle or that?

Answer: twenty-nine seconds.

And how long does the average dog owner take to decide on pet food?

Answer: eighty-one seconds.

And what if research suggested that, the higher the price of a wine, the more the average drinker enjoyed it? And what if the industry told you that the key to selling wine lay in seduction?

On a cold, wet Saturday morning, the rain falling in sheets, we presented the first SonVida at our local wine store in Washington DC. For a few moments, waiting for the storm to ease, we sat in the car outside, holding hands. We had come to this particular moment, after a decade of much joy and some grief. Going retail. The final leg of our rare journey.

Sonia had presented the news live to virtually every country on the planet. I had more bylines than I cared to remember. Neither of us claimed to be shy about selling ourselves. But retail? Nerves kicked in. We spent the final minutes talking about the blend of label, name, brand that we had conceived, and the words we would use about what really mattered. The wine, stupid.

'Don't say that SonVida tastes of this or that,' suggested Sonia. 'Let's not say black fruits, or chewy plums, because if the person tasting doesn't get that on first sip, then it puts distance between us and the buyer and can make them feel uncomfortable. Besides, who knows what a chewy plum is anyway?' Ever the strategist, she concluded: 'Let's use words like elegant, well balanced, lush, rich, all true of Son-Vida, and comfort words. How about: "SonVida, a wine to celebrate with"?'

The grammarian inside me grimaced. Celebrate with . . . ? 'With what?' I asked.

Sonia sighed. 'With their lives, of course. This is the moment when we let go of SonVida, our dream,' she continued, 'and it becomes part of other people's lives and helps them live their dreams.'

I squeezed her hand. 'No, darling, this is when we learn to sell.'

SonVida. How much in a name? Plenty, if you believed the wine industry. Somehow the name of a wine had to evoke place, style, quality. Plus accessibility and friendliness, if you believed everyone who took it upon themselves to advise you. My favourite counsel came from Greg, who had his own vineyard in California, plus a distribution company, a man who understood the romance of the business and the hard-nosed reality. His advice could not have been more down to earth. 'Always keep in mind the guy, or the girl these days, who buys a bottle of wine with sex in mind, to take it back to his or her place after a date. The last thing they want is a wine that he or she can't pronounce!' And with that I understood why German wines had such a *godforsakener harden teimen.*

So, the decision on a wine name? So basic. Yet so important. Alegría, the name of our one daughter and of the vineyard itself, sounded like a natural, but a preliminary search showed it triggered potential conflicts with others. We dallied with the idea of Smith. How many people would be drawn to that name simply by its semi-comic mundanity, let alone the millions who belonged to the global Smith tribe? Yet again, we discovered Château Smiths, one in France, another in Washington State up in the Pacific Northwest. And so we turned to SonVida, a name we had lived with for some years because Sonia had started a small consultancy called Sonvidas after she left CNN. She saw it then as a catch-all for so much. *Sonvidas.* Sonia's lives. *Vid.* Part of my name, and also 'vine' in Spanish. *Son.* OK, but also the final three letters of the name of our youngest, Nelson. I applied that after-date seduction test, and it tripped off the tongue, three simple syllables: *SonVida.* The first sang; the last rang full of life. For *Vida,* I heard *Viva!* The words on the back label formed immediately in our minds:

SonVida is Sonia's life and David's dream. This wine is a story of adventure, friends, love, hope and taking risks. Sonia left her native Argentina to study at Cambridge. Years later, she returned with her British husband, David, to build a vineyard high in the Andes: at 1,029 metres, their vineyard combines climate, soil and altitude to produce wines of intense, elegant fruit, with the smoothest of tannins. Classic wines for today, tomorrow, and a decade from now.

David had a dream: a vineyard, a house and a wine that would change their lives. Here it is. SonVida. A rich Malbec, full of life, from our vineyard. Enjoy.

What was in a label? Plenty again, according to our new friends in the wine business. The name spoke to the head, the label to the heart, so they said. And given the fact that the average buyer did indeed spend less than thirty seconds on selecting a bottle of wine, hard to underestimate the imperative to produce an eye-catching label. The traditional French way, usually a mosaic of words detailing full name and title of producer, locale, region, appellation, quality of wine, Cru or no Cru, often that final stamp saying '*mis en bouteille au château*'. That wordy document had been supplanted in the New World by modernist, minimalist, image-based simplicity.

Cloudy Bay: and you saw just that, a silkscreen sepia version of a cloudy bay off the South Island of New Zealand. Meridian Wine: and you were treated to a distinctive mosaic of watercolour art, a ship here, a beach there, a soft sunset on that one, a shimmering waterline on another one, speaking to the beauty of California's Central Coast. Or Yellowtail: less subtle certainly, but still unforgettable with its yellow kangaroo on a stark, black background, as in-your-face as Australia liked to be. At its most effective, this was recognition through image, not words.

We had bought a view a decade before, and the vista remained at the core of our adventure, the dream given new life every time we arrived on our land and woke up to look at those mountain peaks, and the vines that now stretched as far as the eye could see in front of the Andes. We agreed on the image that went with SonVida, a black-and-white sepia shot of vineyard in foreground, house centre-stage, but both dwarfed by the majesty of the snow-capped peaks, the original being a photograph I had taken from the entrance to our land, my tripod on top of a friend's minibus. Below, a bold, bronze SonVida, capital S, capital V, the two captured as well in a striking red dot in the middle of the bottle. SV. SonVida.

Finally, the mother of all issues. Price. And there the debate never ended, given the swings and roundabouts of a global economy in recession. But as we sat in the car outside the wine store that day, waiting to make our début in retail, the debate was over. Too late to tinker with the package by then.

Yet. Hit the pause and reverse buttons. The two of us had been intrigued by something a trifle obscure but nevertheless rather revealing, an academic study that generated few headlines but sparked debate in our marriage. We had fine-tuned name, label, words, and picked our way through the bureaucracy of barcodes, export licences and approval from the viticulture agency. And then the US National Academy of Sciences, no less, published a quiet bombshell of a report. Dr Antonio Rangel, from the California Institute of Technology, concluded that if people were told a wine was expensive while they were drinking it, then they really did think it tasted better than a cheap one, rather than merely saying that they did. Dr Rangel came to this finding, published in the scholarly *Proceedings of the National Academy*, by scanning the brains of drinkers while giving them sips of wine.

The brain scanner showed that the activity of the brain that registered pleasant experiences increased in line with the stated price of the wine. For example, when one of the wines was said to cost ten dollars a bottle, it was rated less than half as good as when folks were told it cost ninety dollars a bottle. The higher the price put on a wine, the more people seemed to be interested in it, to value it and to enjoy it.

'So you put a decent price on a wine,' Sonia concluded, 'and people want it even more.'

Yes, darling, I kept thinking, but what if people stop buying at a certain price point?

We did informal testing, with winemakers, winery-owners, wine buffs, and price estimates for SonVida fluctuated, not widely, but enough to make us realize that we were out of our depth when it came to marking up a final number for our wine. Your most valuable asset, your house, was worth whatever the market bought it for the day you sold, we reckoned. So we took SonVida to the professionals who sold in the market we knew best, Washington DC, and we said: 'Tell us what you can sell it for, not what you think it's worth.'

And that's how we walked into the store that Saturday lunchtime, ready to do retail on SonVida. At twenty-two dollars, ninety-nine cents a bottle. Plus tax.

# Retail Politics

Sonia greeted everyone with a warm smile and, comforting thought, no hint of nerves now that the moment had come. 'For me, this is a wine to celebrate with,' she said, pouring clients a small tincture of SonVida, then offering them a nibble of cheese and cracker thoughtfully provided by the store. 'It's a wine to feel indulgent with.' Stay on message, *mi amor.* It worked.

Art, a middle-aged banker with a girth to match, sipped our wine slowly. 'I have been drinking Argentine reds for a couple of years now, and I enjoy them. I'm beginning to think some of them could be great wines,' he judged, stopping to look down at the label, taking in the first line, no more, of the words on the back. 'SonVida, Sonia's life and David's dream.' He took another sip. 'But this is excellent, good balance, smooth, rich finish, almost French.'

I launched into a mini-explanation of how we sought balance above all, rather than first impact, how we had urged the winemaker to give it smooth finish rather than fruit-forward explosion, until Sonia intervened with a look that said: Too Much Information, capital letters.

'Thank you for that, yes. It's certainly smooth, and glad you like the finish,' she interjected, smiling at the gentleman. Agree with the customer, you idiot, her face said. The customer's always right.

Art took a case.

Julie, Ann and Margaret, three sixty-somethings who clearly met in the wine store on Saturday afternoons after a girls' lunch, had all spent time in Argentina. 'We loved Mendoza. I can see the landscape on your label in my mind's eye, from being there,' remarked Ann.

'This is a terrific Malbec, and I know many of the best Malbecs,' interposed Julie, obviously the lead spirit in the group. 'How long have you been doing this?'

I started the history lesson from back in the days of the onion and tomato field, explaining how the land had been vine in the 1930s and 1940s, before it was ripped up in the 1970s because grape prices were so low. No, No, No, my wife's face declared, stop talking about tearing up vineyards. No Negative Information, capital letters.

'It's been a dream of ours, to make a wine, ever since we found that special place,' Sonia remarked, cradling a bottle to show everyone the label, and the image of vineyard, house, mountains. 'You know, because you've been there, how rare and beautiful the Andes can be in Mendoza.'

Julie nodded, so too her friends. The connection with the client had been made, the deal had been sealed. Julie, Ann and Margaret took two bottles each.

And then came Mark and Jane, two twenty-somethings who had time for each other, for some research and for holding hands as they wine-shopped on a Saturday afternoon. Time as well to ask questions and absorb answers. 'How old is the vine?' I explained how we first planted in 2002. 'How long in the barrel?' I replied that SonVida had spent twelve months in barrel, qualifying for Reserve status. 'What kind of barrel?' Mainly French, I ventured, but a little American new oak. Sonia overheard that and stepped in.

'This is a wine to enjoy on one of those special moments,' she said, pouring them both a sip more and darting me a glance that said Enough. 'We hope you enjoy it.'

Mark and Jane loaded six bottles into their shopping-basket. I helped them.

My favourite moments represented the fine line between success and failure. I spent a good ten minutes with an elderly gentleman named Mark, whom I recognized as a one-time celebrity lawyer in Washington, patiently taking him through the where, when and how of SonVida, unattended by Sonia because she was dealing with a whole group of clients.

'I love Malbec. I think it's an untold story, and this is fabulous Malbec,' he concluded, savouring a last, long sip of SonVida. 'But I don't buy twenty-two-dollar bottles of wine.'

'Thank you for enjoying it with us,' I said, biting my tongue.

Joanne, a bubbly, athletic dynamo, dressed in sports clothes with a bright-red bandanna, oozed positive energy from the moment she pushed her shopping-cart towards me. She knew little about our grape, or Argentina, or red wine for that matter. 'I usually drink whites,' she offered as an opening remark. I opted for the Sonia track.

'We like to think of this as a wine to celebrate with,' I suggested, presenting her with a small cup.

'I'm all for that,' she replied, looking down to check the price.

Joanne took a bottle and, after a helter-skelter circuit of the store, picking up cheese, salami, smoked salmon and a six-pack of beer, she returned. 'We have a birthday to celebrate,' she told me. 'I'll take another bottle. Would you sign one for me?'

Suddenly it hit me. I remembered the unbridled joy of seeing the first copy of a first book, touching it, reading the jacket blurb over and over, savouring the moment. A book was for today, tomorrow, hopefully a decade on. In your dreams, a book stood the test of time. So too a wine. I waited for Sonia to finish yet another sales pitch.

'Just take a moment to savour how far we have come with this,' I kissed her discreetly.

'And how far we have to go,' she replied, giving me one of her puckish winks and turning to another gentleman waiting for a free taste of wine.

American sport relished statistics. Baseball, the national pastime so defined, boasted averages for almost everything. The percentage linking how many times a player went up to bat, and how many times he hit the ball. The percentage of how many times the pitcher threw the ball, and how many times he gave up a home run. The percentage of how many games a team played, and how many times they won. So if the New York Yankees were playing .500 ball, it meant they had won 50 per cent of their games, and so on. And if Babe Ruth hit .300, it meant he put bat to ball successfully three times out of ten. I judged, during that afternoon of doing retail, that Sonia batted about .900, namely, she succeeded in selling nine times out of ten. Me? Let's just say I stopped counting when I fell below the 50 per cent mark in the first hour.

How could that be? I had brilliant retailers in my family, true retail genius in my DNA. I knew about it first hand from childhood.

Take my great-grandmother, Betsy Keefe, immortalized by a picture that hung on my dining-room wall, showing her in her finest hat and coat, kissing Julie Andrews on the opening night of *My Fair Lady*, Theatre Royal, Drury Lane, 30 April 1958. I knew my great-grandmother as a feisty, combative octogenarian, usually, when my mother and I visited her in the late 1950s, to be found in the snug bar of the local pub, my job being to take her arm and help her home to her apartment, where my mother cooked a solid meal for her. A woman of extraordinary independence, her story spoke to living on the cutting-edge of change. Born into poverty, orphaned at seven when both her parents died of tuberculosis, starting work at eight, married at sixteen, she had entered a world where a woman had no vote, little or no freedom to choose, and few rights. She left us after a life on the barricades, in my mind symbolized less by the vote, or a woman's right to making choices, more by the way she went to the pub on her own, something that would have been unthinkable when she was a young woman.

George Bernard Shaw, the playwright, had known Betsy as a flower-girl, one of two sellers who provided him with the knowledge, the vernacular and the mannerisms to create Eliza Doolittle in his play *Pygmalion*. It first appeared in 1913, when my great-grandmother was twenty-eight, at the height of her undoubted powers. Hence her invitation to present the bouquet one opening night in 1958, when *Pygmalion* became *My Fair Lady*, the musical with Julie Andrews as Eliza and Rex Harrison as Professor Higgins, the pedant who sought to make a noble lady out of a cockney flower-seller.

# Not Bloody Likely

All her life, my Nana Keefe sold flowers from her 'pitch', as the flower-stand was called then, at the top of Villiers Street, next door to Charing Cross station, waking up before dawn to buy her flowers at Covent Garden market, then selling them for as many hours as it took to secure enough money to feed her family. This Eliza Doolittle did not marry Freddy, or take Henry Higgins his slippers. She had sixteen children, starting as a sixteen-year-old bride with my grandmother. Able to read a little, but never able to write, she did retail all her life. My mother recalled her vibrantly in the 1920s, persuading a gentleman that he needed a buttonhole carnation for himself or a posy for his girlfriend, or a bouquet for his wife. On Wednesdays and Sundays she took her basket to Charing Cross Hospital, waiting patiently for customers on the two visiting days the hospital allowed back then. After my great-grandfather, nickname 'Midget', got drunk one Friday night, so the family folklore went, he took the King's shilling and signed up for the Great War in 1915, leaving Betsy and her young children for the Western Front. When she met someone else, her husband was sent a 'Dear John' letter informing him of her infidelity, and, as custom dictated, he was given two weeks' leave from the trenches to return home and deal with the family crisis. That, according to my grandmother, meant giving his wife 'a good hiding', presumably the rite of the age to remind a partner of marriage vows and the inalienable right of the male. Instead, Betsy showed him the door. 'Not bloody likely,' I imagined she told him. 'Not bloody likely,' the phrase used by Eliza Doolittle in Shaw's original stage play, catching the eye of the censors and removed after opening night.

If my great-grandmother spoke to retail born of necessity and the search for survival, then my grandfather simply had the knack for selling. The only man I trusted as a young child, Grandad had a rare adventure after leaving school at twelve to work in his parents' fruit shop, round the corner from the British Museum. Conscripted in 1917, then dispatched to the killing fields of Ypres and Passchendaele, he served a year in the trenches with the Middlesex Regiment, before he deserted early in 1918 and fled into a nearby Belgian village. What followed, by his own account, represented the most tumultuous period of his life. He fell in love with a young woman named Bertha, he learned the French language, he spent serious amounts of time hiding from the military police, who had orders to shoot deserters without trial. He also learned to drink good wine. My youth was peppered with images of my grandfather ordering a burgundy red, Pinot Noir, and a white Graves from Bordeaux, a classic blend of rich, honeyed Semillon and crisp, acidic Sauvignon Blanc in syncopation with his careful selection: roast lamb with his red burgundy, oysters with the white Graves. To a child, he seemed to take awfully long lunches.

Only in my sommelier days did I come to understand what acquired tastes those wines represented, how keenly he understood the pairing of wine and food, and how deeply he had been influenced by his time in Europe. 'Remember, son, that the Germans are just like us, they belong to humanity too. They have the same hopes, and dreams, and fears,' he told me as I embarked on a heavily subsidized school trip to the Rhine, part of a post-war government campaign in the 1960s to introduce the next generation of Brit to Germany and its people. 'And the Germans have much to teach us, if we open our eyes to them, free of the memory of war. Remember we are one humanity.'

In January 1919, a few weeks after the Armistice that ended the war, the British Army distributed leaflets in Bertha's village, promising amnesty for deserters, and repatriation to England, in exchange for dishonourable discharge from the army and a brief spell in military prison. The deadline set was 31 January 1919. 'The most difficult decision of my life,' my grandfather told me. 'Europe, or England.' He took the amnesty, left life, love and fine wine behind him, returning to London to meet and marry my grandmother, the flower-seller's daughter. Amazingly, he went back, with his wife and children, almost every year in the 1920s to Belgium. They met Bertha, by then married with her own family. My mother remembered the village turning out for them, banquet tables laid and a long afternoon of eating and drinking that stretched into an evening dance. I thought of my grandfather as the first European I ever met, and cried buckets when he died of a massive stroke after yet another fabulous long lunch.

The man did retail with little or no effort apparently. I always sensed that he delighted in the cut and thrust of selling in the market place. In the 1930s, he established himself as one of London's original, mobile betting shops, a so-called bookmaker, working the streets of his childhood around Covent Garden market, Leicester Square and Holborn, taking bets from those who held accounts with him, one step ahead of the law, I imagined, and blessed with the capacity to take care of himself, seeing as he had been an army boxing champion, fighting in the light-weight class, in his war years.

Then he sold fruit. Like his mother-in-law, he woke up before dawn until well into his sixties to get to Covent Garden; he would pick his produce personally, then take it back to his store, where he lovingly laid out his window presentation by hand. I recalled him, always, as a dapper man in shirt and bow tie, persuading his women customers to go for the golden delicious apple and the lush Shemouti orange. He peeled the orange, offering a slice as if it were *foie gras* or caviar.

So I felt a little humbled that Saturday afternoon as I watched Sonia by the stand dedicated to SonVida. By closing time, I started finding my voice, and the rhythm that went with clinching the sale. 'We think of it as a wine to celebrate with, or to share memories.'

One gentleman explained that he was buying a bottle for a friend who had just lost his wife. 'I'm going to tell him that he will love the story of you two on the outside of the bottle almost as much as the wine inside.'

I was taken aback, we had been lucky, Sonia and I.

We were still alive, and still together.

If only my great-grandmother and grandfather could have seen us. How much wine did you move, they would have wanted to know as we packed up empty bottles, and boxes, cleaning up the remains of cheese and crackers. Well, Nana and Grandad, we sold 22 cases, 264 bottles of SonVida, in one afternoon.

Not bloody likely.

# UnCorked 2

Whether I wanted to admit it or not, we had gambled hugely on our dream. We had taken a major risk with our future. We bought a farmer's field 5,000 miles from where we lived, and within a year the country it was in collapsed, making our investment worth a song. We had doubled-down on the bet by planting vine, then watched us lose a sizeable portion of our young plants to two hailstorms. Tired of rolling those dice, we upped the ante and invested in expensive netting to protect the vineyard. We had wagered again when we built a house, believing that the dream had to have a roof, as well as vines, to survive and prosper. The ultimate bet lay in making a wine, and taking it to market, in the midst of the worst global recession since the Great Depression.

Yet rarely did I question why we had done this. Rather, I came to celebrate that which I had not seen when we embarked on the dream. How the experience changed us. How the land taught us patience, the age-old secret of the farmer to watch, work, wait, pray, to watch in the changing seasons carefully, because each season gave the earth, and the plant, and the grape, its special quality, one year never exactly like another. How the place educated us to understand the globe around us in a way we never understood before, even though we had travelled the world, teaching us about environment and development, sustainability and conservation. How the business led us to appreciate that sometimes the setback happened for the best. That often you learned so much through mistakes made. That occasionally dropping the ball turned out to a blessing in disguise, a disaster avoided, a path not to be taken. That we had good problems to solve, not just bad options to take. Above all, we grew to appreciate how the people around us gave us so much more than we could ever give them, their time, their talent, their loyalty, their advice, their wisdom, surprised that people like us wanted to live among them, but accepting us as members of their community.

Two baby-boomers, enjoying the blessings of existence in one hemisphere, who sought a new chapter, a fresh challenge, another frontier elsewhere. Two professionals from one arena who asked themselves whether they could make it in another. Two people who had a half-formed dream, and the freedom to take it to fruition. A couple who trusted each other's judgement enough to believe that, together, they could shape a legacy that would long outlive them. SonVida, Sonia's life and David's dream. In truth, our dream came true.

F. Scott Fitzgerald wrote at the end of my favourite American novel, *The Great Gatsby*:

> Gatsby believed in the green light, the orgastic future that year by year recedes before us. It eluded us then, but that's no matter – tomorrow we will run faster, stretch out our arms farther . . . and one fine morning –
>
> So we beat on, boats against the current, borne back ceaselessly into the past.

The dream did not elude us. We ran faster than we had ever done in our previous lives, but we saw the destination. We stretched out our arms, as well as our bank balance, further than we cared to admit. And one rainy afternoon in Washington DC, embraced by friends, but also by those we had never met before, we sold our first wine looking forward. Not borne back ceaselessly into our past, but looking forward to many more vintages in the future.

SonVida. What's your dream?

# And so it goes . . .

*Christmas, Altamira*

A good neighbour called just as our families from London and Buenos Aires arrived at the house for the holidays.

'Has Christmas come early, or what?' said José Manuel Ortega, Spaniard, founder and driving-spirit behind the O. Fournier winery about ten miles away. In our remote stretch of the Uco valley, ten miles apart meant you were neighbours; indeed, the restaurant at his winery, run by his wonderful wife Nadia, was our favourite locale. 'Have you seen it?' he asked again, consciously winding me up as only close friends could when they bore good news. 'It's fabulous.'

'Seen what?' I replied. 'What's fabulous?' Maybe he was jet-lagged. I knew the fellow spent his life on planes, with vineyards in Argentina, Chile and Spain. 'I know it's been a long, difficult year for all of us, José Manuel, but you're not making much sense.'

'OK, I hope you're sitting comfortably,' he laughed. 'Then I'll begin.' (*Pause for effect.*) 'The great Jancis Robinson has put you on the map, my friend. She's made you wine of the week. Wine of the week, in Christmas week, *amigo*. Doesn't get much better than that.'

Surely not. Jancis Robinson? The Jancis Robinson who Sonia thought was the smartest woman in wine? I had refused to put Broadband, or Wi-fi, in the house. For the first time I regretted it. I threw on a respectable pair of shorts – Christmas was predictably hot – and drove quickly down our rocky dirt roads into La Consulta, heading straight for CyberMundo, our only internet café. Along the way I bumped into Jorge and Lalo, businessmen, local personalities and mates. Jorge, owner of the town's best clothing store and real-estate wheeler-dealer, had made me a member of the all-male, Friday-night dining club that gathered at his farm to cook out, drink too much and laugh at the Englishman's Spanish. *Los delincuentes*, I called them, Spanish for 'rogues'. Lalo the bookshop owner, president of the pueblo's football club, once arranged for me to play a few games for the veterans team. I considered my team-shirt a treasured item, and the ribbing I took from my team-mates an honour, my point of arrival in my new home.

'*Inglés*, what are you looking so happy about?' enquired Jorge, mischievous grin spreading across his beard. 'Did your wife put that smile on your face?'

'If only you knew,' I ventured, my expression hinting at something truly special. Sonia would understand. Ah, the Argentines and their one-tracked minds, I thought, parking quickly and telling them I'd join them for a *cafecito* in a while.

The CyberMundo, barely painted, with grubby terminals and a slow Broadband connection, did not lie. The web pages loaded far too slowly, but there it was. Jancis Robinson's review of SonVida, posted online for her readers world wide.

'David and his Argentine-born, Cambridge-educated wife Sonia, a former CNN newscaster, are based in Washington DC, David working with the UN,' she wrote. 'But their début vintage SonVida Malbec Mendoza represents the fulfilment of a dream: to make wine . . . ' So she liked the dream, I told myself. But there was more.

'I must say I was very taken by their first wine, which seems to have real freshness as well as the velvety seduction of high-altitude Mendoza Malbec.' Velvety seduction? That was a line my rogue Argentine mates would enjoy.

'There's no excessive heat or sweetness to this wine. It has a really appetising quality – thoroughly wholesome and with a nice savoury note on the finish.' Not sure what she meant by 'savoury', but it sounded awfully good.

She concluded: 'This wine is worth looking out for. And it is fun at this holiday time of the year to consider the story of the dream behind it.'

Ladies and gentlemen, whatever else we would or would not do with our lives and crazy risks, one of the world's finest palates had patted this needy son of a single mother on the head. One of the world's most respected wine writers had sniffed, sipped, swirled our creation. I concluded that she didn't spit, she enjoyed. One of the journalists I truly admired for her independence and her integrity had validated our quest. The relief flowed through me.

I printed up a few copies, dashed across the street to see Jorge and Lalo briefly at the local coffee house, the haze of cigarette smoke reminding me how far away I was from Washington DC. 'Do you mean there's someone out there who actually likes that miserable wine you keep serving us?' remarked Jorge as he gave me the biggest hug, and I attempted to explain Jancis's review, struggling to put velvety seduction into Spanish. 'English women clearly have no taste,' added Lalo, as he put his arms around me.

By the time I reached Finca Alegría, Sonia's BlackBerry had flickered into action. Congratulations from wine writer Joe Fattorini in the Yorkshire Dales, freezing that Christmas. An inquiry from a wine distributor in Oregon, wanting to know how he could purchase a few cases of SonVida. A typically gracious note from our mentor and friend, Laura Catena. 'Well done, such a nice review. Happy Christmas.'

We took a walk through the vineyard. Remembered our first few hours in that place, both of us quite child-like in our infatuation, when we kept stumbling on onions, and tomatoes, and zucchini buried in the dirt, stopping the toddler Alegría eating them. How many times we were out of our depth, trying to understand Malbec clones, or the double Guyot pruning system, or the meaning of malolactic fermentation. Our first harvest, so close to disaster, Sonia an inconsolable wreck, talking to herself and the heavens as the rain poured down, and David, harvesting as he squelched more grape than he cut, cursing in Spanglish.

'There's a storm coming in,' Sonia noticed, as we returned slowly to the house to find the kids playing ping-pong with my brother while my mother and my in-laws shared a pot of afternoon tea. 'A heavy storm.'

Within a few minutes the roof echoed to the sound that represented the rat-tat-tat of rain falling to earth as *piedra*, ice stones, hail. 'Not again,' said Sonia softly as we stood in the gallery of the house, holding hands once more.

I remembered what Jancis Robinson said to me, years before, when I told her that we had suffered two separate hailstorms in our early years, losing 30 per cent of our young plants just when we expected to make some money at last. 'I couldn't handle that kind of stress, that's not for me,' Jancis said, lifting my spirits when she added, 'Hopefully you've used up all your bad luck.'

Hopefully we had. Certainly that afternoon in Christmas week we had a lucky escape, with hardly any damage as the storm passed through our part of the valley in about twenty minutes. But two hours south, in the wine district of San Rafael, a handful of vineyards were largely destroyed. Two miles west, one of our neighbours lost a plot of newly planted Malbec. Nature was arbitrary and indifferent, missing us, hitting him.

Who would be a farmer?

Well, I would.

Correction.

I am a farmer.

My journey is over. And tomorrow beckons.